THE Multimedia Scriptwriting Workshop

THE Multimedia Scriptwriting Workshop

Douglas J. Varchol

SYBEX®

San Francisco • Paris • Düsseldorf • Soest

Associate Publisher: Carrie Lavine
Acquisitions Manager: Kristine Plachy
Developmental Editors: Damon Dean and Dan Brodnitz
Editor: Alex Miloradovich
Project Editor: Linda Good
Book Design Director: Catalin Dulfu
Book Designers: Jack Myers and Tracy Dean at Design Site
Book Illustrator: Jack Myers at Design Site
Technical Artists: Catalin Dulfu, Tony Jonick
Desktop Publisher: Tracy Dean and Tania Kac at Design Site
Production Coordinator: Alexa Riggs
Indexer: Matthew Spence
Cover Designer: Adrian Morgan at Red Letter Design
Back Cover Designer: Richard Yee at Design Site

Library of Congress Card Number: 96-67495
ISBN: 0-7821-1839-9

Manufactured in the United States of America

10 9 8 7 6 5 4 3 2 1

Warranty

Sybex warrants the enclosed CD-ROM to be free of physical defects for a period of ninety (90) days after purchase. If you discover a defect in the CD during this warranty period, you can obtain a replacement CD at no charge by sending the defective CD, postage prepaid, with proof of purchase to:

Sybex Inc.
Customer Service Department
2021 Challenger Drive
Alameda, CA 94501
(800) 227-2346
Fax: (510) 523-2373

After the 90-day period, you can obtain a replacement CD by sending us the defective CD, proof of purchase, and a check or money order for $10, payable to Sybex.

Disclaimer

Sybex makes no warranty or representation, either express or implied, with respect to this medium or its contents, its quality, performance, merchantability, or fitness for a particular purpose. In no event will Sybex, its distributors, or dealers be liable for direct, indirect, special, incidental, or consequential damages arising out of the use of or inability to use the software even if advised of the possibility of such damage.

The exclusion of implied warranties is not permitted by some states. Therefore, the above exclusion may not apply to you. This warranty provides you with specific legal rights; there may be other rights that you may have that vary from state to state.

Copy Protection

None of the files on the CD is copy-protected. However, in all cases, reselling or making copies of these files without authorization is expressly forbidden.

To the first circle, to the seven of you—
your costume changes were a constant
source of delight.

To the next level out— Mom, Dad, Ron,
Susan and Lauren.

Acknowledgments

I would like to thank my agent Vincent Panettiere, my wonderful editor Alex Miloradovich, and the troops at Sybex: Damon Dean—whose idea this book was—Linda Good, Shelby Zimmerman, Dan Brodnitz, Alexa Riggs, and Catalin Dulfu, as well as Tracy Dean and the crew at Design Site. I would also like to thank Fred Frumberg for starting this whole thing off; Lori Lieberman and Kay Schaber of Industry Alliance at the Writers Guild of America, west; and Cheryl Rhoden, Vicky Summers, and Scott Roeden of the Public Affairs Department at the Guild for their terrific support. And special thanks to my many friends and colleagues of the Creative Media and New Technologies Committee—whose support and discussions I could not have lived without—and to Tom Sarris of Lucas Arts, John Porter of Voyager, David Swofford of Origin Systems, and Dany Brooks and Ric Neil of Electronic Arts.

Contents at a Glance

Table of Contents

Introduction

I heard somebody say once that trying to get a film made in Hollywood is like watching paint dry. It's slow, and nothing moves. Then along comes Adobe Premier, and suddenly you don't need a major motion picture studio. Which leads me to what this book is about: the amazing world of multimedia and the emerging media business.

> **If you've been a misfit most or even part of your life, and even if you've only felt a slight twinge of a damp, drizzly November in your soul, you'd probably make a good multimedia writer.**

Where I'm Coming From

Before you dive into the first chapter, I want to make a few points about where I'm coming from and the point of view you'll be getting in this book:

- **I'm not an academician:** I don't teach this stuff anywhere to anybody. I just try to figure it out and do it, and I use every bit of my life experience in the process.
- **I'm not a computer person:** I'm computer literate—and can even write a little bit of code—but it's my nature to do something for the romance of it, in the "once upon a time" or "it was a dark and stormy night" school of story telling.
- **I'm not a conformist:** The diversity (which can be read as instability) that my approach portends is exactly (at least *I* think) what the multimedia industry needs—creators from all walks of life, with all sorts of daily adventures to bring to bear on the discipline of making meaningful experiences (call it art if you like) that people are willing to pay good coin of the realm for.
- **This isn't an internet or on-line book:** However, much of the material I'll be discussing will probably work just fine in the internet and on-line realms—just think transference.

Where You're Going To

So what's this book about really? Well, it's three books in one—and then some.

- **Part One: Getting Started**—deals with esoteric stuff like theories on the nature of interactive multimedia, and some more practical issues like what's already out there, how to work within the existing landscape, and where ideas come from.
- **Part Two: Learning the Basics**—is a bit more technical but also tackles things like the "creative muse," who's actually out there to buy your creations, and how to shape your ideas into a winning pitch. There's also lots of valuable information on writing and style (how to stimulate your imagination without stimulants) as well as a treatise on interactive scripting models.
- **Part Three: The Anatomy of Success**—covers the nuts and bolts of the whole thing: detailed deconstructions of three CD-ROM products that are on the market (*Psychic Detective, Pyramid: Challenge of the Pharaoh's Dream,* and *Wing Commander IV—The Price of Freedom*) with charts, diagrams, script samples, and screen shots galore. We pull these products apart and see if our interactive scripting model works on them.
- **The Appendices**—are small gold mines of practical information and far-reaching resources. Appendix A contains the complete text of a proposal and demo script for an interactive game called *deusX: Ghost in the Machine.* Appendix B is a compendium of things to read, people and places to contact and information on the Writers Guild of America, west website and Interactive Program Contract. Appendix C lists all the people who contributed their talents to creating *Psychic Detective, Pyramid,* and *Wing Commander IV.* Appendix D contains crucial information about how to access the contents of the CD-ROM.
- **The CD-ROM**—is the disc (inside the back cover of the book) that features demo versions of an extremely valuable piece of software. John Truby's *StoryLine Pro* is the tool used by some of the top writers in Hollywood. It will coach you on the fundamentals of good storywriting. See Appendix D for installation instructions and hints.

Sound like fun?

PART 1

1

Getting Started

CHAPTER 1

What Is This Thing?

"SMART QUOTE"

"The life of a screenwriter of an interactive film is much better than the life of a Hollywood writer because by making an interactive script, you build a better mousetrap, you become indispensable. Because you know how it all fits together long before the rest of them do."

Michael Kaplan—co-creator/screenwriter, *Psychic Detective*

What is this thing called multimedia that everyone's going on so much about? Well, like a recipe, it makes sense to think of multimedia as a whole bunch of individual media mixed together in some Caesar salad-like fashion or another: moving pictures, art/design, writing, sound, choreography—what have you—all media and all methods of communication.

The Interactive Environment

Multimedia writer and designer Michael Utvich says, "Multimedia simply refers to an environment. The distinctive characteristic of multimedia is interactivity. It is the mechanism that allows you to move between the various media—the fact of the media themselves is not interesting."

Interactivity is the distinctive defining characteristic of multimedia. It is that which let's you jump from video, to art, to the written word, back to video, to whatever.

In the interactive movie *Psychic Detective,* deconstructed in Part Three of this book, the user has the ability to make many deliberate edits, bouncing all over the place, changing location and point of view. John Sanborn, one of the creators and the director of *Psychic Detective* feels very strongly that there is "a tremendous amount of subliminal power that the user gets from editing the movie." From interacting—the distinctive characteristic of multimedia.

In the age of the personal computer, within every home we now have the potential for multimedia experiences that are characterized by interactive participation. These experiences may be captured within CD-ROMs, brought to you via on-line services, or plucked directly from the heart of the internet itself.

Nothing New under the Sun

Combining the various media is nothing really new—big yawn. It's been happening for ages, almost since mankind crawled from the primal ooze. Ancient story tellers around campfires rattled on rattles and banged on drums to underscore the dramatic moments of their singing for their supper routines. Theater since its inception used words, music, movement, lighting, costumes and special effects to get points across.

Back in the sixties, and continuing right up to his death a few years ago, choreographer Alwin Nickolais created incredible mixed media dance presentations. He was the first to place dancers in body bags (to hide the individual ego of the dancer, and highlight archetypal movements and shapes), deluge the stage with slide projections (designed and hand-painted by Nickolais himself), and immerse the audience in compositions of his own haunting synthesized sounds. Definitely multimedia.

Up-Close and Personal

When a computer gets taken home, it usually doesn't go in the living room or the recreation room, it goes into a study or the bedroom. Home PCs, for the most part, go into highly personalized spaces, and by extension, multimedia experiences—characterized by interactive participation—are also very personal happenings.

Get out your ego-be-gone spray and use it. Your responsibility as a multimedia writer is to your audience. If you want to be successful in this business, never forget them.

The point is, if you're going to be scripting multimedia experiences, be mindful of the intense personal level on which your audience will be participating. The first lesson of this book is to never forget your audience. Don't think of them as the great unwashed masses who should be so lucky that you've thrown them a crust of your genius.

Far-Away and Distant

A further interesting thought on interactivity, and perhaps slightly at odds with the above few paragraphs, comes from a white paper called *The New Space of Communications, and Interface with Culture and Artistic Creativity,* prepared by Don Foresta, Alain Mergier and Bernhard Serexhe for a September, 1995 Council of Europe meeting. The paper discusses the new communication space growing out of the synthesis of network, computer and television technology and the role of artistic creativity in its evolution.

Like false Gods, beware of false interactivity—or at least don't get caught writing any of it.

Foresta, Mergier and Bernhard write: "Interactivity means one individual talking to another. For industry, and very often industry working in the new technologies, interactivity means man and machine. So-called interactive television, CD-ROM's, video games, only allow interactivity with some pre-designed process, a series of predetermined givens and not with a real human being on the other end. This is false interactivity and will only add to the frustration of a public looking for real exchange. All these types of so-called interactivity are short term and will inevitably add to the problem of communication in our society, the problem of personal expression and of the evolution of the identification of each of its members. Communications technologies in these instances will increase the alienation of individuals and not overcome it."

Interesting, yes? Certainly something to mull over.

The storyteller can bring a tremendous amount to what some people refer to as "dead end, cul de sac loops of pre-designed interactive material." If the multimedia interactive experience is well written and executed—where the user is compelled to think, discover and feel—wow, what a rush.

Trudging the True Path

I believe good books, music, film, television, art and stage plays can assist in the "evolution of the identification" of society's members. All these things can help individuals find personal expression. I see a movie and say, "Hey, I can write something like that." I hear a great band play, "Man, I can do that riff." Maybe you can and maybe you can't, but it gets people thinking. Which brings me to the purpose of this book—how to bring the true spirit of human interactivity to the experience of interactive scriptwriting.

So, to get you in the mood and on the road to thinking like an interactive writer/designer, let's take a look at some history, a little literature, and perhaps a dab of esoteric philosophy.

The Theory of Interactivity

Do you remember that between the ages of zero up until around twelve months you existed in a timeless state, that objects changed their shape and form with the slightest movement of your infant head? This was discovered around the turn of the century by child psychologist Jean Piaget. As your baby brain developed, objects became fixed and space and time took on very distinct coordinates.

> **As a child, did things seem rather magical? Did the Tooth Fairy leave money, the Sandman pile a beach on your bed, could toys talk, and dolls come for tea?**

As Shlain Sees It

Leonard Shlain in his elegant book, *Art & Physics, Parallel Visions in Space, Time & Light,* points out, "This category formation—space, time, and object permanence—was so ingrained in Western sensibility that until Einstein no one could conceive of the world in any other way. Einstein's incredibly simple yet sophisticated theory [Theory of Relativity] posits a view from a light beam that can be conceived by adults only with great difficulty but is the perception of all infants in their prams."

If you're serious about writing for multimedia—and to get you to start thinking differently—Leonard Shlain's "Art & Physics, Parallel Visions in Space, Time & Light" is a good place to start. As Shlain writes, "the thesis of this book is that revolutionary art anticipates visionary physics." The artist sees things first, and then the physicist comes along and puts the numbers down on paper as to why it is so.

Shlain further goes on to make the case that a true artist is in possession of a space-time consciousness that is "all-at-once knowing." A view very much like that of sitting on the head of a light beam, cruising along, keeping up with the starship Enterprise—space, time, past, future and present are all one.

Riding the Light Beam

For the first twelve months of your life then, you viewed the world as if you were sitting on the head of a light beam—time and space merged, past, future and present were one. Sounds just a little bit like an interactive multimedia experience doesn't it?

Does playing a futuristic "Myst"-type interactive experience with ultra-fast processors and total immersive virtual reality create an environment where time, space, past, future and present have the capacity to be one?

To follow this thinking for a moment, let's make the extension that users of interactive multimedia environments can command past, future, and present with the click of a mouse. Since you can skip ahead, go back, pause, go ahead again, time and space have become totally relative, depending on your mood and the quality of the interface/navigation system.

Back to the Future

Again, when you're first born, time and space is sort of like one "thing," objects change position and form with each breath, the inner and outer of who you are isn't even a concept yet. You're just you, all over the place. And then slowly this begins to change. The outside world will have its way with you, and make you part of it. Mom, dad, brother, sister, dog, all became personal spaces that you learn to deal with. The linear alphabet and linear numbers force their way into your consciousness—up, down, left, right—symbol next to symbol after symbol all meaning something supposedly powerful and important.

Certain mystics say not to worry—bifurcation of the brain is a necessary evolutionary process to give mankind some interesting worldly experiences. So go ahead and be confused, it's perfectly natural.

Childhood magic starts to disappear and you become interested in investment banking. For most of us in the West then, the left and right brain way of thinking kicks into gear, becoming like two trains heading out on different tracks, with our confused soul/identity on the station platform trying to figure out which one to jump on board.

Hypertext Happenings

Dr. Charles Ponce, author and practicing San Francisco psychotherapist, is fascinated with the concept of hypertext. Hypertext of course is a direct result of the evolution of the computer, and it is where key words in a text are linked to other text, where in turn key words in this new text are then again linked to even more texts. The linking characteristic of hypertext is further extended to the internet, where linking to nodes of information is the main mode of transport in so called cyberspace.

In cyberspace, you jump (link) from one place to another, roaming over vast distances, touching upon subject after subject, with method to your madness, or just plain random madness in your hopscotching—the choice is yours.

For Dr. Ponce, this ability to link at will is very much analogous to how our baby brains saw things before we became official members of the human race. Space, time, past, future and present were all one. Hypertext, for Ponce then, is old familiar territory. We've been there before, we lost the ability to "do it" (tossed out of the Garden of Eden), and now PCs have given us this ability back—and we love it. We can't get enough of it, and the hypertext concept is a big part of a multimedia experience.

Node Knowledge

To bring us back down to earth and relate these ramblings to scripting for multimedia, let's resolve things into a few salient points:

- **Start thinking differently:** Shake out those orthodox cobwebs of how you see the world—why does left have to be left, and right, right? Start thinking associatively.
- **Never forget your audience:** Your audience, in general, has come from a certain place. Once upon a time all of us were seeing the world as if we were sitting on the head of a light beam. (If nothing else, it's a wonderfully romantic notion.)
- **Use the medium:** An artist (a writer/storyteller) has the capacity to "see all, hear all, know all at the same time" (head of a light beam position) and express this point of view in a medium (multimedia, in our case) so that everyone else can experience it.

Interesting, no?

Shifting with the Paradigm

What's a paradigm shift? A cool new way to look at things differently, that's all. A frequently used example is Gutenberg's invention of movable type—around 1455—in the early part of the Renaissance. Almost over night, books were all over the place. Information was getting out and into the hands of all kinds of characters. People could suddenly go off and read stuff on their own and make up their own minds as to how they thought things were or should be. The invention of movable type was the beginning of the end of the dark ages.

> **At this very moment, personal computers, on-line services, CD-ROMs, ISDN lines, video conferencing, etc.—the bells and tinker toys of the so-called super information highway—are presenting human kind with a paradigm shift, which actually started about a hundred years ago.**

What's So Different

And here we are again, almost at the close of the 20th century, in another paradigm shift. Technological advances in telecommunications and computers (especially the PC and the internet) have made the following things very different for us:

- **Communication:** Telephones, faxes, teleconferencing and email has totally redefined our personal communication space.
- **Information:** Via the internet, a huge amount of information—in the form of words, pictures, numbers, sounds and ideas—has become available to large numbers of people at a relatively low cost.
- **Perception:** How we view the world—the space we inhabit with other objects—has been radically altered by:
  - The tele-distancing of images from afar—a lot of people saw the Earth from the Moon for the first time in the history of man back in 1969.
  - The digitizing of so-called reality, and the computer manipulation of it (e.g. the morphing and/or 3-D rendering of objects on a computer screen).

I can't live without a fax, and I can't live without email. I've got a number of long distance email relationships that are more emotionally intense than some relationships I have with people I see daily—and with whom I'm supposed to be emotionally intense. Go figure.

Putting Things in Perspective

The digitizing of reality and its manipulation via computer brings up some intriguing historical and philosophical issues. For instance, perspective was known by the Greeks and Romans, but with the onset of Christianity, which placed more of an emphasis on the spiritual as opposed to every-day reality, artists lost interest in depicting the real world, and perspective was largely ignored until the 14th century. Then along came the Italian artist Giotto Di Bondone (1276-1337), who created a number of paintings using the concept. The upshot: Paintings now had depth—a third dimension—and it kind of blew everybody away. Here was a mind-boggling take on the representation of reality that common folks hadn't seen before.

Extending this idea to the present day, 3-D computer modeling and morphing has produced startling images (or views of the world) as mind blowing as perspective

Putting Things in Perspective (continued)

perspective was to the people of the Renaissance. Just think of the special effects in some of the movies that are out there today. We love this stuff so much (look at the box office numbers) probably because it shows us a view of the world that we've never seen before.

Of course, the down side question is: Do special computer effects create a valid view of the world? When perspective became widely used during the Renaissance, many people hated it. They said it was a false view of the world, and that it was too egotistical, because the truth of the painting was not in the painting but in the ego of the person viewing it at a particular point in space.

But then again, what is the *right* view of the world? Who can really say.

Where the Scripter Fits

Where does the scripter fit into all this emerging media paradigm shift hoopla plunked on our doorstep. On the internet, the biggest complaint is that there's too much information, and that it's difficult to find what you really want. And when you find what you want, there isn't enough of it—or it's badly, and boringly presented.

Very clearly the mission of the writer/designer dealing with the internet is to find ways to present information in a coherent and entertaining fashion. It's a big job, and somebody's got to do it.

On a more general note, I believe the storyteller fits into the 20th century communications paradigm shift to help make sense of it all: the tale, the myth, the story—entertaining and old familiar ways of retaining and transferring important social, psychological and cultural information. It's crazy out there, and the familiar sign post of a well told tale can settle your stomach, and brace you for your next venture into the unknown realms of cyberspace.

Literary Linchpins

As we have seen, the thesis of Robert Shlain's *Art & Physics, Parallel Visions in Space, Time & Light* is that revolutionary art anticipates visionary physics. By analogy, it is interesting to note that literature has been using the concept of multimedia storytelling long before the idea of a personal home computer became the glimmer in some marketing guy's eye. So, if you're going to write for multimedia, to round out your perspective, let's do a quick tour of some of my favorite pieces of prophetic literature.

The Most Incredible Thing

Back in the mid-eighteen hundreds, Danish author Hans Christian Andersen, who specialized in children's tales, wrote a story called *The Most Incredible Thing.*

In brief it goes like this: One day in the kingdom a declaration was made, "whoever could accomplish the most incredible thing was to have the king's daughter and half the kingdom." "What a deal!" the people thought, so everybody set out to try and come up with the most incredible thing. Some folks ate themselves to death. Street urchins tried to spit on their backs. All sorts of things were put on display, but the people generally agreed the most incredible thing was created by one inventive young man, who devised: "A huge clock in a case, remarkably contrived inside and out. At each stroke of the clock appeared living pictures that depicted the hour. There were twelve performances in all, with movable figures and with song and speech."

Sounds Like a CD-ROM to Me

There was even some interactivity.

The clock struck one, and Moses came out and wrote down the first commandment on a tablet; the clock struck two, and Adam and Eve materialized, totally happy without owning any clothes; at three, the three Wisemen appeared; at four, the four seasons—and so on and so on—and everybody in the kingdom generally agreed that this was the most incredible thing. So they gave the young inventor the king's daughter and half the kingdom, and on their wedding day—and this is where the interactivity comes in—a fellow stepped out of the festive crowd and cried, "Hold on a second, I'm about to do the most incredible thing." Whereupon he took an ax and smashed the magical multimedia clock into about a billion pieces, and declared, "See, told'ya, I've done the most incredible thing."

Well, the crowd was pretty much speechless. Yeah, everybody agreed that this certainly was the most incredible thing, smashing art to pieces. So the destroyer of the clock was declared the winner and given the girl and half the kingdom. They had to do it because the law was the law, and he *had* after all, done the most incredible thing.

Cute Story Huh?

Oh. FYI, the young clock inventor gets the girl and half the kingdom in the end because as author Andersen puts it, "The body had been smashed to bits [the clock], but not the spirit. The Art Spirit had returned as a ghost, and this was no joke." How the story exactly ends, I'll leave it to you to read and find out the details yourself.

I think there's a lesson here somewhere for the folks that fund the National Endowment for the Arts—but that's another story entirely.

The Glass Bead Game

In 1946, Hermann Hesse's *The Glass Bead Game* (known also as *Magister Ludi*—original German title *Das Glasperlenspiel*), which some people call his greatest work, won him the Nobel Prize for Literature.

In *The Glass Bead Game*, Hesse creates a futuristic world, hundreds of years past World War II, that contains the province of "Castalia," wherein resides a community of scholars, monks almost—though not of any established religion—who live, work and breath exclusively in the realm of human mind and imagination. And the primary method through which these fictional characters exercise their minds and imagination is in playing The Glass Bead Game.

Now the best way to describe the game (at least as I see it, because in the more than four hundred pages of the manuscript it is never really described in detail) is that two people would sit down, and drawing upon all the world's knowledge of the arts, philosophy and sciences—the core ideas that represent man's wrestling bouts with the world as we know it—would make up puzzles for one another.

Let Me Elaborate

If I lead off in the game, I might give you the opening ten notes of a symphony, combined in some fashion with half of a sonnet, maybe the signatures on the Declaration of Independence, and a cropped photograph showing only Mona Lisa's smile. It would then be your job to expand on this puzzle, following a precise set of rules, giving back to me my original puzzle, plus your elaboration of it, plus a whole new potential puzzle for me to solve. This rolling conundrum would be tossed back and forth, ever growing, twisting and turning onto itself, until finally one of the players would create an obvious ultimate solution, becoming the winner of the game.

Did You Get This?

"The Glass Bead Game," Hesse writes, "is thus a mode of playing with the total contents and values of our culture. All the insights, noble thoughts, and works of art that the human race has produced in its creative eras, all that subsequent periods of scholarly study have reduced to concepts and converted into intellectual property—on all this immense body of intellectual values the Glass Bead Game player plays like the organist on an organ."

Now, here's the interesting kicker, Hesse did not hypothesize a high tech society for his Castalia—there are no starships, lasers, or computers even in this fictional land.

Think Tibetan Monastery

Hesse never actually describes the medium that The Glass Bead Game is played out in, you sort of get the sense that everything is written down in a series of elaborate formulas, representing music, art, poetry, science, law, logic, history, etc. In a way then, the glass bead game can be thought of as a method in which all the great minds of the last 50,000 years could get together, have snacks, and toss a few ideas around to see what they could come up with.

Hesse's Glass Bead Game is really a high-end (content wise) networked Doom-type game. Two people enter an imaginary environment, and instead of throwing bullets and rockets at one another, they dip into a database of universal ideas and concepts, and present one another with bits and pieces of a conundrum. And the one who gets blocked in first—can't extend or solve the puzzle—dies.

The upshot then for me is that Hesse, in the mid-forties, was describing an elaborate, super mental, multimedia interactive experience. Take *The Glass Bead Game* out for a spin sometime and decide for yourself.

The Alexandria Quartet

Another piece of literature that I'm particularly fond of, and which has antecedent multimedia hints, is Lawrence Durrell's The Alexandria Quartet.

In the late 1950's Durrell wrote four novels, *Justine*, *Mountolive*, *Balthazar*, and *Clea*, about pre- and post- W.W.II Alexandria, Egypt, and populated with some of Western literature's most memorable characters. The quartet's about steamy love and twisted relationships. Durrell writes, "Alexandria is the wine press of love." Three of the novels (*Justine*, *Mountolive* and *Balthazar*) describe the same set of circumstances, from three different points of view. The fourth novel, *Clea*, takes all the characters from the first three novels and moves them forward in time.

The Alexandria Quartet was a conscious attempt on Durrell's part to play with the Cartesian coordinate system—an XYZ axis, with the fourth axis being time.

This, without a doubt, is a model to be considered for an interactive multimedia fiction experience. I discuss this in greater detail in the second part of this book, but in brief, every character will have their own take on what happened, and will be perfectly happy to tell you all about it.

Having a large data storage capacity will allow for detailed character-centric levels that can be fully explored before moving forward in time. You can circle around the same plot points, and see them reflected through the eyes of the various characters.

This is also known as a "Rashomon" structure—made famous by Japanese Director Akira Kurosawa's film *Rashomon* (based on two Ryunosuke Akutagawa short stories, *Rashomon* and *In a Grove*) where you get to see the same murder take place from numerous points of view. You even get the murdered guy channeling from a medium telling you how things went (a mixed media presentation?).

Possession

A contemporary work of fiction (1990) that I think is a must read for anyone serious about writing for multimedia is A.S. Byatt's *Possession*. (Thank you Michael and John for bringing it to my attention.) This is a marvelous tale that truly breaks down the boundaries of time and space. Part mystery, part love story, *Possession* starts out in present day, where gradually, through the discovery of a cache of old love letters and journals, the secret love life of two Victorian poets is revealed.

> ***Possession*** **is a book—words on paper you hold in your hand—but for me it was an interactive multimedia experience, and this is only one of probably many examples in literature that have hints of multimedia elements in them—possible interactive fictional forms that can be studied and adapted to interactive multimedia expression.**

Author Byatt switches from forward narrative to love letters, to journals, to the actual works of the poet's, creating a text-based three dimensional character mosaic spanning over a hundred and fifty years of time. To me, the author's technique was absolutely interactive, because I kept going back to earlier sections of the book to re-read certain poems as more details were revealed—making the earlier poems much fuller when read the second time through.

Should You Write This Stuff?

Before we ramble further into this adventure, let's talk a little bit about who should write for the multimedia business. What kind of profile are we talking about here?

Well, as I'm fond of saying to just about anybody I meet, I think everybody should write, and can write. Like chicken soup, it's good for you. The flip side of this concept being of course you'll hear a lot of so-called professionals going on about "talent can't be taught, only technique." Yeah, I guess, but I'm not absolutely sure that's true.

We need more communication in this world, not less. And I suspect PC multimedia

Should You Write This Stuff? (continued)

authoring tools are going to open the door to a lot of people who never really thought about expressing themselves before in any manner whatsoever, with, for the most part, a lot of this expressing happening with words and story structure form, as well as video, graphics and sound. Though your true "blow your mind" genius interactive writers are probably those kids who can't read this book yet, or who aren't even born.

It'll be interesting, don't you think, to see what kind of artists are created when future babes (not "babes" as in valley-speak—babes, tiny girls and guys) have immediate access to virtual reality interactive experiences from day one on taking up residence in the cradle. A wonder to behold? Let's keep our fingers crossed.

For professional writers who are thinking about taking the multimedia plunge, you shouldn't hesitate a minute. It's all part of keeping up with the learning curve, and it just means a trillion new markets (potentially) have opened up where you can ply your wares. But if you're still thinking—gee, I don't know if I can write interactively, let me tell you a quick story.

The very first time I went on an interview for an "interactive" writing assignment, something interesting happened on the way to the forum. On the assigned day, bright and cheery with polished sneakers, I presented myself for inspection. I smiled, they smiled. Numerous filmmaking and writing awards, professional feature script writing assignments under my belt, they asked, "yes, we suppose you can write, but have you ever written for interactivity before."

I paused.

Do I tell the truth? The squirrels furiously peddling away in my brain. And then suddenly I had this vision of a feature film script I had just finished writing, all fifteen drafts piled up next to my desk.

Three feet high, easy.

And each draft slightly different. Four or five potential endings. Scenes that had been written three or four ways, labeled "A," "B," "C," and so on and so on. The moods of characters, from major and minor, tracked through all the drafts—a touch more tenderness here, harder there. No, no—they walk out of the left hand door, instead of the right hand door. Dammit, they have to be doing this in the backseat of a '59 Chevy, not a station wagon.

I suddenly grinned at my interrogators.

Should You Write This Stuff? (continued)

Had I ever written interactively before, you ask? Well, let me tell you a little story—and I told them about my recent fifteen screenplay drafts, and when I was finished they responded with a thoughtful, "never thought of it that way before."

So the lesson here then? Even if you're writing a love letter or a postcard, and you change your mind and cross something out, it's a potential interactive choice you've just created.

You change your mind all the time when you write and also when you think. So then don't be afraid to write interactively—It's perfectly natural.

CHAPTER 2

The Multimedia Landscape

"SMART QUOTE"

"I jumped in because I wanted to see where it [multimedia] would go. It's kind of scary in a way because there are no guarantees... it's not a closed field the way TV series writing is to a large extent. There's a lot more freedom, and as a writer I find that part appealing. I think there are a lot more opportunities."

Carolynn Miller—screen and multimedia writer

If you want to be a writer/designer for the new media industry, you are going to have to know a little something about what the development, marketing, and distribution aspect of this landscape looks like. To fly blind is not smart—even though I must confess I was flying blind myself for a while. Eventually, in order to make sense of what I was doing, I had to pick up on some of the subtleties of what was going on out there. So if I can learn something about marketing and distribution, you can too.

> **It is not an over-statement to say that the new media industry is so new, and so volatile that many things change in a very short time.**

Take Care Out There!

New developers are opening up shops all the time and just as quickly going out of business. Publishers create interactive divisions, and no sooner do they get them staffed than they're handing out pink slips and shutting them down.

A writer friend of mine recently spent about four or five months placing a CD-ROM project with a company on the East coast. My friend was about to go to contract when the three staff executives that were pushing the project from inside were suddenly fired, along with about thirty other people in the company.

> **In volatile times, things are also fluid. Nothing in this business has been set in stone yet, and if you're clever, very careful, talented, persistent, obsessive—to an almost unhealthy degree—opportunities do abound.**

A couple of months ago I was at a multimedia trade show standing in line waiting to pick up my entrance badge, when suddenly I looked up, and there in line behind me were a handful of people recently let go from what some people were calling only a few months ago the "hottest new multimedia development company in Los Angeles." It looked like an unemployment line.

It's Business as Usual

Joanna Tamer, President of S.O.S., a company specializing in distribution and business development strategies to new media developers, publishers and distributors, and a person who's been involved with the multimedia industry since its beginning, says this to a writer/designer, "...remember that this is a business. And within the next two or three years, when the infrastructure is built, channels are open and ubiquitous products can flood the market, you are still in a business where somebody wants to know if they can make money off of your talent. Don't forget it.

"This is not altruism. There's no altruism anywhere in new media that I have seen. There is value system increase. There are people concerned about the kind of content that gets delivered. But there's no altruism that I've seen anywhere."

Some Statistics

What kind of an audience does the CD-ROM title industry have? How many of them are out there? And how many of them will there be in the future?

Hardware Wise

Joanna Tamer, writes in her March 1995 article for CD-ROM Professional, *Consumer Titles: The End of the Pioneering Era,* "...at the Computer Electronics Show in Las Vegas in early January 1993, a panel of distributors placed the installed base of multimedia-ready machines in the home (MPC and Mac) at 900,000." She then adds that by end-of-year 1993, the installed base of multimedia-ready machines in the home on MPC and Mac quadrupled to 3.6 million units.

Inteco Corporation, a company specializing in marketing studies for the new media, states in their February 1995 marketing report that "the Installed base of home PCs running Windows, with MPC-2 compliant CD-ROM drives, will be over ten million in the US by early 1995. The publishing opportunity on this platform will grow rapidly. By 1998, 42 million drives and 65% of home PCs will be available to play CD titles."

By 1998 a lot of people are going to have CD-ROM drives, and many of them are going to be looking for titles to play in those drives.

Titles That Do and Don't Fly

And the good news gets even better, but it does carry a hint of responsibility with it. Inteco Corporation's report further states, "The largest unknown factor in realizing the market potential for CD titles beyond 1998 is the ability of authors and publishers to create a wide choice of high-quality, attractive titles."

The finger is pointing at you creators, you writer/designer types and you "would be" writer/designer types. There appears to be the potential for a huge CD-ROM title market beyond 1998, but this market will only be there if the titles are compelling and satisfying.

Unfortunately, the market today is loaded with many titles that are nothing more than "shovelware." If you look at the various marketing surveys that are available, in general, and very roughly, between 3,500 and 4,000 titles were produced during 1994, and of this lot, only between 200 and maybe 600 sold more than 3,500 units. Hits like *Myst* and *7th Guest* of course sold many more.

Dollars and Sense

Even with these rough numbers it is obvious that competition for the consumer dollar is very tough. According to Becki Walker, of Walker and Associates, a multimedia marketing firm based in Venice, California, "in order to successfully launch a title today you need a minimum marketing and public relations budget of around $250,000." This just gets the title out and into the market place, it doesn't guarantee that it will sell.

What will make it sell is if the consumer perceives value in it. And part of this perception of value is directly related to the title's concept, and the compelling execution of that concept.

With any kind of luck, there ought to be plenty of people out there in the future who are willing to buy quality CD-ROM titles.

The Players

The players within the new media industry can be broken down into the following four categories:

- Artists
- Developers
- Publishers
- Distributors

The Artist

The artist is you, the writer/designer. You are a content provider. In this landscape you have the option to do one, or both, of the following:

- You can conceptualize new titles from either your own ideas, or from other intellectual properties that you have access to, and script/design these projects out fully—all the way through to gold master (the final CD-ROM disc from which all others will be copied).
- You can become a "for hire" writer who is brought in to write a script from somebody else's concept—generally after much of the initial design work is done. You can also be brought in to write additional scenes or dialogue, write instructional boxes, manuals, or fix somebody else's writing.

As a creator of new title ideas, you'll probably get greater control (and even satisfaction) over your artistic life, as well as a bigger share of the financial pie. Being a writer for hire can also be fun, educational, and even remunerative if you luck out with the right project.

The Developer

A multimedia developer is very much like an independent production house in the film world. The developer is responsible for physically making the CD-ROM title—taking the original concept and turning it into a gold master.

How They Do It

A developer makes money in two ways:

- As a "for hire" shop, where publishers contract them to develop and physically make the title
- On their own in-house CD-ROM title line—where the developer usually finds a publisher to take these in-house titles to market

A developer usually has a permanent staff of people, which may include producers, programmers, art directors and animators. In general, they also have a lot of computer equipment to help get the job done.

Where You Fit In

As a writer/designer you can be hired by a developer for a specific writing assignment (i.e., writing a script, writing dialogue, etc.), or you can pitch the developer a title concept they might be willing to put the money up to make. If they like your idea, but they don't want to fund it themselves, they may help you find a publisher who will provide the financing. Developers and publishers tend to have strong ties in this way.

If you pitch a title concept to a developer and they like it, but they don't want to fund it, "or" help you find funding, they might just hire you as writer/designer on one of their own projects.

Screen and multimedia writer Carolynn Miller says this about pitching projects to developers, "...it's not just that we're trying to sell the project—we're also trying to sell ourselves, and we're also learning as we're doing it."

The Publisher

A multimedia publisher for the most part is exactly like a print publisher, and many big print publishing houses now have multimedia divisions. Hollywood studios have also jumped onto the multimedia band wagon, because it's one more way in which they can exploit the intellectual properties they already own. Disney's *The Lion King* CD-ROM for example.

Their Thing

A publisher's responsibility is to press, package and market the title. It is their responsibility to get the product out into the market place, and to make sure the consumer knows that it's there. A publisher is also a place where you can go to pitch a title concept.

Your Opportunity

If they like your idea, want to put it into development, and you don't have your own development team, they will most likely hook you up with a developer they have worked with before who has a proven track record.

If the publisher really likes your concept, but doesn't want to fund it for some reason, they may recommend you as a writer/designer on another project they are developing.

The Distributor

It's probably not an overstatement to say that without the distributors, there wouldn't be much of a CD-ROM industry. You can create the world's best CD-ROM title, but if you can't get it to market, what good is it?

Bearing the Burden of Risk

Joanna Tamer writes in *Emerging Distribution Models for Consumer Interactive Media,* Apple Computer Inc., 1994, "The role of any distributor is to

Bearing the Burden of Risk (continued)

warehouse and ship products to retailers and to serve as the 'banker' in collecting receivables from major chains and a vast array of smaller, independent retailers. The distributor carries the credit burden, administers the infrastructure for invoicing and collecting receivables from the channels, and pays the publisher 60 days after receipt of goods, although it may take the distributor 90 to 120 days to collect.

"Distributors risk bad debts from retailers."

Distributors will usually place products in the following outlets:

- mass merchants and discounters
- software retail stores
- consumer electronic stores
- office and warehouse stores
- superstores
- video rental stores
- music stores
- book stores

In the film world you can often look to a distributor to provide advance funding for a film based on a screenplay, and the commitment of lead actors and a director to the project. In the multimedia world, distributors will not even discuss the idea of an advance—at least not today, anyway.

As the CD-ROM market matures, it would not be surprising to find that distributors are advancing money to independent developers on certain hit guarantee titles—"Myst II" type projects, for example.

Putting It All Together

Kim Bogan, editor/publisher of *The Interactive Multimedia Source Book,* says that the 1995 edition lists 1,285 developers, 448 publishers, and 55 distributors. So as you can see, between the developers and the publishers there are a lot of places out there to pitch title concepts.

It should also be mentioned that some developers are also distributors—Electronic Arts, for instance. Other developers bypass a publisher altogether and deal directly with a distributor. And some of the larger publishers have their own distribution divisions entirely.

It's all enough to make your head spin at first glance, but easy enough to figure out with a bit of study.

The Distribution Cycle

Maybe it should be called the "cycle of the beast," but a little knowledge of the retail cycle can be very helpful in planning your title pitch strategies. The Consumer Market Cycle Calendar, shown here, gives you a good idea of the phases of development a title has to go through in order to reach the market place.

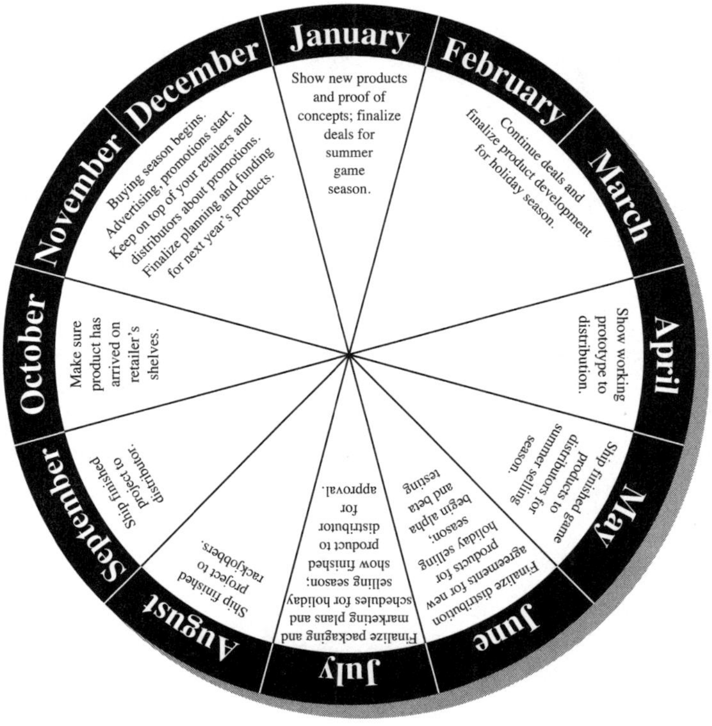

Consumer Market Cycle Calendar

Courtesy of Joanna Tamer and Apple Computer

Tis the Season

Key time points on the calendar are:

- **January**—title funding must be in place
- **February**—title development must begin
- **April**—title prototype ready to show buyers

Like in the film industry, there is a summer release season, as well as the Christmas release season. During the summer, games and products targeted for children out of school are often released. At Christmas time, the products tend to be more general in nature.

> **Joanna Tamer writes in "Emerging Distribution Models for Consumer Interactive Media," Apple Computer Inc., 1994, "as the market broadens and the channels become more efficient, titles will be released on a year-round basis more like records and books."**

If You're Naughty or Nice

In the not too distant future, in hand full of years or less, the channels of distribution will be broad enough that you can walk into any bookstore, go to any section that your heart desires—fiction, history, psychology, gardening, or what not—and find a CD-ROM title specifically created for that genre. This is potentially a CD-ROM writer/designer's dream come true.

> **Somebody is going to have to make a product to fill this obvious great need, and it might as well be you.**

The Title Chase

If you walk into a store that sells CD-ROM titles, you're usually confronted with a lot of big boxes that have a lot of writing and pictures on them. At first glance this all seems a little confusing, but these titles can usually be broken down into a few major categories.

Walker & Associates, a marketing firm who maintains a CD-ROM title database, has identified the following categories:

- **Edutainment**—these are mostly children's titles that teach learning skills in an entertaining manner. Remember how you learned your ABC's by singing them? If you make learning fun, kids will pick up on the material. Examples would be Broderbund Software, Inc.'s *Just Grandma and Me,* and Davidson & Associates *Math Blaster: In Search of Spot.*
- **Infotainment**—these are learning titles for adults, and are usually related to things that adults do, such as hobbies or self-improvement. Two examples are: Moon Valley Software's *ESPN Sports Shorts,* and Computer Directions' *Fitness Partner.*
- **Games**—these are titles presenting pure entertainment, like Virgin Interactive Entertainment's *7th Guest,* and Mindscape/Software Tools' *MegaRace.*
- **Reference**—dictionaries, encyclopedias and databases like ZCI Publishing's *Dictionary of Crime,* and Compton's New Media's *Compton's Interactive Encyclopedia.*
- **Education**—these are often titles that promise to teach you something like a foreign language or all about a science. Examples are Voyager Company's *Poetry in Motion,* and Applied Optical Media Corp.'s *Language Discovery.*
- **Business**—these are general titles that can help you with a business (word processing, spread sheet, and data base programs like Claris' *FileMakerPro* and Microsoft's *Word*) or specific titles that show you how set up a small business and prepare your own taxes.
- **Adult**—these can be "spice" or X-rated titles. Examples would perhaps be something like: *Belinda Does Dallas in High Heels* or *Will Donny Rhythm for You Tonight?*
- **Clip n' Graphics**—this is clip art (graphic art, sound, or photographs) that often may be used in your own projects for the price of buying the CD-ROM. Examples are: Interactive Publishing's *250 of the World's Greatest Music Clips,* and Aris Entertainment *Media Clips: Deep Voyage.*

As the distribution channels open up, the big CD-ROM boxes we're seeing today are probably going to go away, and CD-ROM titles will be sold just like their CD music brothers—in jewel cases only. Before too long, retailers simply may not have the space to accommodate the larger packaging.

CHAPTER 3

The Creative Concept

"SMART QUOTE"

"I think that there will be a time when you do an interactive movie, and nobody questions why it's interactive and the choices come up and people make their choices."

Michael Kaplan—co-creator/screenwriter, *Psychic Detective*

First off, let me start out with a little story. In the past year or so, while foot-dancing my way through many conversations with multimedia producers over lunches, dinners, in hallways and at conferences, I've heard horror story upon horror story from many of them, who, upon interviewing writers for a job, have discovered that these writers:

- Were totally ignorant of what titles were on the market
- Have played *Myst* and want to do something just like it

If you want to write a children's title, play children's titles. If you want to develop a game, play games. If you want to create a data-base title around all the dates you and every member of your college senior class have experienced in the past five, ten or twenty years, familiarize yourself with some data-based CD-ROMs.

If you think you'd like to be a serious writer/designer for the multimedia industry, in particular, for CD-ROM—please do yourself a favor and play the things. And playing "Myst" a couple of times doesn't count.

It only makes sense, because doing this kind of preliminary leg work might just make you realize that you're not cut out for this kind of writing.

Where Ideas Come From

Walt Whitman in *The Song of Myself* wrote, "I am wide, I contain multitudes." Take Walt's advice to heart. Yourself contains you—your past, your present, your likes and dislikes. Your passions, your fears, your loves and delights. The things that make you cry, or laugh, or make you get mad and want to jump up and down and say "NO MORE, DAMN YOU!" These are the things you want to write and create about. These are the things that mean something to you.

Ideas, for the most part, are about ten cents a dozen, and there are two places to find them: look at yourself, or look at the universe around you.

You Know You

Ray Bradbury in his essay on the creative process *Run Fast, Stand Still...* (*Zen in the Art of Writing, Essays on Creativity* by Ray Bradbury, Capra Press, 1990) tells how he had this habit of making lists of titles. He didn't worry about writing the story or anything; he just kept making lists—lists of all sorts of things that touched a core in his soul.

The Lake
The Night
The Crickets
The Ravine
The Attic
The Basement
The Baby
The Crowd
The Night Train

These simple words raked across his heart and mind, evoking deep memories and powerful sense impressions. Eventually some of these titles—even after a long time—became the catalyst for a number of his best short stories.

Know thyself. A healthy exercise is to look in the mirror each morning and really see who's staring back.

Through the Looking Glass

And if suddenly you find you've exhausted all of your "you" possibilities, then just turn your attention to the universe outside the front door. It's a big world out there: Huge, amazing, complex and horrifying too.

Turn on CNN and run for cover. Drive out of town at night and look up at the stars. Go to Paris and see the tower where they kept Marie Antoinette before they confiscated her head. Touch the Pyramids. Wander out to the desert and look for mushrooms or UFOs. Sail the wine-dark seas and wonder what the mid-oceanic ridges look like.

Ideas abound, and sometimes they even run up and bite you on the leg when you're not looking.

From First Lie to First Love

Here's an example of how a CD-ROM title idea came to be.

Last winter I was in Paris for a few weeks and rather blue because things were not going well—my career (what else?), money, love, you name it. There seemed to be a gray cloud over everything. I decided to escape to Amsterdam for the weekend. I wanted to get away and think, get away and come up with an idea for either a new screenplay or multimedia project. On the Friday afternoon train to Amsterdam, working my way through a bottle of wine, I kept thinking about lies, and about betrayals. About how we all lie, about how some people seem to lie more than others. And suddenly I was determined to make this my new theme. Perfect. I was going to explore the process of lying from cradle to grave—prove to myself, once and for all, that we were all born either liars, or poets.

I entitled my new project: *The First Lie.*

As you can tell I was in a pretty sober mood. Paris, the movable feast that it is, does that to you sometimes.

Well, I spent the weekend in Amsterdam, wandering the museums, haunting the bars and clubs, absolutely convinced that I was onto something with my "The First Lie" project. I had great plans for it. I still wasn't certain if it was going to be a film or a multimedia project, or what, but it didn't matter. I could see the Armani line of T-shirts and coffee mugs already. I could even see a line of talking male and female dolls that told a little white lie every time you pulled the string. How could I miss?

On Sunday I left Amsterdam and trained back to Paris. The next day I flew home to Los Angeles. My first night back I walked into a dear friend's apartment and she pushed a book under my nose: "Here, take a look at this." I looked, and the earth moved beneath my feet.

No joke.

It was a beautiful book cover, and across the top the title read: *The First Love Stories* by Diane Wolkstein. And I knew instantly that this was to be my next

From First Lie to First Love (continued)

project, and it was to be done in multimedia. *The First Love Stories* contained seven short stories based on the first love myths from seven world cultures—Shiva and Sati from India; Psyche and Eros, Greco-Roman; Tristan and Iseult, Celtic-European; and more. They were shocking and mysterious tales—joyous, humorous and ribald too. Very good adult material.

And my instincts said multimedia, not linear film, because there were too many levels to explore. Lawrence Durrell wrote in *The Alexandria Quartet*, "Love. Four letters, each letter contains volumes."

I wanted to get these love stories out from the pages of the book, and I didn't want to be limited in the presentation of them. I also felt strongly that a user would be compelled to explore them in an interactive fashion because the experience would illuminate so much about themselves. Love, after all, is an immersive experience.

So from the "first lie" to the "first love" I went. Life is strange that way.

To end this story, I called up author Diana Wolkstein, told her what I wanted to do, received her permission, put a creative team together, and the rest is history. Further along in the next chapter is a copy of the "Walking Paper" developed to pitch *The First Love Stories* project. Take a look at it.

Yours versus Theirs

In general, there are two kinds of ideas—your own, or somebody else's. So let's stop for a moment and briefly discuss the pros and cons of whether it's better to come up with your own ideas, or license the other guy's intellectual properties.

Protecting Your Intellectual Property

Robert Cohen, former Vice President of business affairs for Harmony Gold, a film production and distribution company in Los Angeles, says this about intellectual properties: "Because of the nature of an intellectual property, there is no good definition of an intellectual property. However, it is frequently considered to be an expression of the mind." This expression can take the form of a stage play, a screenplay, a musical score, a photograph, a work of graphic art, *or* a multimedia concept.

Mr. Cohen further comments, "...society has determined that through trade and commerce, additional intellectual property rights are created, hence trademark." Trademark, in essence, is the proprietary interest in something that is sold or traded. "Not only has society created the concept of trademark," Mr. Cohen continues, "but it has also created the protection of intellectual property through copyright and trademark registration."

Here are a few ways you can protect yourself:

- *Federal Copyright:* You can copyright your intellectual property with the federal government by filling out the proper form and sending an original to Washington.
- *Common Law Copyright:* You can also copyright by common law when you send an original copy of your intellectual expression to yourself by registered mail. When the registered envelope arrives, leave it sealed and put it in a safe place. The unopened, registered seal indicates that the material inside was in existence on the date the envelope was mailed, as well as that you claim ownership to the material inside. In order to enforce a copyright, however, your intellectual property must be registered with the Federal government.
- *Writers Guild Registration:* Writers Guild of America, west, in Los Angeles has a literary intellectual property registration service. For a fee, a copy of your literary property will be sealed in an official Guild Registration Envelope, time-dated, and placed in a vault. Your time-dated receipt has a registration number on it that you can put on the title page of your property. According to the Writers Guild of America, west handbook, "Registration does not confer any statutory protection. It merely provides evidence of the writer's claim to authorship of the literary material involved and of the date of its completion." You don't have to be a member of the guild to use the service, and it's relatively fast and inexpensive.

Protecting Your Intellectual Property (continued)

- *The Paper Trail:* In addition, if you have a lawyer or an agent, you may also protect your ideas by creating a paper trail with them. Send them copies of your treatment/documentation, have them date stamp it and put it in your file. This again establishes your authorship and a date of completion for the work.

The point of all of this is: If you want to use someone's expression of mind, provided it's protected, you have to seek their approval, and when they grant you approval, you have to work out some kind of licensing agreement. Licensing agreements are too complex and confusing to go into here, so if you're interested, see your lawyer or an expert on the subject. And remember, the above discussion is for the United States only. Copyright and author's rights in Europe and the rest of the world can fill another book.

Your Own Pro and Con

Your own ideas are the expressions of your mind, and if you write them down and get them out into the light of the world you can copyright them. It doesn't cost you much initially to develop your own ideas, and you don't have to go through the time and money hassles it usually takes to license the other guy's stuff.

On the down side, if you're not a high profile name—famous author, actor, real estate developer, or whatever—your concept will not have a built-in audience. Developers and publishers like built-in audiences, because, based on prior famous-name hooks, they can usually anticipate a certain level of sales. Of course, having a brand name attached to a project is no guarantee for success in the market place. Just look at some of the titles that were built around rock stars over the past few years. A number of them only sold a handful of copies.

It doesn't take a rocket scientist to see that lack of sales is often directly related to the lame interactive concepts used in the products. Consumers tend to shy away from shovelware.

If you don't have any multimedia credits, developers and publishers will give great pause when thinking about buying your ideas. Your concept will have to be dead-on good to get in the door. This problem, however, can be mitigated somewhat if you team up with other people who do have credits. See the section in the next chapter about putting your creative team together.

The Other Wise Guy's

Some one else's idea may already be well formed and a proven concept in the marketplace. If the property has worked, then it probably has brand name recognition. Once again, developers and publishers like this. Just take a look at the success of Dr. Seuss and Richard Scary books. Popular books have large audiences, and these audiences seem perfectly happy crossing over into the land of CD-ROM.

When you add a multimedia dimension to a popular, well executed product, it can greatly enhance the linear experience. Consumers perceive this as value and are willing to pay for it.

The cost to obtain an intellectual property can be quite high, however, and legal and licensing fees can quickly break your bank. Any one, or any entity, who has title to an intellectual property has heard all about computers and the fabulous super information highway by now, so rest assured, they know the value of their material. Of course, if you are a deep-pocketed publisher or developer, you simply pay the price and get on with it. If you come up with a good product, you'll probably make some money in the end.

Where brand name intellectual properties don't seem to work too well is when a feature film is turned into a CD-ROM. Here again, a big problem seems to be in interactive execution. It is simply not enough to show clips from a film and then dump the player into some lame interactive arcade game. That's cheating.

If a studio wants to create an interactive experience based on a movie, it obviously makes sense to go back to the core movie concept, and take a fresh approach to things.

Ghetto Opinions Abound

Propaganda Code and Sony Imagesoft developed a super new engine for the *Johnny Mnemonic* CD-ROM. The script was written from ground zero, they shot their own footage, and they didn't use any clips from the original film. Sounds like a formula for success. Well, maybe.

I was yaking with a *tres* serious gamer the other day and brought the *Johnny Mnemonic* CD-ROM up. I had seen it in development before it hit the market, and I kind of thought it might be a gamer's delight. When I asked him if he had played it, I was surprised when he responded rather firmly that no, he hadn't, nor would he ever play it. I gave him a look and explored further. I told him about its really cool interface, how they shot their own footage and didn't use any clips from the movie either. "Won't you even give it a try?" I asked. "No," came his now very terse reply, "I don't play games based on Hollywood movies."

Everybody's got an opinion, but this opinion I hadn't really heard before. Staying away from something because of the perceived media hype surrounding it? Yeah. I suppose. I've done it myself lots of times with movies, plays, and concerts. Would I do the same thing for a CD-ROM? Probably. And will this kind of attitude stop Hollywood from making interactive stuff from movie material? Probably not—just look at the sales of *The Lion King* CD-ROM.

A Good Place to Start

If you're just starting off in the field and don't have money to option a property, develop your own ideas first. It's good for you, great practice, and who knows, one of them might even hit. If you do manage to get hold of an intellectual property without mortgaging your first born, absolutely make sure you can explain to a developer or publisher (as well as to yourself) *why* this product should be interactive, and then develop your plan of action accordingly.

Whether it's your own idea or a licensed intellectual property, it's how you execute the concept that ultimately counts.

PART 2

Learning the Basics

CHAPTER 4

Preparing Your Ideas

"SMART QUOTE"

"Our biggest problem was how do you take the best aspects of games, the best aspects of movies, put them together, and get customers from both ends of the spectrum involved?"

John Sanborn—co-creator and director, *Psychic Detective*

For the purpose of the following discussion, let's assume you've developed your own idea and now you want to get it ready for a pitch meeting with a developer or publisher. First off, if you haven't done so already, take your concept and write it out, quickly—every bit of it. Don't hold back. Put down everything you can think of and *don't* talk about it with friends, lover or wife.

Develop your idea into a two or three page rough treatment, and don't worry about such things as getting the interface exactly right, or how many discs it will take, or compression rates, or what kind of royalties you're going to get when it finally reaches the market. Just do it. Once you have the concept down in rough draft—rough, because it most certainly is going to change—then it's time to climb down from your fortress of solitude, and take a look at what's out there on the market.

You need to know what's already on the market, and I can't stress this enough, because there may be half a dozen products already on the shelves just like the title you've created in your rough treatment.

Knowledge Is Power

If you know what's on the market, you can then decide to either abandon your idea and move on to something else, or change it in such a way so that it's unique. Distribution expert Joanna Tamer explains in *Emerging Distribution Models for Consumer Interactive Media,* Apple Computer Inc., 1994, "It is important not to be the third or fourth title similar to other visible titles. Retailers will not tend to take the third product in a given genre (i.e., dinosaurs), much less the fourth, unless the publisher or distributor has enough influence with the retailer to obtain shelf space for the product."

So how do you find out what's out there? Easy. Go look.

Surfing the Marketplace

The obvious places to look for what's already out there are the retailers that sell the stuff and the magazines that are devoted to it. There are also a couple of not-so-obvious places—like on-line forums and marketing services. Let's take a closer look at each of these.

Retail Therapy

Cruise the major retailers—Comp USA, Virgin Mega stores, Egghead Software, and so on—and search for titles that look like your idea. If you find any, read the box, jot down the publisher and developer, the systems requirements, and what the copy says about the concept, paying particular attention to the features listed. The features are important. They give you some idea about the thinking that went into the product. If possible, have the store demo the title for you, and try to get through at least one screen or environment—that's usually enough to give you a sense of what the product is all about.

If the product is close to your concept, buy it and take it home for study. Remember, you'll want somebody else to buy your product someday too, not just demo it!

Clare Munn, producer/writer for San Francisco multimedia developer The Penga Group emphatically declares about this method of gathering information, "Act like a student, spread your papers on the floor and sit down and make notes. And get to know the sales people, buy them coffee, take them to dinner, do anything to get them to demo products for you. And ask them questions about the products too, and listen to what they have to say."

Turning Pages

New media magazines are important. You should certainly read *Wired*, *Multimedia Producer*, *CD-ROM Professional*, *CD-ROM Today*, *Morph's Outpost,* as well as a host of other computer/entertainment/game mags that are out on the newsstands. Some of these magazines are also available on-line. All of them are filled with up-to-date industry information, and many of them contain CD-ROM reviews. *CD-ROM Today* is a good one for reviews, and *Red Herring* does a nice top ten review with each issue that should be part of your reading list.

Cruising magazine reviews will sometimes give you very specific information on the product, and this info can be critical to know if you're developing a similar title.

Additionally, new media magazines are sometimes bundled with a CD-ROM that contains half a dozen title demos. Looking at these demos is a quick and inexpensive way to review a lot of product. Even though the demos are not the full-blown versions of the title, as I mentioned earlier, all you really need to see is one or two screens, or environments, and you can pretty much figure out what the rest of the experience is going to be like.

Going On-Line

Going on-line is a great source of information. Bruce Onder and Jeff Sullivan, the writer/designers for Activision's *The Great Game* CD-ROM title regularly surf the on-line game forums, listening for what's hot, what's not, and why it's hot or not. This helps them see what's good and bad about a core game idea.

"You can see patterns," explains Jeff, "You can see what things should be in a game, and what things should not be in a game. And these are things that are going to divide gamers and non-gamers. And this knowledge helps you decide what to include, or what not include in your game proposal." Important information if you desire a hit title.

Yahoo—I've Found It!

I asked author friend and obsessive net surfer Lauren Deutsch to tell about doing a CD-ROM title search on the internet. Here's her report.

One of the ways people have searched the earth's surface for hidden water sources below the crust is with a divining rod, originally a "Y" shaped piece of tree branch, more recently a metal rod. Lightly held horizontally by the twin branches, if the stem dipped toward the ground, it told you: "Yahoo—dig here!"

The divining rod of the NET is Yahoo too! I connected to this fun search machine via Netscape for info on my latest ROM project on Chinese Medicine. I wanted to know what was out there and in what form. Yahoo can be found at:

http://beta.yahoo.com/docs/info/

At the Yahoo home plate there is a search button, so I double-clicked and I'm now hot on the path of gobs of info. There's a place to type in the key words of the inquiry: CD-ROM. This turned out to be too broad a question—777 matches were found. Then I realized that "chinese medicine" would be a simpler second level search, so I changed the request.

Yahoo—I've Found It! (continued)

At first I didn't pay attention to the string of possibilities and got hundreds of listings of everything from "Chinese" to "medicine." Then I tried the "all keys, a single string" (as per the search engine) typing out "Chinese medicine" versus "Chinese" and "medicine." Pay Dirt! Not only is there info from 6 Chinese medicine sources, but—Ta Da!—there was a CD-ROM.

Yahoo's search page is also an on-ramp to other search engines. Open Text Index netted 102 pages of information (including that CD-ROM) via a simple search with "Chinese medicine" phrase requested. Lycos search (check the options so you can do "and" in your string of key words) gave me 43 hits, but no CD-ROM! Ditto for my search via EINet Galaxy, a net in itself with 2 docs found via Galaxy pages, 1 via World Wide Web, 0 through Hytelnet, and 15 through Gopher. There's another link to "other searchable materials and directories." My ALIWEB search was a bit more personally confusing. I got too far afield in Chinese culture and Western medicine, but I'm sure if I gave it a bit more thought (read: education), I'd be successful.

Good news and bad news? I returned to the one CD-ROM find, clicked on it and was treated to a teasing example (with illustrations), table of contents, and a way to order the CD and other titles. A mad clicking frenzy netted not only an order form, e-mail address and info about the distributor, but other CD-ROM titles which they market.

I will also be rooting through the other finds to see what's new and/or what information they have found. Don't just rely on one resource. No one knows everything, but with the NET we can ultimately find everything that's recorded on it.

Lauren Deutsch

Use It or Lose It

There're a lot of ways to use the on-line services and the internet to search for existing title information. It's real easy to use a host of internet/web search engines like *Internet Sleuth*, *Web Crawler*, *Web Voyager*, etc. to search on a subject. If you're on America On Line, *Redgate* (keyword "Redgate") allows you to search through a database of over 10,000 software products for both the Mac and PC, which include CD-ROM titles. They claim to update this database on a quarterly basis.

If you do pull up a CD-ROM title profile, it's wise to remember this information is usually provided by the developer or publisher.

Develop and Promote It

At this point I also want to throw out, albeit briefly, the concept of using the internet to develop and promote your CD-ROM title idea, with the ultimate aim of getting funding (or being discovered by a Hollywood talent agency like The Spot). Depending on what materials you've created for your concept, you can post these materials for the entire internet to see on various user groups, chat rooms, forums, etc. You can also have your very own home page where you can make it available to a select group of people or, again, the entire world.

Home Is Where the Heart Is

I asked Tony Winders and Alan Wallace of the Interactive Agency, an internet public relations and marketing company based in Los Angeles, for some tips on how to set up a home page to promote a CD-ROM concept.

- *Step one*—Says Tony: "Remember that what you're doing is re-purposing content. You've got your core idea in your head, and maybe down on paper, or in a demo, or slide show, whatever, and now you have to focus it for a home page. What's the short-form of the idea you want to get across, and what graphics and/or demos are you going to use to support it." "And you also have to decide who your target audience is," adds Alan. "Do you want everybody on the internet to see your concept, or do you want your url address [the internet address of the site] to be like a private phone number only given out to publishers and developers?"
- *Step two*—is building the home page. You can do it yourself or hire a professional. "If you're going to go it alone," Alan says, "then you need a web authoring tool, something like Quarterdeck's Webauthor, which you can download free from the internet [www.quarterdeck.com]. Or you can learn html [hypertext markup language], which is a computer language that interfaces between the server, the internet and the user computer. It tells the

Home Is Where the Heart Is (continued)

home page server to pull this graphic and this text and make it all come together on this page so that when somebody dials in they can see it." The cost to professionally build a home page can run anywhere from a few hundred dollars to over a $100,000. "And these expensive jobs," Tony warns, "aren't necessarily any better than the home made ones."

- *Step three*—is to decide where your home page is going to live. The beast needs to be on a server which makes it accessible to the internet 24 hours a day, 7 days a week. "The easiest thing to do," advises Tony, "is use an internet service provider (ISP) like Earthlink or Webpage. For a monthly rate they'll maintain the site on their system, and some of these ISPs will even build you a home page as part of their service."
- *Step four*—is perhaps the most important. "It's not always the case of build it, and they will come," says Alan, "you need to market your own site." "First and foremost," adds Tony, "put your home page address on your business card, letterhead, forehead even, if you want people to know about it." But again, it all depends on the purpose of the site and its target audience. If you only want publishers and developers to see the site, then do your best to get your url in front of them. Ultimately, they're the ones to reach if you're looking for financing.

Joining the Service

If you're serious about determining what's out there, and you don't have the time to commit to any of the above methods, then for a fee, you can always commission a title search from a CD-ROM title database service. You can search by subject, genre, and title category—like reference, games, or edutainment. You can also choose from among consumer, education or business market segments.

If you do manage to get a publisher or developer to fund your title concept, they will most likely do some detailed market research before the title gets put into full development.

Back at the Beginning

In summation, before you do too much work on developing your concept, you should know if there are similar products out there on the market. You can do this easily enough by looking at products in retail stores, reading reviews in magazines, going on-line and searching the game or CD-ROM forums, and/or commissioning a title search from a CD-ROM title database server.

> **The most useful information for you at this point is the name of the company that produced the product, the product description, and the recommended age range of the user. If you think this product is anything like your concept, then you can track it down and view it before developing your title further.**

Putting a Team Together

Once you have developed your concept and determined that it has a place in the market, I strongly suggest you think about teaming up with other members of the creative community. You want to do this because partners can bring important assets to the project that can make the difference between a funder saying yes or no.

> **Putting a creative team together is an important step in preparing your concept for pitching to a funding source.**

Two to Tango

There are any number of combinations of people you can team up with. The following are a few suggestions:

- If you don't have any multimedia credits, team up with a writer/designer who does.
- If your concept has a lot of animation, go find yourself an animator who'd like to be involved with your project.

- If you're an animator with a multimedia concept, but not a good writer, go find yourself a writer to call partner.
- If you're a computer programmer with a dynamite engine and a good set of characters but you can't draw or write to save your life, go find an animator and a writer.
- Programmers and technically oriented people can make good partners.
- Creative directors are priceless to team up with.
- Multimedia producers and business affairs professionals are also a good match.
- People with investment capital can be very nice to dance a tango or two with.

One of the basic themes of Ernest Hemingway's novel *To Have, and Have Not* is "you can't go it alone." As Hemingway's hero lies dying from a bullet wound on the stern of his fishing boat heading out to sea, he comes to the realization that sometimes you need help, sometimes you need people, and that you can't go it alone. It's not much different in the new media business.

Reality Checks

When approaching potential partners, you'll have to convince them that you and your project are something they want to get involved with. If they're even remotely ahead of you on the learning curve, they're probably up to their ears in interactive projects already. So good luck. But if you do convince them to hang out with you, then you'll have to make two immediate mental adjustments:

- You'll probably have to share creative control.
- You'll definitely have to share the almighty financial pie.

Don't get frustrated when you can't find acceptable partners right away, take your time, be thoughtful, "patience" should be the drill sergeant's mantra marching through your mind.

Needless to say you must choose carefully when sharing a table with a partner, or partners. Select people you feel comfortable with, and because they have some artistic, technical or professional skill to bring to the experience.

Doing It Douglas' Way

On *The First Love Stories* project, I didn't have an easy start putting a creative team together. After I received the green light from the author, I knew I didn't want to tackle the project alone, it was too big and complicated, and I was already involved in another project, which was limiting my time. I needed buddies, and I needed them quick.

I spent three, maybe four months waving the book at different people. Finally, I settled on my first team member, a producer-type—our mutual excitement was high, we were determined to get this project done. Soon, however, after two or three months of very little action, I realized my producer-type was over-extended with other projects, and wasn't going to work out. We parted on friendly terms and I started up the search again.

Soon I found myself a co-writer/designer. This writer then brought in a high profile new media pro who would act as executive producer. We all three settled on a small multimedia design firm called *Omnivore,* located in Long Beach, California, which had four brilliant creative-types as part of the furniture—a programmer, a poet/creative director/designer, business manager, and a sound artist. Two of these folks also doubled as composers and musicians.

So between my co-writer/designer, the new media pro as executive producer, and now these ladies and guys, the book *The First Love Stories* by Diane Wolkstein had a powerhouse interactive creative team as its driving force. Talk about synergy.

Partnering Up

As you become more familiar with the new media industry, you'll realize why the ancient Greeks rambled on about: "As above, so below." This concept is definitely part of the emerging media landscape. All manner of media companies, from film studios to telephone giants, are making all sorts of strategic alliances, and the only way for you as a creative-type to survive in this game is to probably team up too.

In the end, only you can decide if you want to, or need to, team up with someone.

Keeping It Clean

A year or two back, when the new media was first getting up a good head of steam, I saw a live modern dance performance thematically based on the paintings of Grandma Moses. At the same time I was also having discussions with a computer programmer who was developing some interesting ideas about neural networks, and how if one developed a neural network kernal at the heart of a game or CD-ROM title, you could do some pretty interesting things that gave the appearance of artificial intelligence.

Cool stuff.

Long story short, I brought the choreographer, Loretta Livingston, and her dancers together with the programmer and we were going to create a CD-ROM title that would allow a user to create a "convivial interactive dance theater piece." Our plan was to do a lot of video taping of the dancers, breaking their movements and body parts down into discreet packets of motion and form, and use a neural network kernel to reconstruct them on the fly to the whim of the user.

We developed a twenty page proposal, took some meetings, shipped the proposal around to potential publishers, and we got a range of responses from blank stares to "this is brilliant, but I don't know what to do with it." The cautionary upshot comes from screen and interactive writer Larry Tuch: "You're always a little too late, or a little too early. By the time your product is done the technical envelope has moved on—and it's too early because the market isn't there yet. It's a problem."

So how do you handle this seemingly paradoxical situation of wanting to push the envelope but not daring because it's not time yet, because if you're not on the edge, nobody's going to look at you? Simple: Keep clean, keep your head down, and keep moving in the direction you want. You and the market will converge sooner or later.

Documenting Your Pitch

Once you've come up with a concept, determined it has market value, and put together your creative team, it's time to start doing some serious paperwork. Everybody has their own way of doing it. Here's what some the most successful people in the industry have to say about it.

I have been assured many times that there are many roads to heaven, and I believe—after much talking to pros in the new media industry—the same idea holds true for styles of pitching and documenting interactive products.

Joey's Way

Multimedia consultant Joanna Tamer succinctly points out that you would pitch a multimedia project the way you would pitch an independent film project. "Traditionally, the creative walks in and says, here's my concept, here's my genre, here's my story board, here's a leave behind treatment."

The Reel Won't Do It

John Sanborn—co-creator and the director of *Psychic Detective,* which is deconstructed in Part Three of this book—says, "I don't know what makes a successful pitch. The only thing I can say about getting new projects made is that never in my history has my reel ever gotten me a job. I think it's my ideas, my personal presence, my perceived history as a creative person that's done the trick. My reel's too idiosyncratic, it's not fashionable, it's not this, or it's not that. In terms of interactive pitching, the best calling card Michael [Michael Kaplan, screenwriter and co-creator of *Psychic Detective*] and I have is *Psychic Detective.* If we show it, they know we've got the goods. They know we've done something different."

Carolynn's Collage

Screen and multimedia writer Carolynn Miller explains her method for pitching an interactive project: "My writing partner and I just recently put together a proposal and we've been having a lot of success taking it around. It's just on paper. We did visuals with it. It's not a prototype. There's nothing that actually moves."

Carolynn's document is about twenty pages long and uses big type and "a lot of white space." She and her partner believe that the fewer the words, the better. They have a cover page that outlines the concept, another page that talks about what the user would see first when entering the environment, and what the experience is like being in there. They also talk about the interactivity. "And we have visuals of the main screen we did by cutting pictures out of magazines and making montages," adds Carolynn.

Carolynn Miller says that one of the reasons she can get away with a paper presentation and not a prototype of some kind, is that her credentials, and those of her partner, are pretty substantial, "If we had not had those kinds of credits, we would have needed something more."

As their concept is actually for a series of four discs (four separate products) with a character that links the discs together, they have specific, one-page descriptions of each disc. They also include a matrix figure showing some of the branching possibilities, and a four or five page sample script that shows the interactivity. "If you click on this, this happens, or this dialogue is said," Carolynn comments. "It just gives people a pretty good idea of what it might be like to negotiate through one path of it."

Bruce and Jeff's Excellent Approach

Writer/designers Bruce Onder and Jeff Sullivan's initial pitch-document is often a very comprehensive piece that covers every aspect of the product. "We do what some people call a loose spec of the game," Jeff explains, "we talk about how the interface is going to work, the story line, the characters, we give examples of how the characters work—how the game works without giving it all away. A lot of times it's about fifty pages."

The bottom line with Bruce and Jeff is that if whoever they are pitching to gets what they're trying to do right away, they know they're in for an easier time.

Bruce and Jeff include marketing and business matters, too, like budgets. They try to cover every question that someone would have about the product, at some level or another of detail. Jeff adds, "since this is only a proposal, but a fairly detailed one, it's more than a pitch—but less than handing them a spec document and saying here, produce this, please."

They often work with artists too, sketching out characters or interface art where appropriate. "A picture is certainly worth a thousand words. Describing a simple four face button control that follows you around gets very complex if you tell about it—but if you show it, it's like 'Oh, I get it.'"

Appendix A in the back of this book includes a portion of a pitch document Bruce and Jeff prepared for a game project called "deusX: Ghost in the Machine". An overview explains The Story, The World, The Characters, The Backstory, The Look and Sound, and The Interface. A script segment gives you a real good idea of how you would go about putting a game concept down on paper.

For the Rest of Us

As we have seen, Carolynn, Bruce and Jeff use paper documents for initial pitch meetings. They don't feel it's necessary to make a more elaborate multimedia presentation, but they have serious credentials and perhaps can get away with less.

Other writer/designers create slide shows. These contain basically the same material as a paper treatment, text and visuals. Instead of a paper medium, however, everything gets put on a floppy disk so it can be played on a computer to simulate the CD-ROM experience. Still others go full out and use an authoring tool like Director or Authorware to create a multimedia presentation many times more elaborate than a slide show, with hot spots where point and click interactivity can take place.

The Walking Paper

In *The First Love Stories* project, the creative team decided that initially two documents were needed to sell the concept:

- A two page "walking paper" (see *The First Love Stories* shown here in sidebar format)
- A longer treatment version with visuals

The First Love Stories

Once there was a time before love;
then, love begins...

So begins Diane Wolkstein's retelling of some of the world's most famous tales of romantic love: of Tristan and Iseult, Psyche and Eros, Isis and Osiris, King Solomon's Song of Songs.

In soaring prose and poetry, Wolkstein retells tales of sacrifice and obsession that fired the imagination of ancient peoples, just as they touch on our attempts to find and keep love today. They are perfect source material for the next wave of CD-ROM development, that which takes us beyond games and encyclopedias into a true exploration of "*multi* media."

We propose to take Wolkstein's stories—the Song of Songs certainly, probably Tristan and Iseult and some Native American legend to begin—and re-create them in a melange of sound, images, and interactive options that is immediate, compelling and erotic.

This is a rich, sensual experience. While the stories can be approached directly (with well researched sidebars into the history and context of each), archetypal tales like these deserve more.

As with love itself, the primary experience is one of *immersion.*

Voices matched to each story wash over the user in a tumble of words. Behind them like a whisper is the story in the original language. Behind that are the sounds of ancient cultures: the street, the market, the battleground, the bed.

Original music—whether modern or the recreation of some ancient sound—runs through each story, unifying and enriching it. The screen is fluid: fragments of text highlighted like images surfacing from a pool, color itself that shifts with the mood, video that highlights rather than chronicles—a piece of clothing dropped, the texture of a lover's skin, the arch of a neck, the tautness of a bare back.

In this celebration of transcendent love, the interactivity is more than just hypertext. It's emotional and psychological. The user will be able to influence the design and flow of sound and images for a playback that, like a love poem, can be a gift from the user to another.

Diane Wolkstein is one of America's premier story tellers. We want to bring her tumble of words and images to CD-ROM, to capture in other media the art Wolkstein brings to her work.

The First Love Stories (continued)

But a CD-ROM on a PC is, well, personal. On a PC this title should be intriguing, the first love stories blended with the first music delivered through our highest technology. But consider the television monitors of the emerging settop market. A settop begs for two or more participants. "Love Stories" is a product at its best when *shared.*

We believe that *The First Love Stories* is not just compelling art, but strongly commercial as well. To maximize the commercial possibilities, the title will be designed for easy internationalization. To control development costs and for ease in porting the program across platforms, we intend to make this series of titles using available tools. Properly marketed into the right channels, this title can be extremely successful.

How It Happens

The First Love Stories walking paper is an excellent example of creative team effort, or why you can't really go it alone in this business sometimes. Once a decision was made to produce this piece, I was only able to write down the key points (because I was in the middle of doing something else). Co-writer/designer Lonon Smith provided the rather good prose, myself and the rest of the gang reviewed what he wrote—adding, of course, our own three cents worth of constructive this or that—and then Lonon quickly made the necessary changes. So with a minimum of collective effort, we had what we needed.

The "walking paper" is simply an overview of the concept—short and engaging, something a busy executive can read in a matter of minutes and "get" what you're trying to do. In the television and film industry, a walking paper is sometimes called a "leave behind."

Why You Need One

The advantages of having a walking paper are multifold:

- It can be easily faxed or emailed to a developer or publisher prior to a pitch meeting so they are prepared for the concept you're coming in with.
- In *The First Love Stories* case, the source material was a book, so we could also send the book to prospective funders with the walking paper attached.
- You can leave the walking paper behind for a post-pitch review by the publisher, and any of their staff who weren't able to attend the meeting.

The longer treatment version, with visuals, is the document you would actually bring to a pitch meeting, and talk through with the publisher.

Prototypes and Demos

Prototype, (sometimes known as *proof of concept*) and *demo* are two other terms you'll also hear thrown about on the multimedia street. In many cases these terms are applied to title concepts that have been put into some form of development. For instance, you've pitched your concept with a treatment and visuals, and the publisher says "Yes, we like it. Here's some money, go build a prototype."

A prototype is usually about 2 or 3 minutes long, and it shows the main interface and at least one screen (or scene) that illustrates your basic interactivity. It can have music and/or a sound score. A prototype shows the aesthetics of your concept and the visuals that you pitched in your treatment. It also proves that you can make it. Along with the prototype, the publisher will want a budget of what it will take to get the concept through to a gold master.

If the publisher likes the prototype, they will probably fund you to the next stage—the demo. A demo is usually about 5 or 6 minutes and involves an entire environment (chapter) in which all of the interactivity is shown, and one or two main characters are fully drawn out. If the demo is successful, you'll probably receive full funding for the project.

Prototypes and Demos (continued)

Some creative teams will go ahead and create a prototype, or even a full demo, and use it as a pitch piece, not even bothering with a paper treatment. When executive producer/designer Roger Holtzberg pitched *Pyramid* to the Knowledge Adventure staff (one of the deconstructed titles in the Third Part of this book), he made a three foot high model of a pyramid, complete with pull-out ramps revealing seven storyboards that represented the seven levels of the game. Roger is also rather famous (infamous?) for hiring actors, with full makeup and costume, and taking them into a pitch meeting to make his point.

What to Make and Take

There may be many roads to heaven, but, usually, there are three basic types of pitch documents you need to find funding for your title:

- A "walking paper," or "leave behind"
- A treatment, with visuals
- A floppy disk slide show, authoring ware produced prototype, or demo

Bits and Pieces

There are a few essential elements you need to have in your pitch documents in order to make them winners. Most of these elements are obvious, a few of them are less so, some of them may be done with the written word, and others with audio or visual aids. Here's the basic checklist:

- Title page, listing principle artists
- Overview of the concept, probably with branching diagrams
- Who the target audience is
- Marketing data, if available
- The aesthetic—the look, the tone, and the feel
- Story line
- Brief character descriptions of major characters
- Role of the user
- What the interface is like, non-gender specific if applicable
- Types of interactivity

- How the game play works without giving it away
- What the music and ambient sound is like
- What technology will be used
- On-line components, if any
- Brief bios of principle artists

Buzz Words and Other Business

The following are some important suggestions and key buzz words that should at some point be included in your documentation:

More Better Titles: Figure out a way to make a series of titles, three at least, from your concept, and pitch it that way. Use a theme, or a main character to tie the discs together. *The First Love Stories* project has a disc (a separate product) being made from each story in the book. The cost to make the first title will be higher than the cost on subsequent titles because of two things: a) the first title is a start-up operation, and, b) the first titles' budget includes the price of the engine, which contains all the programming code that makes the title work. Developing an engine, or any other programming features for that matter, is expensive. Once you have paid for all of this, you'll want to make use of it again.

Pitch on a Plate: If your concept is applicable to multiple forms—which means if your CD-ROM title can also be a comic book, a cartoon or sitcom TV show, a movie, a book, a play, or if any of the main characters can be put on lunch boxes, or sold on T-shirts or shower curtains—then it should be presented and pitched that way. As Joanna Tamer reminds us, "The new media industry is very familiar with the concept of cross marketing of ideas. This is a plus for your project."

Downloadable Doom: Plan to produce a "light" or modular version for marketing purposes—in addition to the full version. Marketer Becki Walker, of Walker & Associates, insists, "you should be able to pull some of the artwork out, as well as some of the puzzles—so you can download them over the internet. And make sure your characters have strong personalities. If they have that, then you can clearly and easily create brand identity."

Slang-Free in Sweden: Mention that you will prepare your title for the international market place, meaning you will take care to avoid slang and obscure cultural references. And that the product will be designed and coded with modular language strings for easy insertion of foreign languages.

More Bang for Your Buck: If you talk about budget, try to keep the costs down. Don't attach an unrealistic price to your title, or publishers won't touch it.

Marketing Matters: If you have professional marketing data available, use it wisely in your presentation, and try not to let it seem like it's driving your core concept.

By Way of Example: Look at *The First Love Stories* walking paper and you'll see that a number of the previously discussed items are covered, albeit briefly, in a word or sentence or two, but they are addressed. The treatment is where you can elaborate on them. Additionally, carefully go through Jeff Sullivan and Bruce Onder's overview from their *deusX: Ghost in the Machine* proposal (see Appendix A at the back of the book). Here too, a number of the items we've been discussing have been elegantly woven into their document.

Passionately Talking Giraffes

To elaborate a bit on marketing issues, I did an interview for an interactive writing assignment recently, and during the interview I asked a question about what kind of characters where being envisioned. I was immediately barraged with a mound of marketing surveys that clearly showed to the executive in charge that consumers preferred talking giraffes over talking elephants 10 to 1. So we're going to use giraffes, she said, smiling.

I think I looked baffled. Giraffes. Yeah, I suppose. At least in that survey. Ultimately, and what this executive sort of forgot, I guess, is that it's the passion at the heart of the concept and its execution that really counts. If the core idea has a seriously huge elephant wearing a tutu dancing over daisies to classical music—well, why change it to a giraffe because of a marketing survey?

In other words, use your marketing data to support your concept, not batter it into an ugly stepchild that no longer looks like the fair-haired concept you began with.

Going with the Flow

For completion, so that you can get a look at how an interactive title can be presented in a flow-chart diagram, I have included one from *The First Love Stories* project.

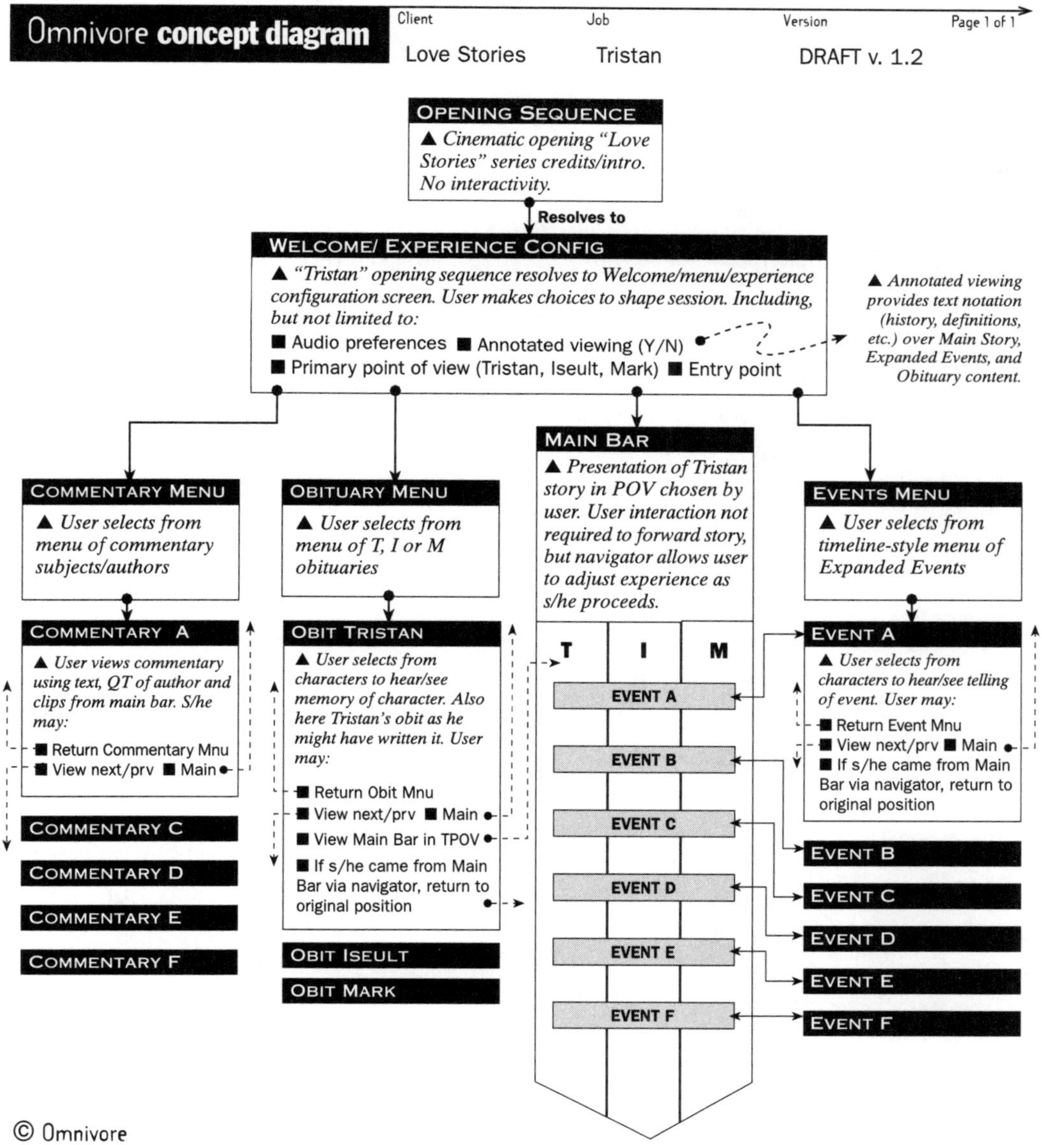
Omnivore concept diagram
Client
Love Stories
Job
Tristan
Version
DRAFT v. 1.2
Page 1 of 1
OPENING SEQUENCE
▲ Cinematic opening "Love Stories" series credits/intro. No interactivity.
Resolves to
WELCOME/ EXPERIENCE CONFIG
▲ "Tristan" opening sequence resolves to Welcome/menu/experience configuration screen. User makes choices to shape session. Including, but not limited to:
■ Audio preferences ■ Annotated viewing (Y/N)
■ Primary point of view (Tristan, Iseult, Mark) ■ Entry point
▲ Annotated viewing provides text notation (history, definitions, etc.) over Main Story, Expanded Events, and Obituary content.
COMMENTARY MENU
▲ User selects from menu of commentary subjects/authors
COMMENTARY A
▲ User views commentary using text, QT of author and clips from main bar. S/he may:
■ Return Commentary Mnu
■ View next/prv ■ Main
COMMENTARY C
COMMENTARY D
COMMENTARY E
COMMENTARY F
OBITUARY MENU
▲ User selects from menu of T, I or M obituaries
OBIT TRISTAN
▲ User selects from characters to hear/see memory of character. Also here Tristan's obit as he might have written it. User may:
■ Return Obit Mnu
■ View next/prv ■ Main
■ View Main Bar in TPOV
■ If s/he came from Main Bar via navigator, return to original position
OBIT ISEULT
OBIT MARK
MAIN BAR
▲ Presentation of Tristan story in POV chosen by user. User interaction not required to forward story, but navigator allows user to adjust experience as s/he proceeds.
T
I
M
EVENT A
EVENT B
EVENT C
EVENT D
EVENT E
EVENT F
EVENTS MENU
▲ User selects from timeline-style menu of Expanded Events
EVENT A
▲ User selects from characters to hear/see telling of event. User may:
■ Return Event Mnu
■ View next/prv ■ Main
■ If s/he came from Main Bar via navigator, return to original position
EVENT B
EVENT C
EVENT D
EVENT E
EVENT F

This was done by Kate Cohen of Omnivore, our art director/designer/poet on the project. In this diagram she's rather nicely laid out the various domains and interactive elements of the universe we'll be creating for the story of Tristan and Iseult, the first disc in the series. I can't emphasize enough how helpful these flow-chart diagrams can be in getting your point across.

In the Afterglow

Carolynn Miller tells us, "This is the most paranoid field [multimedia] I've ever been in. Everybody is always making everybody else sign nondisclosure agreements. I believe that there are always a lot of similar ideas kicking around, and it's execution that is going to make the difference."

So, should you be afraid to leave your documents behind? No. Never. You should not be afraid to leave anything behind. Certainly protect your ideas by copyrighting them, or registering them with the Writers Guild, or establishing a paper trail with an agent or lawyer. But don't be afraid about leaving documents behind. Or even about posting them on-line for that matter.

Time and time again you will hear new media pros shout from the rooftops, "Ideas are cheap, execution is expensive—but great execution is priceless!"

As Joanna Tamer advises, "Don't worry too much about people stealing in cyberspace until it's proven that people are really doing it." If you worry about it too much, you're never going to show your material to anyone.

Nondisclosure Nonsense

Let's touch briefly on the subject of nondisclosure agreements. At some point, sooner or later, if you're serious about a career in this business, you'll invariably be asked to sign one. They're nothing to freak out about, just part of the turf.

A nondisclosure agreement basically means you will not talk about, or use, what the other side tells you during a meeting. If they give you paperwork, it means you'll keep it confidential and you'll return it if asked. It means you are hearing and/or seeing proprietary information—which is a nice position to be in, and a position you never want to abuse.

If you are asked to pitch ideas cold to a company, then you can probably get them to sign *your* nondisclosure agreement, which protects the ideas you are pitching. (Have a legal expert prepare one if you need it.) At the same time you will probably have to sign *their* nondisclosure agreement, because during the meeting they might casually tell you something that is considered proprietary information. Like a telephone, it works both ways.

If a company wants you to sign a nondisclosure agreement, see if they can send it to you in advance so you can read it over in private. If you want a company to sign your nondisclosure agreement, send it to them in advance too, so their legal department can check it out.

Sometimes nondisclosure agreements can be problematic, so be careful. If you are like me and your eyes glaze over at the mere sight of a legal document—get over it. Get some coffee, go to a quite place, and read every bit of the document carefully before signing it. What you don't want to put your name on is anything that says that what you say or present in a meeting becomes the property of the company you are talking to, or the company has the first right of refusal on it. If you are presented with such an animal, and you still want to take the meeting, just cross out the offending language, sign the document, and hand it in and see what they say. If they really want to talk to you, they will probably accept the document with your deletions.

If you have any doubts whatsoever, seek legal advice.

CHAPTER 5

Defining a Winning Pitch

"SMART QUOTE"

"I learned a lot of lessons in the film industry [about pitching] and if you don't get their attention in a big hurry, you'll never get it."

Roger Holzberg—executive producer and supervising designer, *Pyramid*

Once you have developed documentation for your concept, it's time to come up with a pitch strategy. Carolynn Miller says this about the pitch strategy for a new concept she and her partner recently developed, "We felt we had something pretty hot, and we didn't want to mess it up, so, we proceeded pretty cautiously. The first thing we did was meet with our agents, and our attorneys. We told them what we had, we let them read it, and then we worked out a strategy with them. Our strategy was that we would try people in this geographical area [Los Angeles] first, and not show it to anybody unless we could go in and verbally pitch it first, before we physically left it with them. Because we thought we'd have a stronger chance of selling it by having a face to face meeting."

The Strategy

What follows is an example of a simple, winning, pitch strategy:

- **Make a List:** Develop and prioritize a hit list of publishers or developers who would clearly be interested in your concept. Don't waste time trying to sell a kid's living story book idea to a company that makes only shoot'em up twitch games.
- **Take Your Time:** Don't take fifty meetings or send out treatments to fifty different companies all at the same time. Patience. Remember, as you pitch your idea to different people you will be getting all sorts of feedback, good and bad, and this feedback can then be used to adjust your concept to make it stronger. Don't over expose your ideas too quickly.
- **Customize Your Concept:** Seriously think about what kind of company you are pitching to, and why this company would be interested in your project. If they have done something like it, be able to explain how your product will be a new dimension for them. If it's something different, be able to explain why it would be good for them. Without going overboard, try to custom tailor your concept to the company you are pitching to.

Setting Things Up

Before you can set up a pitch meeting, the two big and important questions are:

- How are you going to find all of these alleged publishers and developers who will give you money to make your title?
- If you find them, how are you going to convince them to listen to your story?

A major part of being a professional in the business is to network. The importance of making friends and establishing professional relationships cannot be stated enough. And don't forget about the various multimedia directories (see the references in Appendix B in the back of this book). They have long lists of publishers and developers, with detailed profiles to help you sort out where you should go with your project.

When you're putting your creative team together, choosing well connected team members is nothing to be ashamed of—if somebody has an "in" somewhere, use it.

The following sections cover three broad networking areas you should seriously consider looking into.

Educational Intros

If you're still in school, have your film, TV and media professors introduce you to the people they know in the business. Insist, it's part of what you're paying tuition for. You should also get to know what an authoring system like Director is all about. Learn how to use Adobe Premiere. Even take a course in writing C++, it can't hurt, and it looks good on your resume.

If you're just getting into the business, but it's a long time since you've seen the inside of a classroom, take a few new media courses at a local university or learning center.

Dive in, get your feet wet, and meet the instructors and your other classmates. Toss ideas around with all of them, and see whether you can get a project going. Again, insist that your instructors make professional introductions for you. If you're any good, and you show a passion about all of this stuff, they'll probably love to do it.

Professional Possibilities

If you live in a metropolitan area, there are probably many professional organizations that regularly give new media seminars. In Los Angeles, where I live, the following organizations (and I'm sure there are many more) routinely do this sort of thing:

The Writers Guild of America, west

Women in Film

The Directors Guild of America

The adult extension program at UCLA

The American Film Institute

The International Interactive Communications Society (IICS)

Seek out organizations similar to these where you live, find out what their seminar schedules are, and go. Go and take notes and ask questions—ask a lot of questions—and at the end of the seminar, introduce yourself to the speaker or to the panelist members. Don't be shy, that's what they're there for. Get their business cards and ask if you can call them later in the week. Most of the time you will find these professionals very helpful and willing to spend time with you.

In the film and television world it is often very difficult to meet the creative or business decision makers who can helm or green-light a project. These decision makers are usually protected by a hefty ring of receptionists, agents, lawyers and business managers. In the new media industry things aren't so bad yet.

Trade Show Fast Tracking

At almost any major industry trade show, you can meet the artists, producers, developers and publishers behind the new CD-ROM titles released each year. Often these VIP's are standing right there on the show floor demonstrating their product, and, in many cases, without an appointment, they are perfectly happy to spend a few minutes talking to you. Introduce yourself, ask questions about their product, and listen to what they have to say. At some appropriate point, tell them you have a title concept you would like to discuss, and ask for a meeting—later that day, the next day at the show, or if they work in the geographical area where you live, some time the next week.

A few of the more prominent, annual trade show/conferences are:

MacWorld Expo, San Francisco

Show Biz Expo East, New York City

Intermedia '96, San Francisco

Children's Interactive Media Festival, Los Angeles

Computer Game Developers Conference, Santa Clara, CA

Windows World/Comdex, Spring, Atlanta

VISCOMM '96, West, San Francisco

Digital World, Los Angeles

Show Biz Expo, west, Los Angeles

Comdex/Fall, Las Vegas.

The Interactive Media Festival (see the references in Appendix B), publishes a very comprehensive calendar of interactive events and conferences happening in the United States and abroad. If you're on America Online, the New York Times site also has a new media conference calendar section. Check any of these sources out, find out what's happening close to you, or not so close to you, and go.

While You're at It

Besides networking, trade shows and conferences are also great because of the seminar tracks they usually offer. Within a 2 or 3 day period, you can very easily pick up a lot of cutting edge information that will improve the chances of your title getting funded.

Judy Geller, Director of Program Development for SOFTBANK COMDEX, Inc., the folks who put on the Windows World Shows and Comdex/Fall, explains, "Conferences are probably your only opportunity to hear from well-known industry visionaries who have been invited to speak. Additionally, they provide an

While You're at It (continued)

opportunity to discover hot new technologies and their applications, as well as they are a great place to network with people who you probably have a lot in common with."

The Meeting

You've created your concept, done your marketing homework, put your team together, produced your documentation, and now it's time to tell somebody about it. The following "pitch tips" can be very helpful when presenting your idea in a meeting:

- **Practice:** Work out what you are going to say in advance. Practice, practice, practice. You must become verbally familiar with your material. Use your documentation as the basic outline for the meeting. Whoever you are pitching to should have a copy of it on their desk so that you can talk them through it. If you are pitching with a partner, or team of people, you should trade off who's going to say what, and work this out well in advance.
- **Be Brief:** Keep it short, interesting, and to the point.
- **Personalize It:** Try to make the meeting a human experience. Without overdoing it, if there is something personal in the office that you can identify with—pictures of kids, a poster, etc.—go ahead and make some comment about it.
- **Stay Positive:** Be comfortable, and positive. Remember, these folks want you to succeed. They need a hot product, and they're hoping you'll provide it for them.
- **Listen:** Pay attention to what the executive you are pitching to has to say. Carolynn Miller quite elegantly advises, "It's an easy mistake to keep talking and interrupt them because you're kind of nervous. We have disciplined ourselves to shut up and listen to what they're saying because it can be really important."
- **Refuse Refreshments:** If they offer you a drink—and you spill some of it because you got a little animated during the pitch—don't wipe it up with your sleeve. Accidents happen. I bring this up because I *have* spilled stuff in meetings. I'm a little uncoordinated to put it mildly. (People bring out their second-string glassware when I'm coming over for dinner.) Better yet, just say no to the refreshment offer, it's safer that way.

- **Meet Early:** If you can help it, don't schedule meetings right after lunch. Big lunch can mean big snooze for some decision makers. I like mid-morning meetings myself. I'm up by then, morning rush hour traffic is history, etc.—but that's me. Try to schedule meetings during the part of the day when you know you'll be at your best. Try not to take a 4:30 meeting on Friday or just before the start of a holiday.
- **Dress the Part:** Consider the culture of where you're going to pitch. Seriously consider what to wear. You're the creative, you're going into a situation where the people are expecting a certain—how shall we say—extra something? It probably is not a good idea to wear a formal three piece suit. That's for funerals or asking for money from a bank.
- **Make an Exit:** Last—and probably the most important item on this list—know when to leave. If you're rambling on endlessly and you see them look at their watch, cut your losses and get out of there. If this happens at a couple of meetings, it's probably not them, it's you or your presentation. Go back and practice some more, or practice in front of somebody who will give you some constructive feedback.

Going to Contract

If they like your idea and want to develop it, get yourself a good mulitmedia lawyer and have them negotiate the deal. It's worth every dime you pay them. If you don't have the up-front money for a legal retaining fee, find the money, or give the lawyer a percentage of the contract.

> **A publisher or developer cannot deny you your right to legal or agent representation. And don't let them intimidate you on this point.**

If the project is big enough, it might also attract the notice of an agent. You pay an agent a percentage of the deal, usually ten to fifteen percent. If you bring an agent or a lawyer to the negotiating table, don't worry if the publisher or developer starts to grumble and make noise about having "outside parties involved." If they do this, they are doing it because they know your lawyer or agent may get you a better deal, and most of the time they do.

> **An endless supply of patience is one of the most potent weapons you can carry in with you when negotiating a contract. If you are even remotely in a hurry, you won't get as good a deal, promise. So be patient.**

Playing Hardball

Whether you use a lawyer or an agent, or negotiate the contract yourself, what follows are just a few examples (not all by any means) of some of the points you should try to cover in your deal:

- Retain as much control over creative decisions as possible.
- Get proper credit for the creative work.
- Protect sequel, merchandising, and other format rights. If later on somebody wants to make a stage show, movie or amusement ride based on your CD-ROM title, you want to make sure you get paid for this, as well as collect a royalty of some kind.
- If you pitch your concept based on a multiple platform strategy, then, in the best of all possible worlds, try to get a separate contract dealing with each platform.

> **If it gets sticky, negotiate only the CD-ROM title rights. Hold back on-line, stage, film, TV, etc. rights for another day. If they let you, that is.**

- If you develop any tools or computer engines in the process of creating your title, make sure your rights to them are protected.
- Make sure you get a part of the "back end," or royalty per unit sold.

Once again, these are only some of the deal points you'll need to look out for—there will be many more, of course, relative to the specific deal. See your lawyer or agent on this.

And Mister Softee Too

After giving you all this cautionary advice, I'm going to make a one-eighty and say *yes,* it's nice to get as much as you can in your deal but don't forget you want it to go through.

One of the most important things that can happen to your career is to get your project done.

> **Some "give and take" is also part of the negotiation equation of going to contract. Get your title out now, and your price, to a certain extent, goes up for the next one.**

If you are only being hired as a writer/designer on a project, most of the previously discussed items still hold true. The Writers Guild of America, west has a one-page interactive contract that's becoming quite popular (see Appendix B). If you use it, and you aren't a member of the WGA, the project you script/design under this contract will probably gain you points to membership in the guild. If you have any questions, call up the Writers Guild of America, west, and ask, or point your browser at their website http://www.wga.org.

> **If somebody wants to hire you as a writer/designer on a multimedia project, take a look at the WGA's interactive contract. You may be able to use this contract in your situation even if you aren't a Writers Guild member.**

The Writing Isn't Fee

A writer's fee is a touchy, but important subject that a lot of people are interested in these days. Let me state up-front that there isn't much data readily available about what writer/designers are being paid in the market place. However, there are two bits of information that keep cropping up that seem to make reasonable sense:

- Compared to the motion picture and TV industries, interactive projects pay hardly nothing.
- As we speak, the compensation rates for interactive projects are going up.

The Writing Isn't Fee (continued)

Rumor has it that an interactive writer may receive approximately 5% of the overall title budget—rumor also adds that this may vary widely. For example, a CD-ROM title budgeted at $700,000 would have $35,000 slated for the writer. Typically, payment would be one-third upon signing, one-third upon submission of first draft, and the remaining upon submission of final draft. The thing to watch out for here is whether payment is on delivery, or upon acceptance. This is negotiable, and something to be very careful of if it is based on acceptance.

If a producer continually wants you to do re-writes because the material in their opinion is "unacceptable", you're in a tight spot. It is entirely within your rights to negotiate for additional money for any extra work they want you to do. Try to work out in advance the exact details of what is expected of you and get it in writing.

You should also get some royalties—a percentage of each unit sold. If they bundle the product you worked on, you should also get a fixed amount for that privilege too. You should also get screen and box credit if you can. You should also be allowed to use the project as a writing/prototype sample.

If you're writing an interactive script, figure a minimum of three to four months to do it in. If you're working on an hourly basis, I hear tell the fee can range between $85 to $100, or higher, depending on your credits. A day rate, in general, can punch in at $500 to over $1000.

Dealing with Rejection

If you don't get a contract, you get rejected. Like nondisclosure agreements, rejection is part of the turf. It can reduce you to a set of nasty ulcers and nail biting fetishes, or, it can be treated like all the stop lights in Los Angeles—there's one on just about every corner, and sometimes they're red, and sometimes they're green. It's nothing personal.

It took me years to stop plunging into serious depression every time some producer, editor, or decision-maker said no to me for one reason or another. In hindsight, they probably had some good reasons for saying no too.

I'm not going to insult you by saying something like "you've got to turn every negative into a positive." You won't hear it from my lips. But one thing you can do to solve this rejection blues stuff, if I may call it such, is to get so damn creative, so damn excited about what you're doing that you don't have time to worry about what the clowns on the next hill over are thinking about you. Have two, three, four, or five projects going at the same time. If one gets shot down, there's another coming right along to take it's place. It's the only way to keep sane.

Get rolling. Get moving. And keep at it. Throw enough mud at the wall, and something's bound to stick.

CHAPTER 6

The ABCs of Interactive Writing

"SMART QUOTE"

"Getting your arms around a big interactive story or movie is like trying to hug a greased grizzly bear. It's big, it's going to be lurching out in all sorts of directions, it's slippery as all hell. If you're not careful, it's going to take off on you."

Michael Kaplan—co-creator/screenwriter, *Psychic Detective*

This is a tricky chapter to write. I'm going to start off with some general creative comments, then work my way into some specific interactive scripting issues. Some of the topics will immediately connect, some of them won't, but once you've made it all the way through, they should hang together quite nicely. Here's hoping.

> **Think of this chapter like a garbage dump of ideas, it'll smell a bit, but you're bound to find a trinket or two you'll like. (For another way to look at it, see the "StoryLine Pro" demo on the CD-ROM and Appendix D for info on how to run it.)**

May the Muse Be with You

One of the best books I've ever read on firing up the creative muse is called *Zen in the Art of Writing, Essays on Creativity*, by novelist and short story writer Ray Bradbury—writer of such classics as *Fahrenheit 451* and *The Martian Chronicles*. My copy of *Zen* is worn and dog-eared, and I thumb through it like my LA Thomas Street Guide whenever I'm uncertain of my creative way, which I admit I am at times.

> **Sometimes I get tired of what I'm writing; I get bored with it. It feels like every corner I turn ends me smack up against one of Herman Melville's damn funeral processions that he talks about in the first page of Moby Dick—and though I used to, I can't go down to the sea anymore for a change of pace.**

Breaking the Blockade

When I'm feeling blocked and just plain bored, I take out Bradbury's book, read an essay, and I'm usually cured. These ten essays were written at various times for various publications over the past thirty years. The earliest one is dated 1961, and no, I don't own stock in the company that publishes Mr. Bradbury's books. So what do these essays have to do about writing for multimedia?

Specifically—nothing. Generally—everything.

Living the Creative Life

Bradbury writes about living the creative life—how to work it, breath it, smell it, feel it, love it, and how to be practical about the whole thing too. He talks about such things as:

- How kids seem to be on the inside tract when paradigm shifts are coming down t he pike.
- How associative thinking (hypertext again) is essential to free you from the shackles of linear thinking.
- How you have to write something like a thousand words a day for a thousand days before anything good really comes out.
- How you never fail if you write—and only fail if you quit.
- How your writer's mind sees the world differently every second of every day (interactive choice).
- How you just have to plain old get out of your way and trust to the crazy voices inside you shouting, "Let us OUT!"

Every one of us is unique, and every one of us has something to say. "How to Keep and Feed a Muse" is my favorite Bradbury essay, because it taps me on the shoulder and reminds me "how fresh and original is each man, even the slowest and dullest."

The Hero's Journey

In my research for this book, which consisted mostly of talking to and taping writers, producers, and other professionals in the multimedia business, I did not necessarily get a strong response when I asked, "well what did you think about Joseph Campbell's Hero's Journey concept and do you think it applies to writing for interactivity?" For the most part, people knew what I was talking about, but they didn't necessarily use the Hero's Journey metaphor when they were thinking about or creating multimedia interactive experiences. I even had one very talented interactive writer (who shall remain nameless) who knew a little bit about it but wasn't particularly interested in learning anything more.

Although my sampling of multimedia professionals, relative to the entire profession, is rather small—30 odd people, tops—I would imagine a great many people out there in interactive land apply Joseph Campbell's Hero's Journey concept on a daily basis. At least I hope so.

In any event, if you're going to write and design for multimedia, you should have at least some cursory knowledge of what Campbell's stuff is all about, so herein lies the skinny.

Mr. Campbell's Take

Joseph Campbell (1904-1987) was a mythologist. He lectured, authored, edited, and translated many books on the subject. Probably his most widely known book is *The Hero with a Thousand Face*s, published in 1949, which has had a serious on-again off-again love affair with the New York Times Best Seller list for the past forty years.

He was on the hunt for universal patterns in the myths of the world, and for the most part found them. Archetypes and archetypal patterns kept cropping up again and again, regardless of the cultural origin of the myth.

Mr. Campbell writes in the Preface to this book that its purpose is to "uncover some of the truths disguised for us under the figures of religion and mythology by bringing together a multitude of not-too-difficult examples and letting the ancient meaning become apparent of itself."

Your Basic Journey

Briefly, and very generally, the hero's journey is this: whatever the myth there's *always* a hero—sometimes male, sometimes female—and this hero usually lives peacefully in a community. Suddenly the community is threatened by an outside force, and the hero receives a "call" to come and help out the community. This "helping out" usually requires the hero to undertake a hazardous journey to a foreign land to bring back specialized knowledge that will save the community. The heroes usually refuse the call, "No way!" And then for some reason or another, they end up changing their mind.

Mentors, Tricksters, and Guardians

Once the journey is underway, the hero often meets a mentor figure who gives him knowledge that will allow the hero to survive the journey. Sometimes the hero meets a trickster during the journey too, and the trickster can really mess things up if the hero's not careful. At journey's end, the hero is usually confronted by guardians of the "gate" where the special knowledge is kept. And these bouncers make it real tough for the hero to enter the joint too. Once inside however, the heroes are "tested" to see if they're worthy of obtaining the special knowledge that will save their community.

Without fail, the basic Hero's Journey story pattern is found in just about every myth you run across. These are powerful story elements that have resonated with people throughout time, all over the world, regardless of race, color, creed or culture. For more on this, see Joseph Campbell's book, "The Hero with a Thousand Faces".

The Linear Story Pattern

The Hero's Journey concept, which provides a model of how to write a good linear story, can be broken down into the following structural elements:

- Your story has to have a hero.
- This hero receives a call to adventure.
- The call is usually refused.
- The hero finally agrees, and the adventure begins.
- The hero hooks up with a mentor who teaches him how to survive along the way.
- The hero is tested and challenged by tricksters and guardians.
- The hero crosses thresholds.
- If the hero passes all the tests and meets the challenges, some special knowledge is given that can save the community.
- The hero returns home in triumph and the story ends.

The Interactive Hero

One of the disappointing things for me about linear media experiences—a film, play, book, music concert—is that they end. They stop just when things are getting really interesting. Maybe it's just me, but I always want to hang around afterwards and see what's happening. If the experience is successful I'm "satisfied"—but I want more. In an interactive multimedia experience you can let your audience do that—have all they want and hang around forever.

So, using the same story elements found in the Hero's Journey concept, your journeying hero can have multiple calls to adventure, numerous mentors that impart secret knowledge, many guardians of many gates, tons of thresholds to cross, as well as multiple tests to take and secrets to learn once you've passed these tests.

Additionally, because the hero is a very changed person at the end of the journey—they've seen and experienced many new things, and are never the same person again—it's entirely reasonable to assume that they are not going to "fit in" once they return home. The old environment is not satisfying enough, so it is only natural for them to receive a new call to adventure. They can't help it.

The traditional Hero's Journey concept can be thought of as being a cycle. The seeds of a never-ending story are implanted by the broadening horizons of the journey, and a never-ending story is almost by definition what an ideal interactive multimedia experience is all about.

So when scripting an interactive tale, it's entirely possible—and maybe even absolutely necessary—to introduce a new character in the third or whatever you happen to be calling your last act (which is something you're told *never* to do in linear media if you want your audience to have a satisfying, "wrapped-up" experience). It would be interesting then, to take a look at the myths Joseph Campbell studied and see if indeed a new character (archetype) is added toward the end of the myth—someone who eventually becomes the precipitator of future adventures. Anybody want to do a Ph.D. thesis on this?

And Hollywood's Too

For those of you not familiar with the business of screenwriting in Hollywood, for better or worse, Joseph Campbell's Hero's Journey story pattern has been embraced by many creative types in the film and television field. Because of this embracement, it would not be a stretch to say that one reason (of many) Hollywood films and tv shows are so successful in foreign markets is that they often contain many of the story elements that Campbell plucked from the great myths of the world.

> **The logic is: If your film's made up of structural elements familiar worldwide, then your film will be familiar to foreign audiences and accepted, which translates into box office success.**

Hollywood films and Mr. Campbell's concepts have been nicely blended in the book *The Writer's Journey, Mythic Structure for Storytellers & Screenwriters* by Christopher Vogler. *The Writer's Journey* is a must read. Mr. Vogler breaks Campbell's Hero's Journey concept into a twelve-point metaphorical model and rigorously lays out how this model can be used to build a solid film structure as well as analyze the structure of any existing film or story. The book also gives you some ideas on pacing, character building, and story structure.

The Hero Conquers Foreign Markets

Jumping back into the multimedia world for a second, if it is even remotely true that the success of Hollywood films in foreign lands is related to Hero's Journey structural elements, then by analogy (and with a big grain of salt because I have no data on this) it would make sense to damn well make sure that these elements are included in interactive multimedia storytelling as well—that's if you want to have a worldwide successful CD-ROM title, of course. It would be interesting to check foreign sales of American CD-ROM product versus storytelling methods/structure used in the product to see if any patterns are showing up.

Beyond Story Structure

What follows is a bit of an envelope-stretching joyride, which attempts to answer the question: "How can I *really* apply these Hero's Journey story concepts to interactive multimedia writing?" So try to stay with me if you can. I think I can make an interesting point or two before you start throwing tomatoes.

Losing the Linear Line

All stories have a beginning, a middle part, and then an ending, right? This seems natural, and the Hero's Journey pattern—pulled down from the myths of the world—seems to show this clearly.

But wait a minute, isn't this linear thinking?

> **We choose to see structure because it's how we've been taught. It's what everybody does. But what if everybody's wrong?**

Joseph Campbell looked at the myths of the world, sew patterns, beginnings, middles and endings, whatever—and we ended up with a model story structure that has "The Hero at Home" and then progresses linearly through trials, conflicts and tests, ultimately returning to the starting point with special knowledge to save the community. I'm not only dumping on Campbell here, this business of structure goes back a long way—probably right back to the first organized ritual ever performed by man and continuing right up to modern film, television, and theater. Structure. Structure. Structure!

The Collectively Unconscious

Something's wrong here. Are we buying into it again? Linear thinking?

Archetypal images associated with myths allegedly come from the collective unconscious. The collective unconsciousness, intuitively (for me anyway) is formless, dreamlike, an all over the place and out there kind of "thing," just like what we supposedly experienced when we were babes in diapers.

> **We didn't think linearly—supposedly—when we were in the cradle. We experienced the world in an amorphous, shapeshifting and totally enchanting way. It was perfectly natural for objects to change shape and size when we moved our miniature heads this way or that. (See Chapter 1 if you're just tuning in.)**

So when we're looking at myths—looking at images from the collective unconscious—why are we coming up with a beginning, middle and an end? It doesn't make sense. Think about it—why choose to see structure? And my serious and obvious response to this question is: We do it because it's the best way to make sense out of the world—otherwise it's all just a mass of confusion.

Lounging in LimboLand

My point is that interactive multimedia experiences give us the opportunity to eliminate the structure crutch. Finally! After all these years. Like chicken soup, it'll probably be good for us. And the first step of getting out from under the structure yoke is to dump the word "story."

No more story! Where you have a story you've got a beginning, middle and an end! Get out your story-be-gone spray and empty the whole can! Hunt down every story in your neighborhood and jump up and down on it until there's nothing but a trillion little pieces left to go whimpering back to story-structure land. Good riddance!

Story has made our lives sane, sober, upright and forthcoming for far too long. Story has given the world meaning and purpose—and beginnings and middles and endings. But wait. Without story, without implied structure—what's left?

Silence.

We slowly turn, and out of the mist rides formless, structureless *chaos*—where even the slightest change in the most simple, whimsical initial condition sets the whole thing whirling off into one great magnificent, cosmic storm of senselessness. This, ladies and gentlemen, I invite you to ponder as *the* genuine interactive multimedia tale-telling model.

Cashing in on Chaos

Chaos theory is the third scientific revolution of our century after relativity and quantum physics. Intuitively, it's a way of coping with randomness, with events so complicated by multiple variables (choices) that nothing makes sense. Chaos theory basically (and very simplisticly) says that where there appears to be total disorder—randomness, madness, whatever—in a system, there is in reality an "over" order. You just have to look at it properly. Metaphorically speaking: "there is method to this madness," but you have to step back to see it.

Chaos theory is a really different way to think about interactive multimedia tale-telling. Of course, I can't prove any of this with a lot of impressive-looking graphs and equations, but I can tell you that I saw hints of this when looking at the *Psychic Detective* CD-ROM (deconstructed in Part Three of this book).

Further gut level proof for a chaos point of view comes from Michael Utvich, who notes that television provides us with "a continuous stream of discontinuous information—discontinuous content. Television turns interruptions into a culture object, the interruptions turn into part of the show." And this continuous stream of discontinuous images is further made discontinuous by clicking on the old remote any time you wish. Channel surfers are us. Seems like a whole lot of chaos to me.

The troika creative team of Kaplan, Sanborn and Simmons is terribly interested in splitting up the film/multimedia environment into finer and finer pieces, and allowing the user to discover their own path of editing an experience together. They are convinced that providing an almost chaotic pool of image, music and dialogue to dip into gives the user a very powerful sense of story completion and satisfaction.

Closing the Loop

Before I close out here, for completeness and for those of you more computer and/or mathematically oriented, I'd also like to mention that along with chaos theory, and sort of subset to it, comes fractal and holographic models of the universe. These concepts, I feel, would make really interesting interactive multimedia tale-telling models too, but a discussion of them is way beyond the scope of this book.

A cautionary note: If you're sitting in front of the money guy pitching your interactive multimedia project—don't tell them you're going to handle the branching aspect by using Chaos Theory. I don't think they'll give you the money.

Resurrecting Structure

After we just got through saying structure is dead, let's take a look at a paradigm that might be useful in helping you script an interactive tale-telling multimedia experience.

The first thing you need is an environment—the universe where your experience will take place. Once you have that, there are three ways you can structure the action within it. You may:

- Explore randomly
- Have constraints, which may be very narrowly defined or contain multiple paths leading to single or multiple conclusions
- Allow both random and constraint-based exploration, with constraints applied as needed

The good news about this structural model is that whatever processing method you choose—random, along paths, or a combination of both—you can always run into sub-environments along the way that have a different processing method than the previously described universe. The even better news, of course, is that these sub-environments can have sub-environments, which in turn may have sub-environments—and so on and so on into infinity if you wish, with each of these sub-environments having their own unique set of rules and regulations.

Essentially then, what we have here is an interconnected world-within-a-world situation—a self-similarity of universes all the way into infinity. This is exactly what fractal geometry is all about.

Confused? OK. You have a universe that you can randomly explore. You see a treasure chest in this master universe. You open the chest, go inside, and a whole new universe is revealed. But it just so happens that in this new universe the rules have changed. You can't wander randomly anymore. For the sake of illustration, let's say that in this new universe there is now a mission to complete, and this mission is tied to a story that has a plot that needs to unfold along a certain set of guidelines. Once the mission has been completed, the user may then be presented with the opportunity to stumble upon another sub-environment, which will present an entirely different universe with a whole new set of rules.

One last note, the situations a user experiences in one of these sub-environments can be uniquely dependent on choices made in the previous environment.

It's just a model. Seriously think about it and see whether you can improve upon it or come up with one of your own. It's good interactive practice.

Just Going for It

As I see it, from personal experience, you can create a story in the following two ways:

- **The Construction Method:** You can start off knowing what the plot and ending are and fill in the details, which is like constructing a building from a set of engineering plans.
- **The Exploration Method:** You can start off with some kind of tangible intangible—an image, a character, a strong action, a memory, a fleeting glimpse of a face going through a door, a smell—and then, with this in mind, sit down and start writing out the story from there.

> **In the Hollywood film trade, a traditional screenplay is about 120 pages long and usually has a three act structure. With each page representing about one minute of screen time, act one usually ends at or before page 30, act two develops the story for another 40 to 60 pages, and act three, the resolution, usually takes up less than 30 pages.**

With an Erector Set

Many professional screenwriting teachers will tell you that the construction method is the way to go. You have to get your plot down first—work out the story beats, the act breaks, the ending—and then fill everything out with characters.

The soul of drama is plot, they would say, echoing Aristotle. We know a person by his actions, so plot first, then develop the characters to execute the plot.

These teachers would also tell you to use index cards or a scriptwriting program to help you structure the plot. Write one scene per card, they'd explain, then you can shift the cards around and see how the scenes play against one another. This sounds like a very sane way to do things—for some people.

> **The construction method actually does produce very sound—good and even great—creative screenplays all the time. The deconstruction of "Wing Commander IV", in Part Three of this book, shows you how an index card method works.**

Or Out of Thin Air

Ray Bradbury (him again) in his *Zen in the Art of Writing* essay says: "Plot is no more than footprints left in the snow *after* your characters have run by on their way to incredible adventures. Plot is observed after the fact rather than before."

> **For Bradbury, plot shows up after you sit down and write something on a blank page.**

I Saw a Face

Here's an example of the exploration method for constructing a story:

- **Put down an image**—*"I saw a face reflected in glass today."* (OK. I just wrote this without really thinking about it—no premeditation what-so-ever.)
- **Expand on it**—*"I saw a face reflected in glass today. A beautiful face. Innocent. Pure. Unearthly, was my immediate thought."* (Great. It's a start.)
- **Develop it further**—*"The lobby of the office building was filled with a lunchtime crowd, people pushing and shoving, demanding to get out into the first spring air after a long dreary winter. I saw her face reflected in the glass door as I was pushing through it."* (Besides the narrator, we now potentially have a second character, a woman, and a place, an office building. See how we're building?)
- **And then keep going**—*"I stopped, startled, as if a vision had suddenly appeared to me, and I immediately turned around—people pushed into me, and I pushed back. And looking over their heads and shoulders, there she was. A young woman, twenties maybe, standing in the middle of the crowded lobby, looking totally lost. Her hair was a golden brown that seemed to shimmer with a life of its own. She was dressed in a white, spring-time one-piece skirt, rough cotton, that looked homespun."* (We definitely have a second character going. But what are the narrator and this woman going to do next?)

- **Letting the story evolve**—*"Suddenly she turned her head, and looked directly at me, as if she knew I was staring at her. My heart skipped a beat."* (OK. They see one another, and a potential relationship is there for the making. Now what?)
- **Until the plot thickens**—*"And then I was roughly pushed aside, slammed into the lobby wall, and when I regained my balance, and looked for her again, she was gone. Just gone. As if she had vanished into thin air."* (A set-back perhaps?)

Remembered a Newspaper Article

After I wrote "I saw a face refected in glass today," a newspaper article I read a year or two ago suddenly came to mind. It was about an arts project in New York City that had been funded to place memorial plaques in the elevators of a new office building constructed over an old graveyard. So the woman in my story is a ghost, and perhaps she rides the elevators day and night, up and down, down and up, and our hero is the only one who can see her. And she sees him.

And Created a Story

This is an illustration of the process of creating a story through exploration. The face in the glass triggered the memory of a newspaper article, which put me in an office building in Manhattan where the hero sees a beautiful woman who takes a serious look at him. He gets pushed aside and suddenly she's gone. Weird. But what happens next? He'll go over and look for her of course, but he won't find her. Then what happens? Two days later he sees her again maybe, across the atrium of the building, coming out of an elevator. Same girl, same beautiful hair, same dress. He stops. She stops, and looks at him—again. This time he breaks into a run and goes for her. And the story goes on from there.

In the Multimedia Way

But what does all of this have to do with multimedia? And how can you possibly compare the process of writing a screenplay, which is very structured, with writing a short story or novel which has much more freedom in terms of its narrative flow? Well, from my own point of view, I feel comfortable creating a story with either the exploration or the construction method. I've written screenplays that started off with a single image, exploring out from there to see what was in the universe, and I've written other screenplays from index cards.

Either the construction or the exploration method can produce some good stuff. This dichotomy, I suspect, is one of the reasons I'm attracted to interactive multimedia, because it can blend both creative methods.

Peak Experiences

I suspect that the ideal interactive multimedia experience is a combination of character-centric and plot-centric situations. The user is able to explore any number of richly defined characters that are totally compelling, that you just want to hang around with, and don't necessarily care that they're not being driven anywhere by some external plot.

Then all of a sudden, something happens to one of the characters that narrows the focus—defines a general path that all the other characters in the matrix respond to—and the whole interactive experience takes on a new shape, vectoring to some distant resolution. After a time things may calm down, and the universe gets back to normal, until the next time the system gets stressed. (This is probably what an on-line fiction system will look like, I bet.)

The Soap Opera Supreme

So, what we're looking at here, I think, is an elaborate soap opera model—lots of plots, and lots of characters all connecting at different points in an amorphous time stream. Such is life. No?

Do we start out writing an interactive multimedia experience with a known plot, or do we let our characters find one for themselves? My hunch is it'll be a tug of war between them, with the loudest voice in your soul winning.

The Cocktail Party Lexicon

Hollywood folks have a tendency to use a kind of shorthand movie speak because nobody seems to have the time to really explain complicated things anymore. For example: "My new screenplay is like *Jaws* meets *Looking for Mr. Goodbar.*" Everybody's seen *Jaws* and *Looking for Mr. Goodbar,* presumably, so without really having to use much brain power, people immediately know that your screenplay is about a lonely loan shark who owns a singles bar.

If you're heading for a multimedia cocktail party, this same shorthand method can be adopted when talking about interactive story structure models—all you have to do is say a key word or two and people will immediately know what you're working on. The following was developed with some help from writer Michael Utvich:

- *Rashomon:* Say this to somebody and they'll know you're working on a structure based on a bunch of characters who've witnessed the same event, that they're probably all lying about what they saw, and you get to switch between their points of view.
- *Let's Make a Deal:* Shout this out, and everyone knows you're working on an interactive that gives the user the choice of three doors—behind door one is a lady, door two a tiger, and door three the opportunity to stand in line all day at the Department of Motor Vehicles.
- *George Burns:* Light up a cigar and say "George Burns," and it's quickly understood you have a character that interrupts the action all the time and makes sarcastic comments directly to the user about what's going to happen in the future. (This one, by the way, is a real good audience involver because it breaks the third wall and actively engages the user.)
- *Soap Opera:* Dish this out, and folks know you have a character-centric universe as opposed to a plot-centric universe.
- *Mystery:* Mutter this one under your breath, and it's clear your structure is based on a user solving a mystery/puzzle and moving through an environment discovering things.
- *Beverly Center:* Tells everyone you're talking about an interactive shopping mall.

The Cocktail Party Lexicon (continued)

So if your interactive project includes an abrasive help character, who actively lets you shift between the POVs of a number of characters who have experienced the same main event, and when it's all over, the user gets to buy T-shirts of the whole thing—well, you can call this structure "George Burns talking to Rashomon down at the Beverly Center." Right?

CHAPTER 7

The Interactive Model

"SMART QUOTE"

"An interactive product involves the individual on a voyage of self-discovery. That's what its function is in the media mix. Products that meet that criteria will succeed, and those that do not, will not."

Michael Utvich—interactive writer/designer

After much thought—and talking to a lot of interactive writers, deconstructing the CD-ROM titles in Part Three of this book, making notes, thinking some more, and transcribing hours of taped interviews—a pattern, a methodology, a set of loose rules, if you will, have emerged as to how one goes about putting an interactive script/design together.

Breaking All the Rules

A serious note of warning before we get into any of this. Theoretical models based on existing creative works are good for only two things:

- Polite banter at cocktail parties
- A jumping off point for your own creative work

Yes, read the deconstructions of *Casablanca, China Town,* or of whatever famous film in whatever How to Write a Film Script handbook happens to be on your bookshelf. Study these models. Read the explanations on how to develop plot and character, pacing and dialogue. It's all useful. Pig out on all the how to books you can find until you can't eat anymore. And then after a while put them all aside, and begin your own work.

You're never really going to get very far in the creative business following somebody else's instructions. Take a look at them, trash them, and then go your own way.

The same is true for this book. The set of rules, categories really, that I lay out on the next few pages are simple, loose, obvious even, and I hope you successfully break every-one of them when scripting your own title.

A Scripter's Mindset

First, I want to lay out some general, *a priori* mindset insights I think you should consider before tackling any interactive scripting job.

No Free Ride

Just because it's multimedia, and interactive, it does not give you license to run riot with half-baked, poorly-conceived ideas and bad writing. Multimedia suggests an artistic freedom that other media do not appear to have—at least on the surface anyway. Working in multimedia is not an easy way out. To be a successful interactive scripter takes just as much effort, control, perseverance, talent, and brilliance as it does to write a book, a play, a screenplay, a choreography, or a musical composition.

Interactive multimedia experiences are just one more part of the media mix. They're not going to replace films, plays, TV, books, music concerts, etc. They're just going to take their place alongside everything else.

I, the Audience

Scripting for an interactive experience is truly writing for an audience that can get their hands on your creative stuff, play with it, and make it their own. That's the whole point of interactives. People don't want to sit in front of a computer for hours on end unless they're involved.

In multimedia, some people say, audience participation is probably more important than content. Truly successful multimedia scripters know their audience well—what they want, how they want it, and how to get them involved. If you want to tell a story and not get your audience hands-on involved, go make a movie or write a book.

A writer in a linear medium is responsible for choosing the beginning and the end of an experience, as well as everything that comes in between. A writer in an interactive medium is responsible for creating an environment, and then creating and organizing choices within that environment that a user may get involved with.

A Voyage of Self-Discovery

I can't jump up and down enough about this one. What will the audience learn about themselves when going through your interactive experience—this is the payoff. Think of the user as a hero on a journey looking for who they are.

> **It takes effort to learn anything, so don't assume your audience doesn't want to think—they just don't want to be confused.**

Forget about being a scripter for a second. Let's just talk about life. Remember, everything that you do, you do because it reveals yourself to yourself. Every moment of your life is a moment of self-discovery. It is, I have proof. But most of us don't pay attention to this little fact. We're so blinded by the details of everyday living that we have no idea who we are or what we're doing any of this for.

If you're going to become an artist, your responsibility to is to go on a voyage of self-discovery. And then once you've figured out a few things, you have to come back to the real world and give the folks you left behind a leg up. It's a sacred trust. And who knows, it might even make you some money.

Paradigm Shift Blues

Don't let yourself go nuts trying to figure out where to pitch your tent on the so-called super information highway. It's a whopper of a paradigm shift all right, but because we're right in the middle of it, we can't see the big picture too clearly yet. And that's OK. It's a process rather than a finalized thing.

> **The scripts for the three interactives deconstructed in Part Three of this book are all different, all unique—and they work beautifully. So in our quest to develop "the" interactive scripting model, maybe there is no such thing?**

So jump in, start creating, and enjoy yourself.

An Interactive Visualization

A good exercise to start training your interactive scripting intuition is to imagine yourself in a familiar, closed environment, and then to observe how you interact within that environment.

Let's go to the grocery store, shall we? Your neighborhood food store is a closed environment that has a specific purpose—to sell you food. Ok. Let's try it. (Note: if you like, you may assume a lotus position, but it's not entirely necessary for this exercise.)

- Visualize the parking lot, all the cars in it, and the front of the store. Got it?
- Park your car and walk toward the front entrance—Oops, watch out for the free rolling carriage somebody just let loose. Say a polite "no thank you," or "I'll catch you on the way out" to the person soliciting donations at the entrance.
- Enter the store and look around. What's the layout like? (Breath deeply now, inhale, exhale, you're almost there.) The checkout counters are in front of you. Aisles and shelves filled with food stuff beyond. Off to the right is the meat department. To the left produce. Way in the back is the beer. How's it looking?
- Now proceed past the checkout counters—Oops! Have to get a cart first. That's right, choose one with four wheels that work. Good. (Inhale, exhale, do you feel yourself bathed in a bright light yet?)
- Push your cart past the checkout counters and now pull out your shopping list. What? You forgot the list. Lose ten points for that one. So that means we have to take a general spin around the aisles and see if we can figure out what was on the list.
- Stop at the nice demonstration lady serving little spam-like sandwiches. Take a handful at least, you'll need the energy for the journey, and who knows, you may need them to bribe the produce guy who's got the freshest cantaloupe stashed someplace in the back.

Ok. Enough. See how this works? You have an environment, a universe, that has a layout, and a set of rules of interaction. Perfectly natural. And wonderfully interactive. Read on, and stand by for a sequel. What else did you expect?

Nuts and Bolts

OK, let's go for the heart of the matter. But before we do that, yet another warning: The following material is not presented in any particular order. It's *all* important. For the sake of your own sanity though, you should probably consider the first three items before the rest.

The Universe

One of the first things you need to do is to define the "world" that you want to create in. Whether you're working with a story line, a story treatment, baseball cards, or a database, you have to ask the question—what's the universe? What's the environment. The Resident's *Freak Show* for example is set in a traveling freak show with some very messed up people running around. *Rebel Assault* takes place a long time ago in a far distant galaxy where the Empire is seriously striking back.

So come up with your universe first. For instance:

- My CD-ROM is going to be about a bowling alley in the Midwest circa 1950's.
- My informational CD-ROM is going to contain all the instructional manuals for all computer printers made by XYZ computer company in 1992.
- My CD-ROM is going to be about a trip to the grocery store to get dog food when a typhoon blows into town.

Visualization Part Two in 3-D

Let's continue with the interactive visualization we started a few sections ago and put some stress on the environment—put some story into the mix—yeah.

- *The backstory:* You just got home from a two week vacation in Bali. You feel rested and look great for the first time in years, but the neighbor who was supposed to feed the dog screwed up and didn't do it, so you have one starving animal on your hands.
- *The mission:* Get dog food at any cost.
- *The stakes:* One dead pooch if you don't do it NOW.
- *The ticking clock starts:* You squeal your car into the grocery store parking lot, but the only parking space open is about to be taken by an old lady in a Silver Cloud Rolls Royce (I live in Hollywood, remember)—you've got to race her to the spot.

Visualization Part Two in 3-D (continued)

And so on it goes from there. Your dog food hunting hero can have all sorts of adventures in the closed environment of the grocery store. The news just predicted an earthquake happening in the next 24 hours, so the store suddenly gets descended on by a frenzied mob of flashlight-hunting crazies. Or the store can get held up by six masked bandits from the local old age home, and your hero has to find a way out—and explain it all to the police later. A tidal wave can come along, tip the entire grocery store upside down, and your hero has to find the dog food section walking on the ceiling of a completely messed up environment.

Hey. It could happen. (Those of you in a lotus position may slowly come out of it now. That's right, inhale, exhale.)

Mapping It Out

The next thing to do is define the boundaries of your universe—the physical and non-physical (historical, psychological, sociological, etc.) constituent elements within the space. In a game, the terms "rooms" and "levels" come into play.

Finding Your Way

Very *Return to Zork*-like, you can have a level where there is a forest, and a path that goes through the forest, and then over a river where there's a mill. You can enter the mill, which has one big grinding room and a cellar that you have to find. In the grinding room there are interactive "hot" spots—a ledger, a mirror, whatever—that when clicked on, give you information that helps you through the game.

The Usual Suspects

The non-physical constituents of the universe are basically the backstory of the place—factors such as:

- The special features of its society (slavery, caste system, nobility, free beer and wine every Friday night)
- The psychologies of the main and minor characters (where they come from, how they relate, who's sleeping with whom)
- The plot or plots of the whole thing

The Rules of Interaction

Once you've defined and laid out your universe, you then have to figure out the rules of interaction within the universe. Will the user be:

- Just an observer, wandering through branches like in a reference title?
- An actor in the universe, with either a first person point of view, like in *Doom*, or third person over-the-shoulder point of view like in *Wing Commander IV*, which then turns into first person POV during the missions?

You also have to determine:

- What spots, or pieces of the universe are going to be "hot?"
- What information will these hot spots contain?
- How many "clicks" per minute (choices) do you want available to the user (too few, it's boring, too many, it's confusing)?
- How will the characters interact with one another?
- How will the characters and the user interact (shout at the screen, wave flags, Vulcan mind-meld)?

The Interface

This can be a tough one, and whole books can be written on the subject. How does the user actually get into the screen and get their fingers dirty with all the stuff you've come up with? For the time being we're stuck with buttons, clicking, and joysticks.

> **As technology advances, we'll obviously have voice and eye (and heavy breathing?) recognition. And that'll help a great deal toward the creation of a more intuitive interactivity.**

No matter what the current state of technology may be, however, all the writers and designers I've talked to keep repeating the same mantra: "An interface should be simple and elegant, elegant and simple." For example, the interface in Lucas Arts *Full Throttle*, is elegant, fun, and awfully simple.

> **The interface is something you must give serious thought to, and the only real advice I can give is: Relative to your genre, go see what other people have done. Once you know what you like and dislike, you can start your design from there.**

The Aesthetics

What's the tone and look of the piece? This is what aesthetics are all about. You've come up with a universe, brilliantly mapped it out both physically and psychologically, determined the interactivity and the interface, and now you have to think about what kind of colors you want to paint the bathroom.

> **Art direction and design is very important. Even with informational products, the aesthetic of how you present your material can make the difference between a boring tech manual, and a manual of printer parts that sings and dances its way into solving your problem.**

What's the mood you wish to sustain? Do you want somber sepia tones, a voice-over with old pictures drifting in and out of the screen, a shoot'em up game with western motifs and/or rocket ships perhaps? Come to think of it, I'd buy a printer that had a singing and dancing manual, wouldn't you?

Music and Sound

One of the things that probably convinced you that *Myst* was *MYST!*—a great experience, a completely believable world, or worlds—was the ambient sounds. Good use of music and sound in a CD-ROM can make for a powerful interactive experience. It helps with the interface—unconsciously bridging the gap between the outer world of reality and the inner world on the screen that you've created—and it helps with the drama and the pacing of the whole thing.

> **Combine the sound of echoing footsteps crossing a stone floor, with dark creepy images, and it's pull-the-covers-over-your-head time. In other words, create an atmosphere your audience can buy into—something that causes them to suspend their disbelief. When this happens, your envisioned universe is a success.**

When you're writing your script, pay close attention to the sounds just beyond the range of dialogue. Write them down, even if they seem weird. Put them in your script as hints for the sound artists—they'll appreciate it. And if you hear a tune, a jaunty little melody, a haunting creature-feature symphony, put that down too. Put it down in words—the composer will understand. Take a hand in the music and sound design, and you'll have a much stronger piece.

Story and Character

Sometimes a story (plot) comes first and you develop the characters around it, or sometimes characters appear, and your story (plot) comes out of what they do. If you have a particularly clever interactive element or audience interface, it's entirely possible to develop your story and characters around that.

> **"Psychic Detective" executive producer Jim Simmons pondered for some time the idea of having users psychically project themselves into the heads of different characters. Thus was born the main character, Eric Fox, the psychic detective, who can transmit himself, along with the user, into the minds of other characters.**

As you are developing, mapping, and setting up rules for your universe, it's no shame to spend time developing a detailed backstory for each character—this will only help when it comes time to write the actual script. You should also take a serious look at the Hero's Journey concept discussed in Chapter 6. You may find this metaphorical model ideally suited to your needs.

The Operation of Chance

Chance is something you may or may not want to have in the universe you're creating. Life, in a way, is a series of accidents. Some pleasant, some not so pleasant. No matter how structured and safe you think your personal reality is, you're completely at the mercy of chance. Terrifying thought? Certainly is. But without sounding like a "six-packed" philosopher, that's what life is all about.

Chance. The roll of the dice. The run of the horse. Will your airplane drop out of the sky today? We think, we act, we believe in one thing or way, then something out of the ordinary happens and suddenly we're thinking, acting, and believing in completely different ways. Evolution through the operation of chance? Pretty risky. But it happens in nature all the time—it's perfectly normal, and it's also rather exciting.

In the interactive script you're creating, the operation of chance can provide some interesting pressures, adding greatly to the value of the experience. Michael Utvich nicely says this about chance, "It can be a functional trigger to create random action that pushes the user into a whole bunch of new problem situations." A whole bunch of new problem situations? God, that's all you need.

The Inference Engine

You build an inference engine into your universe when your universe needs to know something about the user. The universe then uses this info as part of the dynamics of the interactive experience.

Building an inference capability into your script/design is like seeding your world with intelligence. It's artificial intelligence, true, but if done cleverly, with heart and wit, the user will suddenly realize the world you've created has a unique identity, perhaps with a heart and soul.

A good example of just such a beast is the audience profiling device developed by Michael Utvich for the *JD Power's Guide to Automobiles*. The user answers a series of psycho-graphic questions, which the program then analyzes, developing a user profile through which the automobile database is then filtered. A more subtle usage of an inference device happens when your environment keeps track of the moves the user makes, and then uses this data to expand or narrow future available choices.

The Technology

Ultimately, when developing your script/design, you'll have to make at least a passing nod to the technology. You can't get away from it—and this is where your computer expert team member comes in handy if you've got one.

The following items are things you should definitely know about:

- **The Platform:** In your initial treatment you should have a line in there that says something like "concept is portable to all platforms" even if you're not quite sure what it means. *Platforms* are the machines your concept/script/world will be played on, like PC or Macintosh computers or 3DO, CDI, Sega, Nintendo, or Sony Playstation gaming machines.
- **The Engine:** You should also know what an *engine* is. You'll have multimedia people ask about this all the time. "What's your engine like?" they'll say, looking you up and down and taking your mettle. Like the engine that powers your car, a computer engine powers the interactive multimedia universe that you have created. It's the seemingly endless stream of computer code and commands that respond to a user when they touch a keyboard—to type a sentence, put an image on the screen, make a sound, or play a movie.

> **Computer engines can be bought right off the shelf in a software store, or you can rent or lease one from a software or development company, or create one from scratch—doesn't matter. One way or the other, you'll need one to power your universe.**

Relative Time

When I say *relative* time, I'm talking about real time versus created universe time. It's probably safe to say that if you're reading this book, you grew up with television and films, and you're absolutely at ease with the TV and filmatic conventions of compressed time, wipes, dissolves, fade to blacks, etc. It's perfectly okay to have a film or TV story that whips back and forth through time, or changes physical location with a simple cut—you're never lost or confused. All this cutting and dissolving adds to the dynamics of the story, propelling you toward some satisfactory conclusion.

Relative time is a shadowy but important new media point. As the technology gets better, I have the feeling it's going to become even more important in terms of delivering a satisfactory interactive experience—probably more so in a dramatic situation than in a game or informational title.

Older and Hopefully Wiser

The recognition of the passage of time in a created universe is important because it lends to the believability of the situation. In the CD-ROM *Pyramid: Challenge of the Pharaoh's Dream* (deconstructed in Part Three of the book) the characters age twenty years as you go through the seven levels of the game because it actually took about twenty or more years (real time) to build a pyramid. Playing the game, however, it may take only seven, eight or twenty hours to get through those twenty years. In other words, game time has physical symbols that show the passage of real time, thus making it believable.

You Can't Go Home Again

In a dramatic interactive situation where you are assuming your user has only a limited amount of time to experience the title per sitting—say no less than thirty minutes and no more that sixty—like a typical TV, filmatic time breakdown. It's probably a safe bet to say that a title, particularly an interactive movie, will work better if all of the possible user choices are moving forward in time. In other words, you cannot go back and eavesdrop on a conversation you passed up the day before in "title time." *Psychic Detective* (deconstructed in Part Three of this book) works great this way. Relative time constantly moves forward, and you have to be quick if you want to figure out what's happening. This certainly makes for a breathless, and satisfying interactive experience.

On-Line Linkages

When you script/design your universe, you must spend some time thinking about what characters, what situations, what elements of your world can be enhanced by an on-line hook up. What if you have a mystery/thriller title whose outcome depended entirely on the ups and downs of the stock market, the daily weather in some obscure spot on the globe, or the price of mare's milk in Siberia? This is not science fiction. It's happening today, and it will only become more common in the future.

> **Being able to connect your CD-ROM title to a real time on-line service will only grow more important as we move toward the millennium. Serious gamers are already playing against remote partners.**

So if you want to write and design for the emerging media, you must consider the on-line possibilities.

In a Nutshell

Let's recap the twelve rules (categories?) of what you need to consider in order to create a hot interactive script/design—remembering, of course, that they are in no particular order of importance. They're all important.

- The universe
- Mapping it out
- The rules of interaction
- The interface
- The aesthetics
- Music and sound
- Story and character
- The operation of chance
- The inference engine
- The technology
- Relative time
- On-line linkages

> **Stay tuned for the next part of this book where we deconstruct some successful products to see how well everything you've read about so far works in the "real" world of interactive multimedia. (For a look at a really effective scriptwriting program, check out the "StoryLine Pro" CD-ROM and Appendix D for info on how to run it.)**

The Show Bible

When you get into the meat of scripting and creating your interactive design, what you're really doing is building what they call in TV terms a "show bible." This bible contains everything you need to know about your creation.

Some of the things the bible for your multimedia universe should describe are:

- Where it takes place
- What the plots are
- How the plots relate to one another
- Who the characters are
- What their backgrounds are like
- How they relate to one another

There's volumes more that can be written on this subject, but if you get started with the items listed here, I'm sure you'll get the picture in no time.

PART 3

The Anatomy of Success

CHAPTER 8

Psychic Detective

"SMART QUOTE"

"You do an interactive movie, and only the strong survive."

Michael Kaplan—co-creator and screenwriter, *Psychic Detective*

This chapter is all about an interactive movie called *Psychic Detective,* which was created for Electronic Arts by Michael Kaplan, John Sanborn, and Jim Simmons. Michael, John, and Jim were the core creative team, with Michael writing the screenplay, John directing, and Jim executive producing.

All screenshots from "Psychic Detective" ©Electronic Arts 1996 and provided courtesy of Electronic Arts.

> **Michael Kaplan refers to writing "Psychic Detective" as "The most exhilarating creative experience I've ever had, but my frontal lobe came close to liquefying more than once."**

Super Sleuths

Michael Kaplan is a professional Hollywood television and film writer (and a member of Writers Guild of America, west) who fled Hollywood three-and-a-half years ago and now resides in Cambria, California with wife Susan, daughter Leah, and Tess the Lab. He wrote for the ground-breaking NBC comedy series *Michael Nesmith's Television Parts,* and co-scripted half a dozen sold-but-unproduced screenplays with his partner, John Levenstein. When pressed, Michael will admit one of them got made by Peter Bogdonovich, and he removed his name.

Entering the interactive field in 1991, Michael contributed material to Canter Technology's *Meet MediaBand,* and worked as head of creative development for a small games company. He is currently working on numerous interactive film projects with John Sanborn, including the sequel to *Psychic Detective.*

John Sanborn is an award-winning film and video artist (originally from New York City) now living and working in Berkeley, California with his wife Sara and a couple of big dogs. His recent work, *Quirky,* a video self-portrait, has been shown internationally at film festivals and has been aired on PBS and the Learning Channel as part of the Independent Series. He is also working as a director with Colossal Pictures to create commercial and interactive works and to develop long-form series for television. John will be directing the sequel to *Psychic Detective.*

About directing *Psychic Detective,* John says "It was like a marathon. It was a tremendous amount to shoot, a tremendous amount to edit, a tremendous amount to score. If you told me interactive meant five times as much work, I'm not sure I would have gotten involved. But in the end, it was five times as satisfying."

Jim Simmons is an executive producer at Electronic Arts. He lives in San Mateo, California with his wife and children, and he began his interactive career designing robotic pets for Nolan Bushnell. Additionally he has produced entertainment software for Hasbro Electronics, Warner New Media, Tiger Media Philips, and Walt Disney Computer Software. Jim will also be executive producing the sequel to *Psychic Detective.* About creating *Psychic Detective*, Jim comments: "This is what it must have felt like in the earliest days of the movie business, when discoveries were being made with a very adventurous spirit by a bunch of renegade creative types.

(See Appendix C for a complete list of credits.)

Who Done It

Psychic Detective-Black Diamond is the story of Eric Fox—psychic wonder kid and very serious slacker—and his adventures with a group of Russian ex-KGB psychic spies. In the prologue, we meet Eric doing his cheesy act as "The Psychic Flash" in the Puka-Puka Lounge. He touches objects for psychometric readings (who owned them last, where they've come from, etc.), which he then announces to the audience. The audience loves it, but Eric thinks it's a joke—only a way to make a quick buck.

Michael Kaplan writes in his story outline, "As far as Eric Fox is concerned, his special gifts are good for one thing only: shortcuts."

In Walks Laina

One fateful night, in walks Laina Pozok, "blonde, exotic, full of secrets" and totally psychic. Michael's outline then goes on to describe their fateful meeting: "She looked at me and some fire exit in the back of my brain swung open," Eric tell us. Laina ups the ante, whispering to him "Touch me. Touch me in the special place." The next thing Eric knows, he's looking through *her* eyes—gazing at his own flustered self. "You can enter the minds of those around you," Laina murmurs. "Even as you walk and speak."

Eric has discovered the power of *transmitting*, trespassing in the minds of those sensitive to his abilities. Laina teaches Eric about transmitting, and then hires him to play psychic detective and help her out of a jam: "My father just killed himself. My sister may be in danger. I need your help."

That Old Black Magic

For the next six chapters, climaxing in the deadly psychic Black Diamond game, the player, with Eric Fox as their alter ego, is taken for a breathless E-ticket ride through the psychic world of mysterious Laina Pozok and her ex-KGB friends and acquaintances.

We meet Laina's sister Monica, their Euro-trash cousin Chad, Moki, ancient Madame Tikunov, deadly villain Max Mirage, and over fifteen other crazy characters who scheme, connive and kill for the coveted *psychic collectors*—devices made of precious metals and gems that can enhance the abilities of any psychic.

Through the use of 740 QuickTime movies, Eric and the player are thrust into the middle of all of this. Their mission:

Help Laina and her sister Monica

Get Eric to face his childhood fears

Ultimately do battle with the villainous Max Mirage

Not get psychically fried

Chapter-by-Chapter

Here's a quick overview of the story, chapter-by-chapter:

- **Prologue**—Eric meets Laina, she teaches him to transmits himself into the minds of other people. She hires him to play dick.
- **Chapter 1**—Laina takes Eric to a cocktail party at the Pozok mansion where all kinds of underhanded dealings are going on. Cousin Chad is murdered. Eric and Laina flee.
- **Chapter 2**—Outside the mansion, Eric and Laina watch as the police arrive. Eric then has three choices: follow Laina, follow Monica, or go with Moki. Eric ultimately ends up at Laina's duplex where she pulls out a psychic collector.
- **Chapter 3**—In Eric's first experience with the psychic collector, his powers are greatly enhanced. He comes out of his experience/trance to find another dead body, and he's quickly thrown in jail by the cops, because they think he did it.
- **Chapter 4**—Eric physically lays in his bunk while his mind psychically hop-scotches around the city picking up important clues.

- **Chapter 5**—Eric is released from jail. He ultimately ends up back at the Pozok mansion where he learns more about the Black Diamond game. Eric and Laina, with psychic collector in hand, head for a showdown with Max Mirage at Miragequest.
- **Chapter 6**—Brandishing his psychic collector, Eric charges into the Miragequest headquarters, where he's confronted by three choices: try and free Monica, convince Sylvia to betray Max, or confront Max directly, ultimately culminating in the Black Diamond game.
- **Black Diamond Game**—The Black Diamond forms a psychic field composed of interlocking diamonds. Eight iconic images—representing thoughts and fears strewn throughout the story—appear on the board. Eric must choose four; Max will take the other four. They then take turns, pitting thought against thought, until only one survives.

The creators have come up with numerous endings to "Psychic Detective", and you can never really die during the piece. The player and Eric can only suffer varying degrees of psychic burnout for doing something dumb while playing the game.

The Concept Backstory

Executive producer Jim Simmons had the concept for *Psychic Detective* on his mind for a number of years. His initial idea called for a character named Eric Fox, who was a young psychic with the ability to jump into people's heads and see what they see and hear what they hear. A mysterious woman enters his life and brings him into a mystery. A good story, and a perfect interactive metaphor.

When Jim Met John

Jim met John Sanborn, and when the two of them sat down to talk about doing a project together, Jim brought the psychic concept up. It just so happened that John had seen a TV documentary the week before on how the Russian KGB had tried to developed a psychic spy network during the cold war. As John recalls: "It's true, the whole premise for *Psychic Detective* is based on fact. They [the Russians] claimed they made psychic collectors too, which would take your powers and amplify them."

The concept for "Psychic Detective" quickly evolved from a psychic who could jump into people's minds with a mysterious woman entering into his life, to a psychic who could jump into people's minds with a mysterious woman connected to a whole bunch of ex-KGB Russian psychic spies. A wonderfully dangerous device called a psychic collector gets thrown into the mix too.

And Along Came Michael

John brought screenwriter Michael Kaplan into the project and the combined brain power, John says, "spun us off into the stratosphere."

For Michael, Jim's initial psychic concept, "...was the nut. The more I wrote, the more I would scrutinize this little acorn and watch it turn into a massive oak. It really was a solid idea because it had a reason for a story and it had a reason for interactivity. Above all, this device of head-hopping is an idea that *wants* to be interactive. Letting the player choose and piece together the story points is far more interesting to me than a conventional, linear approach."

Eric on Steroids

So Michael, John and Jim went to work on developing the concept.

One of the first things they addressed was the concern that Eric was going to come off too passive, that all that the player could really do was be a voyeur by jumping into people's heads. "We quickly threw out onto the table the idea that you touch objects and get flashes," Michael explains, "There would be physical evidence that was 'hot,' which means that if you touched it you got flashes. We also had, and eventually got rid of, physical evidence that was cold. This was like using the CD-ROM database where there would be love letters, journals, and photographs you could actually pursue as well as read."

From Photo Collages

Initially it was thought that *Psychic Detective* would be a combination of still photo collages and narration, with full motion video reserved for when Eric and Laina were together. "We said there would probably be a ticking clock," Michael recalls from a meeting early on with Jim and John, "The further you dove into the mystery, the more it became a race against time. That didn't really happen. The ticking clock was replaced by the fact you kept moving through the piece no matter what. That was something that developed over time."

To Full Motion

As Michael began fleshing out initial story points, John huddled with the Electronic Arts' technical department, and it was soon decided that *Psychic Detective* could, and would be a full motion video experience, where the user's choice-making would be like video editing on the fly.

Where That Takes Us

With that decision made, and after much discussion and brain storming, it was eventually decided that Eric and the user could:

- Transmit into other people's minds
- Touch objects and receive flashes of information
- Respond to action prompts, which would be tied to the timing of the game and allow choices—such as telling a character to "Get Lost" or "Follow Her" or "Ask Her a Question"
- Activate the psychic collector to give Eric and the player the ability to jump into a lot more heads and throw thoughts to influence people
- Play in the Black Diamond game at the end

Death on the Deferment Plan

It was also decided during the first few creative meetings between John, Jim, and Michael that there would be no early deaths, that one false move would *not* cause you to start over again. "Jim hated early deaths," Michael says, "he felt that people secretly hated that, and that we should avoid it." So a default mechanism was devised that would carry the player through the entire experience without dying.

This "no early death thinking," along with the concept that the experience was going to be in full motion video that allowed action prompts to come and go with the natural dramatics of the story, ended up creating the tone and flow of the piece.

Journey to the Edge of Time

"It didn't require a ticking clock," explains Michael, "This was just a train that was going to leave with or without you. When we got into the action prompts, we saw that this was really powerful. That this was going to make the thing move fast. That this was going to give drama to the choice itself, and that in many ways, this was the future."

Pods of Knowledge

The first documentation that Michael produced was a ten-chapter outline, summarizing story, characters, images, and interactive elements. "The way I work is that I collect a pool of ideas, characters, dramatic moments. In the case of an interactive story, player moments are interesting challenges—situations. You're fishing for ideas, pulling one after another into the boat and it's not time to decide what you throw back. Then at a certain point you have to start playing cop with yourself. You have to decide where is the story, what's going to work."

The following two sections are a reproduction of one of Michael's early "Pods of Knowledge" documents, which is how he keeps track of front and backstory beats that are shifting and changing on a sometimes daily basis.

The Backstory

- Black Diamond was a covert psychic arm of the KGB.
- Laina's father, Vladimir, was the head of the group.
- Laina was in the group.
- Horst was in the group.
- Lexi and the Derma Twins were in the group.
- Lexi fled the country with the twins; they were all killed.
- Collectors were built to enhance ability.
- Enhancements included: transmittal, reading history, manipulation, and throwing destructive thoughts.
- The breakthrough moment came when Lexi destroyed a cat.
- Our collectors have never been accounted for.
- Only Vladimir knew how to build them.
- Horst had an accident and "singed" himself.
- Horst and Laina were having an affair.
- Vladimir sabotaged Horst.
- Lexi was manipulating the Vologian government, was running a slave empire, and was found out by Novina Labunka.

- Moki belongs to the American counterpart of Black Diamond. He wanted Lexi to defect.
- Vladimir ransacked his office just before dying.
- Vladimir did not suffer a stroke. Lexi fried the daylights out of him.
- Laina was Lexi's unwitting accomplice.

The Frontstory

- One of Vladimir's notebooks is stolen.
- Monica's boyfriend is stabbed.
- Horst has a collector.
- Horst and mama want another collector to rejuvenate Horst.
- How to use a collector.
- There's a weird bag lady hanging around this story.
- Tesla and Sylvia Bourget are after Vladimir's things.
- Tesla and Sylvia are out and out crooks.
- Moki wants us to spy on the Bourgets. Who are they working for?
- Max Mirage is this big cheese in the background.
- The Republic of Vologia has a new leader: Novina Labunka.
- A big reception and performance is scheduled to honor Novina Labunka.
- Horst is killed and his collector stolen.
- Monica is kidnapped.
- Goldberg the grad student is beaten up for hassling Max Mirage.
- Moki is convinced Vladimir has hidden a collector.
- A servant threw the collector out.
- The bag lady has the collector.
- Moki suspects Max Mirage is Lexi.
- Moki is given a crippling psychic shock.
- The Bourgets offer a collector-for-Monica swap.
- Max Mirage manipulates us. He is Lexi.
- We play a duel of wits with Max Mirage.
- Max is planning a mass vegetablization at the big function for Novina Labunka.

Scripting It All Out

Once the chapter outlines were completed, Michael started writing the script. His methodology was to create a flow chart of all the possibilities within a chapter as determined by the story outline. He then labeled the possibilities, and printed out a blank chapter that was all headings and numbers, thus buttoning up the chapter so that all the possibilities lead to the chapter ending.

The Numbers Game

Once he had this blank chapter of headings and numbers, he then went through it scene by scene, putting in all the necessary technical information, like what prompts would appear, what objects could be touched, or who's head could be jumped into—all the connecting points for the scene. Michael then went back in and really wrote the scenes full out, trying to make them entertaining.

> **"This, without fail," Michael says, "was the process for every chapter. Start big, fun conceptuals, and then get totally rigid, anal, labeled and try and be a writer again under the confines that you've created for yourself."**

Passing the Heft Test

Ultimately, over a six-month period, Michael produced a 900-page script in a slightly altered screenplay format. But a 900-page draft simply would not do. No. Much too much to shoot. So Michael remounted his charger, took up battle again, and reduced the tome to a svelte 600 or so pages.

The opening of Chapter 1 (see the sidebar entitled: Script 8.1) gives you an idea of what the format looks like. "To me," Michael says, "the epiphanal moment always comes when things collapse on each other, and suddenly I realize that two or three one-dimensional characters that each serve a single purpose to the story become one interesting character that serves several purposes. When I plot out things like this, I often begin with 'What role do these characters serve?' and 'What function are they going to have?' The question of depth and character and personality trail along behind, which is quite different from linear writing. Over time the fact that they have multiple functions and secrets and several motivations suddenly makes them interesting, rich, and complex."

"Psychic Detective" was an idea carried around for a number of years, and then one creative mind got together with two other creative minds, and without really understanding where they were going—following their hearts and noses—they ended up with something that really worked. Here again, creative teams are essential, and passion is too.

Script 8.1

1.INTRO

The Game Screen is one large FRAME in which this scene plays.

EXT. MANSION - NIGHT

CLOSE ON a stone gargoyle or lion. As footsteps approach, CAMERA PANS to discover Eric and Laina coming up the front walk.

Laina touches Eric on the arm, drawing his attention high above.

SHOT of French Windows and a little balcony on the upper floor.

LAINA (O.S.)
That's where my
father jumped.

SHOT PANS down to the jagged tips of a wrought iron gate.

ERIC
Yowch.

LAINA
I tell you, Eric.
Vladimir was beaten.
Disgraced. But too
stubborn to just...
give up like that.

She pushes open the front door. As they enter, the door swings shut, and

CAMERA HOLDS on the huge, diamond-shaped knocker.

INT. MANSION/FOYER - NIGHT

On the transition, THE GAME SCREEN BEGINS TO FORM. There are no prompts just yet, but we have entered Eric's POV.

Eric's POV - He and Laina stand in the foyer, peeking in.

Eric's POV - A dark living room with an accent on oppressive East European art. Guests wander and drink, speaking in hushed voices, examining the art work and furniture. In the center of the things is MONICA—a grunge bombshell of 21.

NOTE: As each character appears on camera, their TRANS prompt appears in the TRANS section of the Game Screen. It is grayed-down and fuzzy—not operative until the first tier.

LAINA (O.S.)
My sister, Monica.

ERIC (POV)
Cute.

LAINA (O.S.)
(a tad harsh)
Very cute. Very weak
and gullible.

Eric's POV - Monica is talking to SYLVIA, an icy, elegant woman in a blood red outfit. She is 30ish.

ERIC (POV)
Who's the power
blouse?

Eric's POV - Laina turns to him, a half-smile on her lips.

LAINA
Maybe you find out
for me.

Eric's POV - MOKI, a little rumpled man comes down the stairs.

ERIC (POV)
And him?

LAINA (O.S.)
(not convincing)

```
                         I don't know. Father had
                         many... students.

Eric's POV - CHAD, impeccably dressed and with all the bearing of a fallen
prince wanders through the room. He is 25 years old.

                            LAINA (O.S.)
                         Ach. My cousin Chad.
                         If there is money to
                         be made, he smells
                         it. Keep an eye on
                         him. And Monica.

                             ERIC (POV)
                         Where will you be?

                               LAINA
                         Me, you do not have
                         to worry about.

Eric's POV - She has stepped into the living room, leaving Eric behind.
(Laina's grayed-down TRANS PROMPT appears at this moment.)

(Go to 1.1A)
```

The Deconstruction

Psychic Detective is not an environment game, and it's not a series of puzzles. *Psychic Detective* is a universe onto itself—unique, mysterious, and fun.

The Universe

Psychic Detective is an interactive movie that takes place in a modern-day urban environment. Its genre is mystery/supernatural. It's a universe filled with people talking, reacting, and interacting with one another and the player. It has interiors and exteriors, like rooms of big old houses and grungy street corners. It has character backstory and object backstory, and it uses cinematic language to convey style, tone and plot.

As John Sanborn puts it, "It's a totality that you have to ingest and understand. And then there's the Black Diamond game, which reflects two things: how well you played through the movie and what you learned cumulatively. Put these two elements together and you get the predilection of one of sixteen possible conclusions."

The Interaction and the Interface

There are five basic ways a player may interact with *Psychic Detective*. You may:

- Transmit into another person's mind
- Touch objects
- Use action prompts like "Stop Her" or "Follow Her"
- Use verbal actions such as interrogations
- Use the psychic collector to throw thoughts and influence people, and read psyches to get a person's backstory

There's a sixth way to interact, which is to play the Black Diamond game, but we'll get into that later.

The Psychic Space of Eric's Mind

The interface for all five methods of interaction works through prompts that appear on the screen during windows of dramatic opportunity—in what the creators call "the psychic space of Eric's mind."

If you look at the screen shot shown on the previous page, you'll see a quarter screen "window" surrounded by a rather spacy looking border—this border is Eric's psychic space of mind.

> **In real time, this psychic border pulses, twists, and flexes with a life of its own. The idea is to make you believe you're looking at something just beyond the range of eyesight—that you're looking into some kind of psychic zone.**

Prompting the Action

All action prompts appear on the psychic border. They look like buttons, and, generally, they are little portraits of people. For example, when Eric's face appears as a button at the top of the screen, this means what you're seeing is from his point of view (POV). The other prompts represent people you can transmit into—like Monica, Sylvia, Laina, Moki, and Chad.

Chad Approaches

If you look at the script (see the Script 8.2 sidebar), everything, hopefully, becomes a little clearer. At the top of the scene you're in the mansion living room, and you're looking through Eric's POV (point of view). The script clearly indicates that the transmit prompts are "IN" for all these different people.

Reading down a few lines, Laina crosses to the staircase and disappears. As she disappears, the script says "OUT: TRANS—Laina", which means the prompt to transmit into Laina's head has disappeared. It goes away because she's left the room and you can't jump into her mind anymore. Additionally, Chad's transmit prompt has gone out because he is now directly confronting Eric. The screen shot on the next page shows that these prompts are no longer on the screen.

Chad then starts talking, and in the background, Eric catches sight of Moki slipping up the stairs while Madame Tikunov is coming down. Madame T's prompt is now on the screen, while Moki's has disappeared. In addition, the object prompt "IN: OBJ-Necklace," for the necklace Chad is holding, has come onto the screen.

Script 8.2

1.1A: Chad Approaches

INT. MANSION/LIVING ROOM - NIGHT

Eric's POV - As he steps into the living room, the TRANSMITTAL PROMPTS suddenly begin to glow.

IN: TRANS-Monica **(1.1F) (1st Entrance)**
IN: TRANS-Sylvia **(1.1G) (1st Entrance)**
IN: TRANS-Laina **(1.1H) (1st Entrance)**
IN: TRANS-Moki **(1.1I) (1st Entrance)**
IN: TRANS-Chad **(1.1K) (1st Entrance)**

Eric's POV - Laina crosses to the staircase. Monica watches her with a hostile disbelief. Moki whispers something to Chad.

Eric's POV - As Laina disappears, Chad makes a bee-line for Eric.

OUT: TRANS-Laina
OUT: TRANS-Chad

Eric's POV - Chad is face-to-face with him, speaking with a proud, Slavic accent.

CHAD
A friend of Karelia?

ERIC (POV)
No. I came with Laina.

CHAD
Idiot! *Republic* of Karelia.
The homeland: world of many
lakes, of beautiful bounty.

Eric's POV - Moki slips up the stairs, passing MADAME TIKUNOV, an old woman who is descending. Moki disappears from view.

IN: TRANS-Madame T. **(1.1J) (2nd Entrance)**
OUT: TRANS-Moki

Eric's POV - Chad, meanwhile, has moved into his private space. He dangles a necklace around his wrist.

IN: OBJ-Necklace **(1.1A.c)**

CHAD
For example: genuine
Karelian onyx. Perfect for
your sweetheart?

ERIC (POV)
Might be overkill on
the first date.

OUT: OBJ-Necklace

Eric's POV - Chad pockets the necklace and takes Eric by the arm, steering him towards a side table.

CHAD
Come here. Perhaps you are
a man who enjoys his...
recreation.

IN: ACT-Get Lost! **(1.1A.b)**
STAY: TRANS-Monica **(1.1F) (2nd Entrance)**

```
STAY: TRANS-Sylvia (1.1G) (2nd Entrance)
                                   CHAD
                        A little game, a one-of-a-
                        kind souvenir... Please.

(Go to 1.1A.a (Default),1.1A.b, 1.1A.c,1.1F or 1.1G)
```

The Necklace with a Past

If you were to touch the necklace by activating the necklace prompt, you would immediately be thrown into another scene (see the Script 8.3 sidebar). A shot from this scene shows that all the prompts have gone out and you're now looking at an *object flash.* An object flash is actually a short movie, and according to this script, Laina is given the necklace as a gift by somebody in the past, but she refused it.

After this object flash, you are then dissolved back to the mansion as Chad puts the necklace away.

Script 8.3

1.1A.C: Touch Necklace

OUT: ALL PROMPTS

OBJECT FLASH:

INT. LIMBO/LAINA & LEXI

SHOT of Laina - she's just removed the necklace from a box. It's clearly a gift. She looks at it with obvious surprise, then bursts into derisive laughter. Shaking her head, she tosses the necklace back at...

A crestfallen Lexi.

DISSOLVE TO:

INT. MANSION/LIVING ROOM - NIGHT

Eric's POV - Chad pockets the necklace and takes Eric by the arm, steering him towards a side table.

CHAD
Come here. Perhaps you are a
man who enjoys his...recreation.

IN: TRANS-Monica **(1.1F) (2nd Entrance)**
IN: TRANS-Sylvia **(1.1G) (2nd Entrance)**

CHAD
A little game, a one-of-a-kind
souvenir... Please.

(Go to **1.1A.a** (Default), **1.1F** or **1.1G**)

Where Passive Playing Takes You

If you followed through to the end of the previous scene (Script 8.2) and hadn't activated any of the prompts (remained passive), you would be defaulted at the end of the scene to scene 1.1A.a—"Go to 1.1A.a (Default)."

It's also interesting to note near the end of Script 8.2 that the "STAY: TRANS-Monica (1.1F) (2nd Entrance)" annotation is there to remind the player that Monica can still be transmitted into. The "(2nd Entrance)" part of the annotation means that time has moved on since her prompt first came on at the top of the scene, and that if you choose to jump into her head now, it will be in the middle (or 2nd entrance) of her scene.

Transmitting Monica

If you chose to jump into Monica's head as soon as her prompt button appears, when Eric walks into the room at the top of scene 1.1A: "Chad Approaches" (see Script 8.2), then you would have gone immediately to the first part of scene 1.1F: "Transmit Monica" (see the sidebar for Script 8.4), where it says "(1st Entrance).

If you had waited any kind of time to jump into Monica's head, then you would come into her POV scene about halfway through, at the "(2nd Entrance)" spot annotated in the script.

Groovy Pieces of Psychedelia

The "Transmission segue" at the top of scene 1.1F: "Transmit Monica" is there to indicate that a "groovy piece of psychedelia" needs to go in this spot (come up on the screen) to take care of any jump-cut hiccup that might occur as the computer switches scenes. Also, the "RETURN" annotated at the right side of the page (it occurs three times during the scene) shows where the player will go if they decide to return to Eric's head before the scene has played out.

Monica's portrait button will be at the top, because that is whose, POV you're seeing all of this through. And the buttons for Sylvia, Laina, Moki, and Chad are still there because you can still transmit into them. Eric's button is there too if you chose to jump back into his head.

Script 8.4

1.1F: Transmit Monica

INT. MANSION/LIVING ROOM - NIGHT

Transmission segue.

STAY: TRANS-Sylvia **(1.1G) (1st Entrance)**
STAY: TRANS-Laina **(1.1H) (1st Entrance)**
STAY: TRANS-Moki **(1.1I) (1st Entrance)**
STAY: TRANS-Chad **(1.1K) (1st Entrance)**

RETURN
: 1.1A

(1st Entrance)

Monica's POV - Sylvia is talking to her, but Monica is looking beyond her, distracted by Laina passing through the room towards the staircase.

SYLVIA
...he was hoping to
come in person—

MONICA (POV)
I don't believe it!

Monica's POV - Sylvia turns to see Laina disappearing up the staircase.

OUT: TRANS-Laina
OUT: TRANS-Chad

SYLVIA
Your sister?

MONICA (POV)
Doesn't waste much time.

Monica's POV - Sylvia glances over at Eric and Chad. Monica, however, focuses on Sylvia's Miragequest pin. It is a hologram, and the face of Max Mirage occasionally flickers into view.

SYLVIA
Who's the toy-boy?

MONICA (POV)
(not hearing)
Where's Mr. Mirage?

SYLVIA
Meet him at the tea room. 10:00.

Monica's POV - Still staring at the pin, her voice far-away.

MONICA (POV)
Max Mirage makes me feel good.

SYLVIA
(impatient)
Yeah, yeah.
Everybody says so.

Monica's POV - Moki makes for the staircase, passing Madame Tikunov who has come down from the second floor.

OUT: TRANS-Moki
IN: TRANS-Madame T.**(1.1J) (2nd Entrance)**

Monica's POV - She sounds like she's about to spill tears.

MONICA (POV)
I miss the good times.

SYLVIA
Monica. Focus. Max wants to make you an offer.

MONICA (POV)
To me?

STAY: TRANS-Sylvia **(1.1G)** **(2nd Entrance)**
OUT: TRANS-Madame T.

RETURN: **1.1A.A** or **1.1A.B**

(2nd Entrance)

Monica's POV - She fidgets with the ring on her finger.

SYLVIA
Miragequest would like to handle your father's collection.

MONICA (POV)
Which one?

SYLVIA
His papers. Research. Max Mirage will personally help you categorize.

MONICA (POV)
We would do it...together?

Monica's POV - Sylvia seems to have a hard time with groupies. She tries to smile encouragingly.

SYLVIA
Whatever it takes.

Monica's POV - A commotion erupts on the other side of the room. Madame T. screams at Chad, ripping the board game away from him.

MADAME T.
Idiot! Take your hands away!

Monica's POV - Chad flees towards the kitchen.

IN: TRANS-Chad **(1.2J)** **(1st Entrance)**

Monica's POV - Madame T. hisses something at Eric and heads back upstairs, carrying the board game. HOLD on Eric.

OUT: TRANS-Chad
STAY: TRANS-Sylvia **(1.2G)** **(1st Entrance)**

RETURN: **1.2A**

(Go to **1.2F** (Default—continue transmitting), **1.2A**, **1.2J** or **1.2G**)

Telling Chad to Get Lost

To illustrate an action prompt like "Get Lost", take a look at the end of Script 8.2, where an "IN: ACT-Get Lost! (1.1A.b)" prompt is indicated. The screen shows the prompt as words appearing along with a button portrait of Chad that says: "Tell Chad to get Lost!" If you activate this button, you are immediately sent to scene "1.1A.b: "Get Lost!" (see the sidebar for Script 8.5).

Script 8.5

1.1A.B: Get Lost!

INT. MANSION/LIVING ROOM - NIGHT

OUT: TRANS-Madame T.
STAY: TRANS-Monica **(1.1F) (2nd Entrance)**

STAY: TRANS-Sylvia **(1.1G) (2nd Entrance)**

Eric's POV - He pulls his arm away from Chad, turning to him.

ERIC (POV)
You shouldn't sell stuff
that isn't yours.

Eric's POV - Chad stiffens slightly.

CHAD
Do you know who I am?

ERIC (POV)
Cousin Chad. The
Euro-slacker.

Eric's POV - Chad is caught, speechless for a second.

CHAD
We have nothing further to say.

Eric's POV - He bows slightly and wanders over to the board game, muttering to himself.

Eric's POV - Eric glances around the party. His eye settles on an abstract painting, clear across the room.

Eric's POV - Eric begins to move towards it. He passes Monica and Sylvia.

OUT: TRANS-Monica
OUT: TRANS-Sylvia

Eric's POV - Monica wears a silver ring with a large inlaid gem. She fingers it nervously.

Sylvia has an MQ hologram button on her lapel.

IN: **OBJ-Ring (1.1D)**
IN: **OBJ-MQ Pin (1.1E)**

Eric's POV - The ladies look at him with mild suspicion, then return to their conversation. Eric passes them by.

IN: OBJ-Painting **(1.1C)**
OUT: OBJ-Ring
OUT: OBJ-MQ Pin

Eric's POV - He pauses in front of the picture: an oil painting of the collector vortex.

(Go to **1.1C** (Default), **1.1D** or **1.1E**)

Eric Discovers Art

As the script indicates, Eric tells Chad to buzz off, much to Chad's chagrin, and then Eric spies an abstract painting on the far wall of the room that piques his interest, which he then heads for. As he crosses the room, object prompts come up and go out (the player has the choice to activate these), and eventually Eric settles in front of the painting. Note that the scene's default is for Eric to get a "flash" from the painting.

The Psychic Collector

To show how the psychic collector works (transmitting into other characters' minds over long distances, throwing thoughts, and reading psyches), let's take a look at the last part of Script 8.6 "INT. MIRAGEQUEST/PRIVATE ROOM-EVENING" (see the sidebar). Eric enters a private room at Miragequest. It's his POV, and Sylvia is sitting at a desk. The script indicates the collector prompt comes on—"IN: ACT-Collector (6.1A.b)," and the screen shows this prompt glowing nicely.

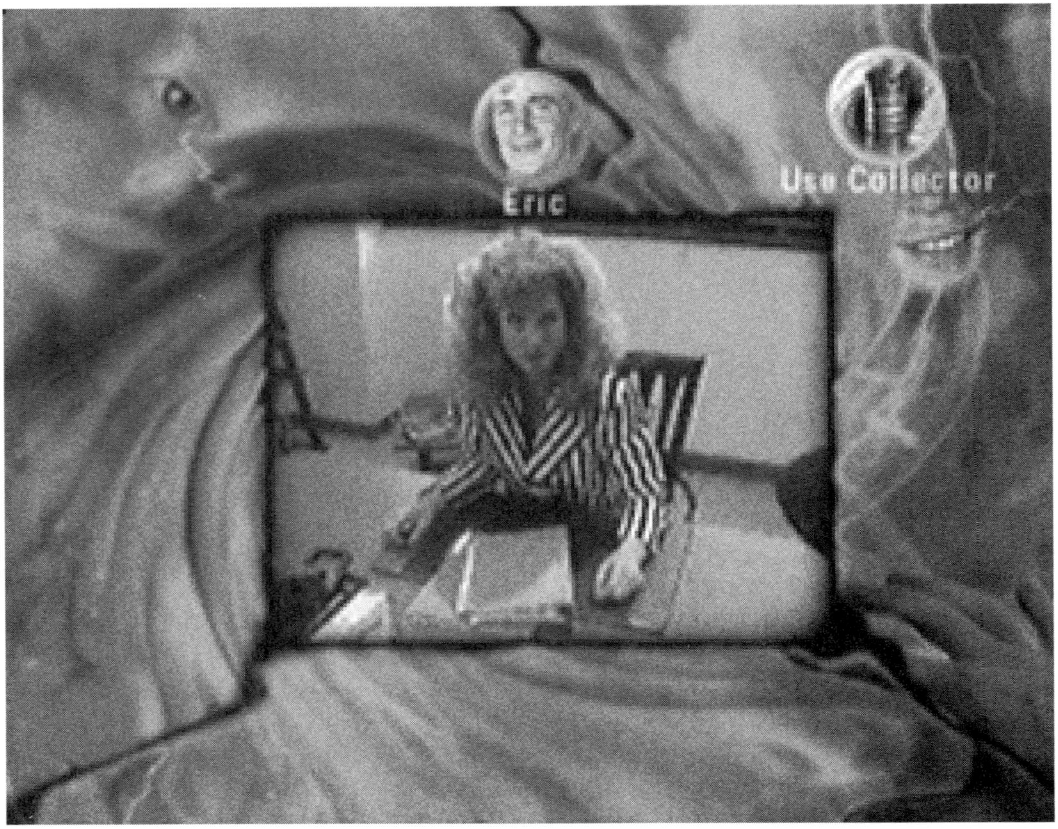

Script 8.6

6.PRO.B: Go to Sylvia

EXT. MIRAGEQUEST/INT. LAINA'S CAR - EVENING

Eric's POV - On Laina.

ERIC (POV)
The Queen Bee is all
hot and bothered. I
wanna rub that itch.

Eric's POV - Laina is clearly disappointed.

LAINA
If you must.

ERIC (POV)
Let me hang onto this.

Eric's POV - He takes the collector from her.

INT. MIRAGEQUEST/1ST FLOOR CORRIDOR - EVENING

Eric's POV - A door: PRIVATE. An empty room across the hall.

ERIC (POV)
Wait in there.

LAINA
I don't—

ERIC (POV)
I got no time for
cat fights.

INT. MIRAGEQUEST/PRIVATE ROOM - EVENING

Eric's POV - Eric enters. Sylvia sits at a desk. We see the blue notebook.
Two pages have already been ripped out.

IN: ACT-Collector**(6.1A.b)**
IN: ACT-Seduce **(6.1I)**(if triggered by 4.2J)
IN: ACT-Seduce **(6.1I.a)**(if triggered by 2.3E or 4.3J)
IN: ACT-Seduce **(6.1J)**(Default version)

Eric's POV - Sylvia glares, hitting a button on her desk.

SYLVIA
You're in the wrong room.

ERIC (POV)
Aw, don't we ever get a
scene together?

Eric's POV - Move off of Sylvia onto a new Miragequest Testimonial Poster. Monica is one of the featured faces.

(Go to **6.1J** (Default), **6.1A.b**, **6.1I** or **6.1I.a**)

Into the Vortex

Choosing the Collector prompt immediately sends us to scene 6.1A.b: "Vortex (w/Sylvia)" (see the sidebar for Script 8.7). The first thing that appears on the screen when you choose a collector is a vortex of rapidly moving images. These images are sort of a preview of the characters you're going to be able to do stuff with when the collector finally settles down.

Towards the end of this scene, once the collector has chilled, prompts collect in three distinct areas. These prompts will allow you to transmit over a long distance, throw thoughts at Sylvia, or read her psyche.

Script 8.7

6.1A.B: Vortex (w/Sylvia)

INT. LIMBO/LIGHTS(REP)

Eric's POV - A burst of colored light hits the screen. Strobing images play, as fast as possible:

INT. VLADIMIR'S STUDY(REP/VAR)

SHOT of Chad being stabbed.

INT. LIMBO/CLOSET/DAD(REP)

SHOT of the cigarette swirling before the face of the screaming boy.

INT. LIMBO/MOKI(VAR)

SHOT of Moki screaming with pain.

INT. LIMBO/BEDROOM(REP)

SHOT of the woman (Eric's mother) grimacing with pain and pleasure.

EXT. DUPLEX(REP/VAR) - NIGHT

SHOT of Sergei being shot.

INT. LIMBO/CLOSET(REP)

SHOT of Eric's father peeking through a crack, then shutting the door abruptly. The Screen goes Black and DISSOLVES TO:

FADE UP ON: The collector vortex. Prompts collect in three distinct areas:

Transmitting from long distance

IN: TRANS-Monica **(6.1C)**
IN: TRANS-Moki **(6.1E)**
IN: TRANS-Madame T. **(6.1F)** (if triggered by 5.3A.1, 5.3A.2, 5.3A.3 or 5.3A.4)
IN: TRANS-Max Mirage **(6.1K)**
IN: TRANS-M-Quester **(6.1O)**

Throw Thoughts

IN: THROW-Affection **(6.1L.a)**
IN: THROW-Aggression **(6.1L.b)**
IN: THROW-Submission **(6.1L.c)**

Read Psyche

IN: PSYCHE-Sylvia **(6.1M)**

(Go to a selection. Default can be random shuffle among the Transmitting options.)

Seducing Sylvia

To get Sylvia to submit, choose the submission button "IN: THROW-Submission (6.1Lc)." We immediately jump to scene 6.1L.c: "Submission (Sylvia)" (see the sidebar for Script 8.8). As the script indicates, Sylvia immediately gets to her knees and "begins writhing with exquisite pleasure," thus allowing Eric to get the notebook he's after.

Script 8.8

6.1L.C: Submission (Sylvia)

A 30-Frame Submission Burst, DISSOLVING to...

INT. MIRAGEQUEST/PRIVATE ROOM - EVENING

Eric's POV - Sylvia's image is subtly manipulated—a quick smudge, a rearrangement of features.

Eric's POV - Sylvia drops to the carpet and begins writhing with exquisite pleasure. She murmurs dreamily, far-away.

SYLVIA
Smear me with the blood from kosher killings. Weird industrial fluids...

Eric's POV - As Sylvia continues to twist and talk, Eric makes for the desk.

SYLVIA (O.S.)
...Make me do unspeakable things with frozen food. Crazy-glue a parrot to my body.

Eric's POV - He grabs Vladimir's notebook, the ripped-out pages, and the brown folder that belonged to Moki. Eric makes for the door, taking one last look at Sylvia, still in her own world.

SYLVIA
I'll be scratched and squawking and bleeding for your thoughts. Oh. And I'm wearing a clown costume...

Eric's POV - A WHITE FLASH as the collector is turned off.

(Go to **6.2C**)

It's Easier than It Looks

When you think about it, the interface for *Psychic Detective* is really pretty simple—just a bunch of buttons that keep showing up and going away, and when they're around, you get to choose some. The way in which these buttons are timed to dramatic action, however, makes them powerful metaphors for the player's ability to dip into the collective consciousness (and unconsciousness) of the characters. They're also a way for the player to navigate up stream, down, or across, for that matter, and have a rich story experience.

> **If all of the above seems pretty complicated, well, it is. But only on paper. The actual movie plays quite nicely, though you do have to be quick of eye and nimble of finger.**

Beyond the Three Act Structure

Starting out, Michael knew he wanted to create a mystery that could be solved in many different ways, so for him, that put the three act structure on hold. There was going to be a beginning, multiple endings, and the middle was going to be something real different.

> "Initially," Michael recalls, "I was just picturing parallel streams moving forward. Early on, we started talking about chapters. We were initially talking about 12 chapters. It seemed like a way to address the material."

Reining the Story In

But the structure couldn't be all parallel streams, there had to be points where all the business had to converge—at bottlenecks. "No matter what happens," Michael says, "Eric goes to jail. There are different ways he can get arrested, different ways that he can be interrogated, but he's going to end up in jail." Having bottlenecks in the structure was also a good way to control the story, to rein it in if it got too wide. "It saved me my mind knowing that there were a couple of life rafts along the way that I could grab onto and fight to bring the story in."

A part of the structure puzzle was worked out in terms of what kinds of experiences the user could have playing this game. "If you're going to have somebody playing this," Michael adds, "it's not enough that it be a passively interesting sequence. There's got to be things to do, and they have to be exciting."

Creating Experience Pods

Eric landing in jail was something that came up in early discussions, because pinning Eric's body physically in one place allowed Eric and the user the opportunity to jump into a lot of different heads. It allows them to literally roam the city at will—a great interactive experience for the player. So from the get-go, Michael knew that he wanted Eric to end up behind bars, and this "experience pod," if you will, greatly determined what came before and after in the story line.

Tagging experiential situations ahead of time helped Michael build the structure of his "Psychic Detective" universe, forcing all sorts of plot points to surface that could then be cleverly tied together.

Eric also has the ability to touch objects and receive information, another great audience experience. Here again, Michael knew that somewhere there ought be a room full of stuff that could be touched—probably in the mansion—only makes sense, right? Therefore, an entire mansion touching-room experience was envisioned, and then all Michael had to do was figure out where along the way Eric and the player could get in there to have some fun.

Varying Styles of Interaction

In general, and totally intentional, the six chapters and final Black Diamond game of Psychic Detective each have a different internal structure and style of interactivity associated with them. Here's how they play out:

- **Chapter 1**—almost all of the main characters are in one location—the mansion—and inside the mansion is where all the action takes place. Eric is able to wander around exploring the environment in his own body, or jump into the heads of different characters and experience the place from their POV.
- **Chapter 2**—the story shoots out in three directions. You're on the street, and have the choice of following either Laina or Monica, or going off with Moki. This kind of "traveling movement" opens up the piece dramatically, giving it a very different feel and interaction than Chapter 1.
- **Chapter 3**—becomes the lesson with the psychic collector. Suddenly things get intensely horizontal, because you now have seven different characters you can transmit into over long distance. You also have three kinds of thoughts you can throw at Laina, as well as the ability to read Laina's psyche. Again, there's a whole different feel here, with some very different interaction.
- **Chapter 4**—yet again has a different kind of structure and interactive feel. Eric's in jail, but his mind is free to wander the city—hop-scotching from head to head as the good citizenry he's hitch-hiking rides with randomly crisscross the city.
- **Chapter 5**—is another structural blow out. A lot of the permutations set up in the first four chapters get played out here, and the screen just fills up with possibilities. For this chapter, Michael explains, "The operating metaphor is scuba diving. If you go underwater there are mesmerizing objects fixed in place, suspended in time, unaffected by what's happening on shore—whenever you break the surface you see that events continue to change on shore. If you stay underwater too long, you run out of oxygen and are forced to come to the surface."
- **Chapter 6**—narrows the story down to where Eric charges into Miragequest and can either free Monica, seduce Sylvia to betray Max, or confront Max directly.
- **The Black Diamond Game**—and all of it ends here (see the following section devoted to this topic).

> **The scuba diving metaphor hits home when you're in the hidden object room of the mansion. If you get lost in the weird visuals associated with each touched object, and if you come up for air too late, the plot has moved on, and maybe a character will be dead. Oops.**

Boy Meets Girl on Psychic Campus

Simply put, Michael's process for figuring out the structure for Psychic Detective was really a fleshing out of the slug line—psychic boy meets psychic girl, girl gets boy to help, boy's helping turns into a lot of conflict, boy and girl face the final battle—in combination with strictly maintaining the rules of interaction for the universe (jumping into minds, touching things, etc.).

The slug line and rules of interaction then acted as creative spring boards for coming up with audience "experience pods," which then fed back into the whole process, acting as major environment points to help further define the story/structure. I suppose it's a bit like walking a tight rope while trying to decide what pole to attach the end of the rope too. And in the end, as the shape of the piece was coming out of the mist, the creators consciously kept the internal structures of the chapters different, allowing for a unique chapter-by-chapter interactive look and feel.

The Black Diamond Game

Michael, Jim, and John turned their attention to exactly what the Black Diamond game was going to be just after Michael finished writing Chapter 1.

"We all knew it was a psychic battle," says Michael, "that you could throw thoughts at one another. And looking ahead, still roughing the story out at that time, I knew there was going to be information you'd find during the movie, or not find... that there was going to be different character states at the end. Was Madame T alive or dead? Laina burnt out or healed? Monica free or a slave? And somehow, all of this had to have impact on the game, and if it didn't, and if all we had was a checkers game, then we were screwed."

Bored Board Designer

One day Michael and Jim sat on Michael's back deck, and with pennies and a roughed out game board in hand began assigning values to different moves, generally "trying to play the game."

"John had no patience for this," remarks Michael, "he went in to my computer, pulled up Adobe Photoshop, pulled up some images he brought with him, and after a while said, 'hey look at this.' He came up with a game board that made the Black Diamond concept very concrete—how it would look and how to ascribe meaning to it."

The First Thing That Happens

The Black Diamond game starts with eight iconic images on the screen. These icons represent thoughts, fears, and even characters that the player has been confronted with during the movie. For example, the image of a lit cigarette may be one of the icons. If it is, it represents Eric's childhood fears, because his father burnt him with a cigarette when he was a small child as punishment for using his psychic powers.

The player then gets to choose four of the icons, and the remaining four go to Max Mirage. Once the choice is made, the icons drift down to the eight diamond shaped places on the game board, and the player moves first—you take one icon (or thought) and pit it against one of Max's. The stronger icon wins.

Power Images and Information

If you had Eric face his fears during the movie, the cigarette icon becomes a powerful image for your side. If you didn't have Eric face his fears, then you can hurt yourself if you use the icon or if Max uses it against you. If you choose Laina's icon, and you healed her during the movie, then she's a powerful icon for your side too. And if you saved Madame T, and choose her icon, it also becomes a plus.

The point of all of this is that when you play through the movie, a tremendous amount of information is revealed (who is afraid of what, who did what to whom, and when, etc.), and the characters achieve different states. (Laina is healed. Monica is freed, etc.) All of these factors have an impact on the Black Diamond game.

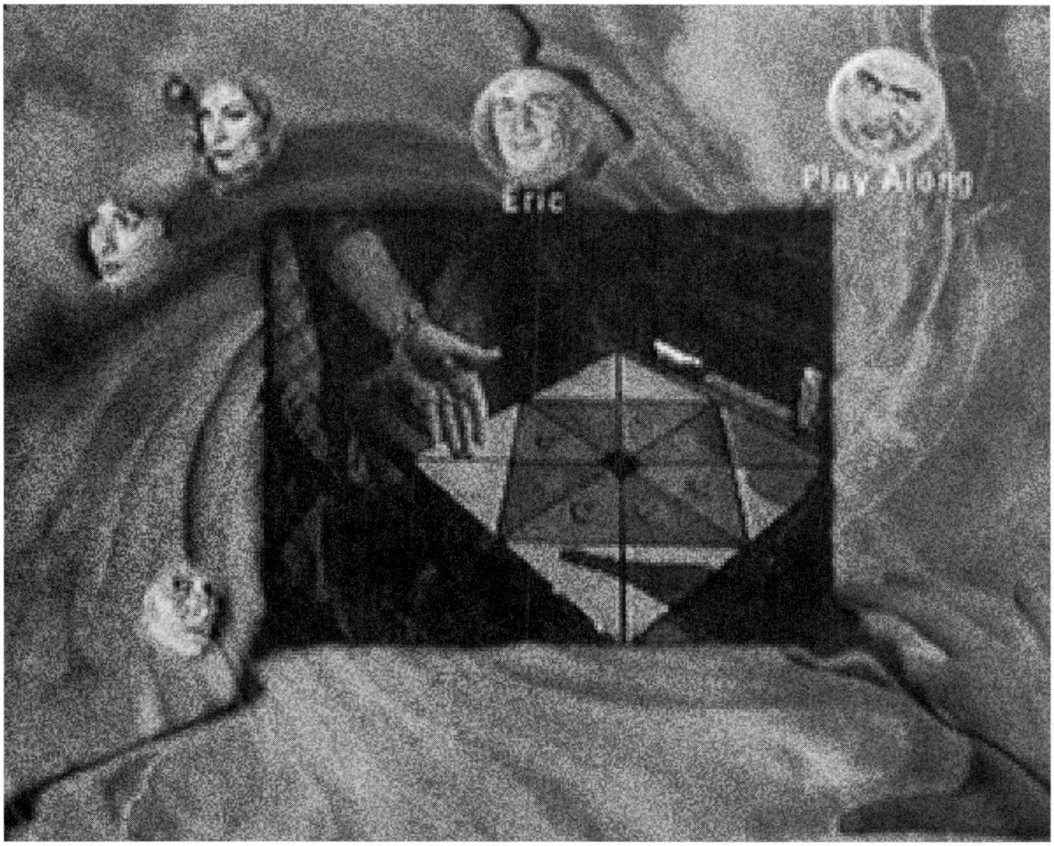

Breaking with Tradition

"A traditional computer game structure," says John, "is that you can't move forward unless you solve a puzzle. That's not what we did. We did something different. The Black Diamond game is a knowledge filter. It takes everything that you've learned and it evaluates how you played through the movie and puts them together. To people, or publishers, used to a win or lose scenario, it's an interesting blurring of the win/lose concept."

> **There are sixteen different endings to the Black Diamond game, five different victories, and five different defeats. There's a draw, and then there's a special draw which opens up to a second playing of the game—and a win, lose, or draw out of that.**

Tone and Character Development

Tone is an important part of character development. And there was a conscious choice on Michael's part to create a tone for *Psychic Detective*—charged up, a bit campy, very pop, sort of like an adult graphic novel. "All these little films [in *Psychic Detective*]," Michael explains, "are like panels in a comic book." And in order for all of the quick change manipulations to really work, Michael felt the story could *not* take itself too seriously.

> **"It was interesting how Jim and the Electronic Arts brass were a little uncomfortable that there were jokes," Michael says, "but over time, they came to embrace the story's funny and quirky tone."**

Arcing the Romantic Karma Points

In addition to tone, a character's arc is a major element of who and what a character is. And arcing a character can be a tricky thing when it comes to interactive writing.

When Michael first started writing the script for *Psychic Detective,* he was very interested in fully developing the relationship between the main characters Eric and Laina. He wanted them to have serious dynamic growth throughout the script. And so while writing, he kept track of what he called "romantic karma points." That is, if you behave properly to Laina at certain points along the way, and do not push things too quickly, you are going to come

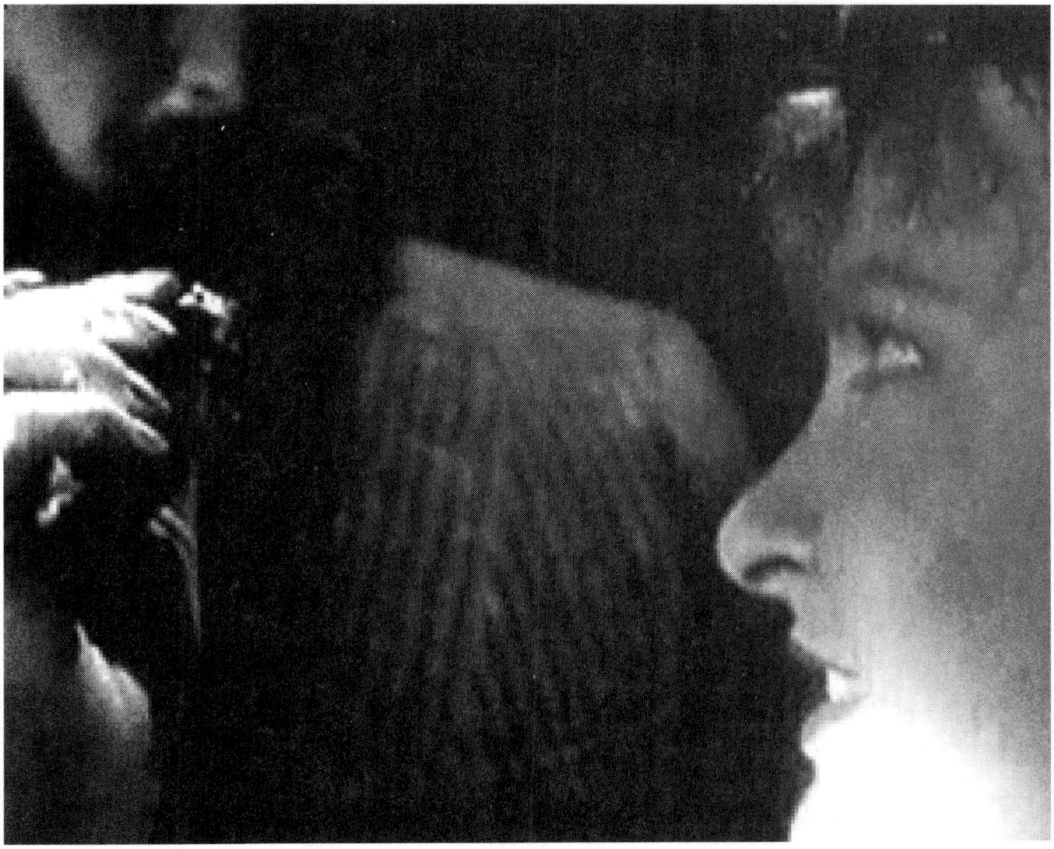

together on a romantic level. If you push things too hard, you'll alienate her.

"In the end," Michael points out, "it just didn't survive the final cut. I had to trim the material from over 900 pages to less than 600. There were just so many overriding plot factors that had become more important than just how had the romantic karma been built up."

Slacker Saves World Gets Kiss

Ultimately, the relationship between Eric and Laina became more simplified. Eric gets a big kiss if he saves the day at the end of the game. But character development wasn't entirely simplified due to disc space and production considerations. Eric's character does arc in a way, and it's the player's choice-making process that makes Eric's arc change.

For example, Eric starts out in the beginning as a callow, wise-cracking slacker. If the player does not interact with the movie very much (chooses a passive role), Eric does not rise to the challenge of the situations he's confronted with. In other words, he takes the path of least resistance (the defaults see to it) whenever he's confronted with a major (difficult?) decision. Ultimately, he's still a callow slacker who ends up losing the game for you.

> **Eric is a much stronger and different character because of player interaction. All of the endings for "Psychic Detective" are in some fashion or another connected to Eric's character growth.**

If the player is very pro-choice, then there's ample opportunity to influence Eric's character. If the player gets Eric to confront his traumatic childhood fears, then these fears are no longer valid, and Eric grows. This growth has even further ramification, because during the Black Diamond game at the end, these fears cannot be used against him.

Codependent Galore

Laina, too, has some growth. She shows up at the beginning as a burnt-out psychic, choked to the nose with guilt. If during the movie Eric can find out why—her backstory—and confront her with this knowledge, she'll be healed, and become a stronger character. She will also become an important ally for Eric when he plays the Black Diamond game with Max Mirage at the end.

In general though, because of the limitation on script length, Michael couldn't really put too many subtle shadings on the various characters, and as he points out: "One of the things that became a challenge was that she [Laina] instantly became a hyper-neurotic, or manic-depressive character because she was reacting to the choices on Eric's behalf."

> **"If he [Eric] decides to do this, she's swooning, getting upset, or lashing out, which makes her an unstable character, and that's unfortunate," says Michael. "That's one of the things that I'd like to improve, because I think that there are better ways of creating characters in interactive situations."**

Scoring Multimedia Music

Because players can "edit" Psychic Detective on the fly, as it were—cutting in and out of scenes like changing lanes on an LA freeway doing a hundred miles an hour—you'd tend to think that scoring music for these scenes and making it all match as you switched from one to the other, would create a symphonic nightmare from hell.

John Sanborn was definitely concerned about this, but, as he's quick to point out, "Each individual movie had its own integrity—as written, as shot, as edited, and, by extension, as scored. This micro integrity, oddly enough, made it work from scene to scene musically." Each movie was scored to have an opening gambit, a strong core, and closure. "If you let the movie just play," John says, "everything cuts together—you come in at the middle of a music cue, and it seems proper."

An Interactive Movieola

One of the unique technical features of *Psychic Detective* is that Electronic Arts created a post-production tool called "Movieola", where the 740 QuickTime movies shot and created for the piece could be assembled and played. John Sanborn points out, "It [Movieola] was a buffering environment. It allowed you to make changes, play it, make some more changes and play it again. You could create a rough cut."

The primary reason for the development of "Movieola" was that early on, John, Jim, and Michael felt that video games were too programmed—"they weren't edited." Their humanity had been stripped from them, and they felt too procedural. They didn't have a movie feel to them.

John further explains, "Unless I sat with the programmers day in and day out, there was no way that he or she could translate what was in the script, although the script is extremely exact, they couldn't translate it into reality because they weren't playing the movie. Programmers don't play it, they assemble the pieces and they sit back and say its done. And then you look at it and say, well, now, I'd like to change that, and change this, and change that."

The Flash on the Cutting Room Floor

The editing process for *Psychic Detective* in general went like this: A trio of editors cut the footage roughly to the script, and using Adobe Premier, John created most of the required special movies, like the object flashes and the vortexes, etc.. In the end, 740 movies were brought into Movieola, where they were treated as 740 different objects. No matter what their length, each movie was considered an object, a separate bit of information.

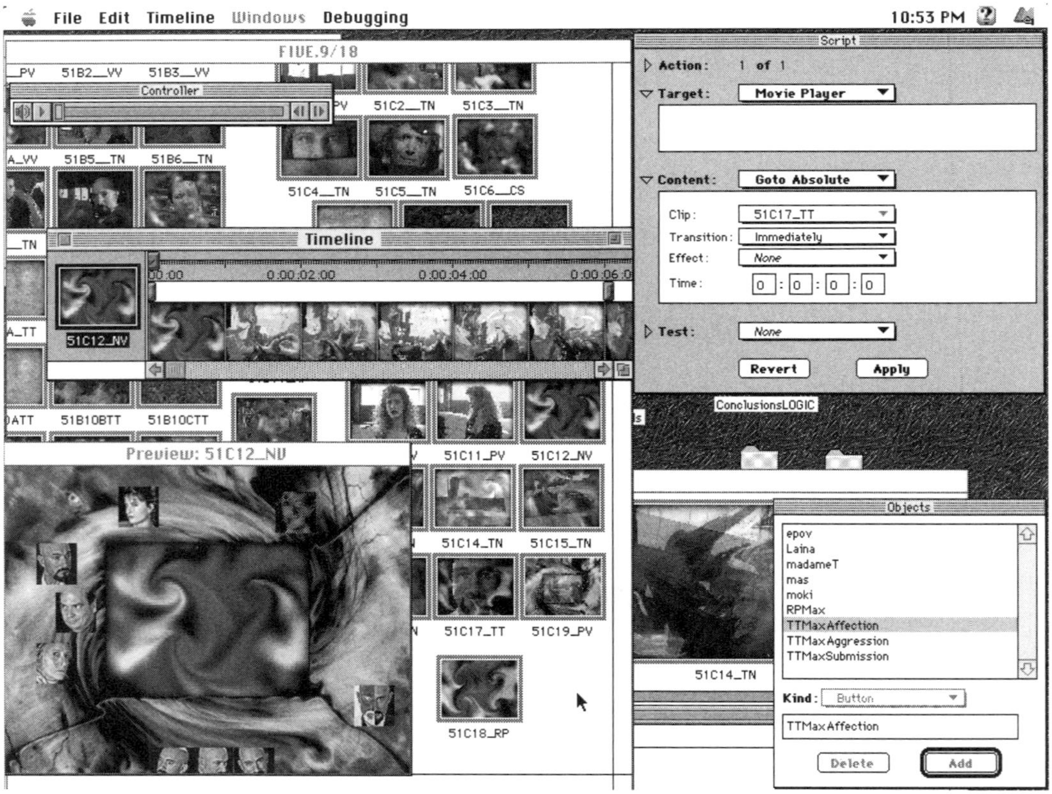

John then set about adding "action tokens" or data intelligence to each separate movie. As you saw, the script contains detailed instructions where prompts are to come in and out, and if you did this, then you went here, or if you touched that object, you got this flash. All of these script-noted instructions were carefully added to the right place, and the right time in the footage by John in Movieola.

> **The real power of Movieola is that it lets you instantly playback a movie you're editing with all its related footage, so you can get the "feel" of the piece. If you don't like it, then you can tweak it until it works. John comments, "So the authoring task falls to somebody who can be as smart as a programmer in one sense but also has the taste of an editor."**

Timing Your Head Trips

Another cool thing Movieola allows creators to do is play with relative time. As a psychic detective you can jump from head to head, but once you are in somebody's head, time still moves forward for the rest of the movie—Michael's scuba diving metaphor here again. So the trick is to make sure the player jumps into the right time frame every time a jump is made. Movieola allows this to happen by relating the time between two clips, which essentially means setting dialogue and action points, so, as John says, "We can have a synchronized dramatic experience that we can jump between."

CHAPTER 9

Pyramid: Challenge of the Pharaoh's Dream

"SMART QUOTE"

"The [Egyptian] cultural details were sometimes so outlandish, they could only be real. For instance, when women dressed for parties or parades they placed little molds of colored, scented animal fat on their heads. Over several hours, the grease would melt into their hair, yielding an ancient Egyptian image of beauty."

Anne Casavant Chaney—writer, *Pyramid*

In this chapter, we're going to deconstruct an educational adventure game for both kids and adults. Aptly named *Pyramid: Challenge of the Pharaoh's Dream,* this game is all about the building of a great pyramid in ancient Egypt. The project is a co-development of Dreamquest Images (the Academy Award winning special effects house for *The Abyss* and *Total Recall*) and Knowledge Adventure, Inc. *Pyramid* was executive produced by Roger Holzberg (who also served as supervising designer) and written by Anne Casavant Chaney. The CD-ROM is published by McGraw-Hill Home Interactive, located in Redwood City, CA—a division of the McGraw-Hill Companies.

Your last journal entry indicates, as per Anne Casavant Chaney's script, "For two weeks I have probed every crack looking for the secret entrance. Now, I think that I have found it."

All screenshots from "Pyramid: Challenge of the Pharaoh's Dream" by McGraw-Hill Home Interactive © 1996 and provided courtesy of the McGraw-Hill Companies.

Pharaoh Makers

Executive producer/supervising designer Roger Holzberg joined Knowledge Adventure in the spring of 1993 and brought with him 15 years of experience in the Motion Picture Industry. As Executive Producer/Designer at Knowledge Advenutre, Inc., Roger has worked on Steven Spielberg's *Movie Maker.* Additionally, he executive produced and designed *The Adventurers*, a digital/global, on-line kid's club and *My First Encyclopedia.* He also produced, designed and wrote *The Discovers,* which utilizes the IMAX movie as a "table of contents," merging the movie with the rich tapestry of Pulitzer Prize winner Daniel Boorstin's best-selling book. He also produced, designed and wrote *Speed* and was the writer of *The Living Sea,* an IMAX film currently in release. His animated feature, *The Last Whale,* is scheduled for a spring '96 release. He is a member of the Writers Guild of America, west.

Anne Casavant Chaney is a writer specializing in educational media. She brings well-researched content and an audience sensitive presentation to her writing. Anne earned her bachelor's degree from Massachusetts Institute of Technology, and maintains great fondness for scientific exploration. She spent two years as director of film development at MacGillivray Freeman Films, writing treatments and scripts for IMAX movies. Anne earned her doctorate in Education from Harvard University in 1993. As a dissertation project, she wrote and conducted a formative evaluation of an educational simulator ride for kids. Her most recent writing assignment is a CD-ROM called *Savage*, produced by Discovery Communications. In addition (as part of the McGraw-Hill Home Interactive publishing team), Philip Bouchard and Dr. Cheryl Weiner contributed design and educational content throughout the later stages of the development and production cycles.

(See Appendix C for a complete list of credits.)

The Pyramid Scheme

Pyramid opens up with a dynamic, movie-style music score, and 3/4 screen video, which puts you, the user, in the role of an archeologist exploring the ruins of an ancient pyramid somewhere in Egypt. It's quickly established that there have been a number of recent and very mysterious disappearances associated with the structure. And your last journal entry states that a secret entrance has been found.

Dare You Enter?

The question is: "Dare you enter?" And the answer, of course, is: "Yes!" Because here's where the adventure and fun begin.

You break through the entrance into a dark tunnel where you are treated to the Pharaoh's Dream—a movie sequence in which the Pharaoh tells of the dream he had when he was a five-year-old boy. The Pharaoh's child-self explains how he saw that within the pyramid's walls "I will become a god. My pyramid must stand forever. Its entrance shall face to the north. My pyramid will be a beacon to the sun god, Amen-Ra, my true father." The child-god ends by telling of a great Master Builder who will come from a foreign land to help construct the edifice, and of course he's talking about you, the player.

A Little Piece of Your Heart

From the Pharaoh's dream sequence, you segue into the "Ghost Room" where you meet the gods Anubis and Amen-Ra.

Anubis is the Jackal-headed, ill-tempered funerary god who doesn't have much time for slackers. When somebody dies, it falls to him to weigh the person's heart on a scale and determine whether the life they led was good enough to allow entrance into the afterlife. He's nobody to fool with, and he immediately grumbles that you're in trouble, and then baits: "Perhaps you can master the tasks of construction?" And if you can't, well, he'll personally see to it that you're entombed forever under a stack of large rocks. Nice guy.

On the other side of the Ghost Room—man-bodied, with the head of a hawk—is Amen-Ra. A bit more mild-mannered, Amen-Ra has power over all life on earth, heaven, and in the underworld. He creates things by naming them—a mighty power to have. "It was I who brought light and life to Egypt," he speaks with fondness.

From Out of the Past

Amen-Ra tells you he's sending you to a likeness of the past, to see and learn the works of his people. And your mission, if you decide to accept, is to return with proof that you have earned their knowledge. He gently warns, however: "Many like yourself have sought the Pharaoh's Dream and failed." And because he's a kindhearted super being, he grants you a helper—the Scarab. A beetle bright with color, and ornate of wing, who really has a lot of better things to do than hang around answering dumb questions from you. And in her beautiful rhyming verse, she lets you know it too.

For scripter Anne, the Scarab character was very important, "I wanted to support younger users and make their path of play as exciting and interesting as that of the older audience members. And to maximize the appeal of this help character to the younger kids, I decided that she would speak in rhymed couplets."

"Seek Isis, Maker of Sunrise, Lady of Heaven," advises Amen-Ra, as he morphs back into stone. When you find Isis, you, as the Master Builder, are thrust into Level One of the game. You are transported back in time—over 4,000 years in the past—and are given the gift of virtual flight—allowing you to swoop, soar, and hover over the pyramid construction site located next to the flowing, blue-green Nile.

Mummy Mall Contractor

On Level One, the construction site is only a vacant lot of high-end real estate for now, but there is a dock on the river for unloading stones from the quarry, a kiosk area, and a camp for the workers.

The gist of the game is that you, the Master Builder, must, through seven levels, build the pyramid.

You're the person in charge, and with the help of your saucy-tongued beetle, you have to figure it all out. Puzzles and tasks abound, but that's not all. Besides having to master such things as how to level the ground before you can begin building (or which direction is true North, or how to lower the Sarcophagus into the burial chamber without dropping and breaking it, and even how to embalm a body by taking the brain out with a metal wire, ouch!), there's an entire story line, with some very real and engaging characters that you have to interact with. And of course all is not well in this ancient kingdom by the Nile.

Venomar and Dendara

The Pharaoh is only five years old at the time of Level One, and the Regent of the land—the person who's ruling the place while he's growing up—is his Aunt Venomar. Now Venomar is a feisty old bitty who turns out to have, just like a real person, a positive and negative side to her personality. On the plus side she's very concerned that the cost of building the pyramid will bankrupt the country, so she's not as enthusiastic as a lot of the other folks around the palace about spending all this money on a five-year-old boy's dream. Crazy nonsense.

As Roger describes Venomar, "she's a cross between Cruella DeVille from 101 Dalmatians and Richard III."

On the other hand, the old gal has a real thirst for power. She likes being pharaoh for the day, and she'll be damned if she's going to give it up to some snotty-nosed kid. So there's a plot under way to eliminate the young Pharaoh at some convenient point in the building of the pyramid. And you, the Master Builder, get drawn into all of the intrigue.

There's also Dendara, the Pharaoh's older sister. She's age eleven at the start of the game—athletic, strong, and independent. Dendara loves working with her hands, and she's a regular fixture at the construction site—working in the quarry, overseeing this or that, helping out where she can, and at times sending you to her friends for critical information. Dendara is wise for her age, and a trustworthy friend to the Master Builder.

And Then Some Time Passes

The building of the pyramid takes place over a twenty-year period, with each of the seven game levels representing a leap forward in time. After each game level, the Master Builder must return to the Ghost Room and deposit with Amen-Ra their proof that they learned the knowledge of his people during that level.

As time passes, the Pharaoh grows up, Dendara becomes a young woman, Venomar gets older and more desperate, and your ever-present helper, the Scarab, feels you have progressed far enough in your Master Builder knowledge that you no longer have need of her—and she dies, passing away into the afterlife. In the scene shown here, Dendara is to the left (in her twenties now), the Pharaoh's in the middle, and sourpuss Venomar is to the extreme right.

"According to Egyptian mythology," Anne points out, "scarabs are a physical manifestation of the sun god, Amen-Ra. When the Scarab character dies in Level 6, she is absorbed into the sun god. From her body, the grain that the player has given to her rains down on Egypt. The parched land greens."

Before You Rediscover Yourself

Ultimately, if you are successful as the Master Builder (creating one of the true wonders of the past and present world), you, as the archeologist, are allowed to accomplish your dream of entering the inner sanctum of the tomb—the first human in modern time to view the glorious remains of the distant past.

Wickedly funny at times, and very high-tech with its virtual flight sequences, "Pyramid" challenges the user to learn the customs and knowledge of an ancient people, as well as to solve the moral mystery of Venomar's assassination plot to do away with the young Pharaoh.

The Concept Backstory

"The original concept," Roger says, "was to do a CD-ROM series called virtual wonders of the world." He then explains that as a kid he was always in love with the idea of time travel and fascinated by other cultures and technologies. He loved the idea of being able to meet people from another place and time, and see what their lives were really about. "And I wanted to create a software series that would allow you to do just that."

Virtual Wonders of the World

As Roger started doing research, casting around for the perfect wonder of the world to bring to life on the computer, the idea of doing a virtual pyramid game really leapt to the surface. "On both the narrative and technological side, it was all there," he says. "Ancient Egypt was a golden age of technology. Many of the basics of what we understand about astrophysics, physics, and chemistry were really developed in that time period—specifically, to build pyramids."

The Spirit of the People

As he explored further, Roger became even more convinced that he was on the right track. He learned that contrary to old Hollywood movie lore, the people who worked on the pyramids weren't slaves. They were normal people of the community—laborers, craftsmen and artisans who did this sort of public works project for a living. As scripter Anne points out: "For many months during the year the Nile flooded its banks, and the farmers who worked the land next to the river couldn't raise their crops, so they worked on building the pyramid."

Building a pyramid was also very much a part of the spirituality of the land. "These people believed that 'real life' took place after life—when they were dead," Anne further explains. "So building a tomb for the Pharaoh was immensely important to them. Taking part in this enterprise reflected well on them and their families, and helped them to secure a place in the afterlife."

> **Roger loved the idea that the only thing that was consumed by the workers during the project was bread and ale. "Not so the foreman could get them drunk so they would continue working," he laughs, "but because making ale was the only way they could purify the water of the Nile."**

And Their Visionary Children

Further enticing *Pyramid* into reality was the concept that many of these great structures were built because of the visions of children. The idea that men, money, and rock were put into play and then roughed into shape because of the dream of a child makes for some powerful story material.

Fusion, Feminism and Family Values

The creative team also deemed it critical that the narrative be completely fused with the game play. A historical supposition was created for *Pyramid* where historical facts were used to build a narrative. "There was a regent who cared for a child pharaoh," Roger says, "and there are historical records of older sisters of pharaohs who loved to work with their hands and be part of the pyramid construction process."

> **"I don't find it a satisfying experience to play a game where you do the narrative for a little while," Roger explains, "and then you pause and do a puzzle that doesn't advance the plot—or the other way around, the plot doesn't advance the game play."**

So the narrative for *Pyramid* was build simultaneously with the design of the game—and Roger wanted a woman writer for the job. He felt strongly that most adventure games, as well as the subject of Egyptology, catered specifically to boys and men. He wanted to break the mold. "I have a ten-year-old daughter and the one thing in the world I didn't want to hear her say after playing *Pyramid* was—Dad it's a boy's game!"

"What attracted me to the project," Anne explains, "was that a very rich and exciting environment had to be created, something really different." She elaborates on this in her original treatment, "While the game can certainly stand on its own as entertainment, there are almost unlimited educational opportunities to teach about the philosophy, math, religion, music, food, dance, science, art and dress of the Egyptian people."

Roger and Anne also discussed in great detail the relatively young target audience—ages 8 to 14 years—and how the game had to appeal to adults as well. "It is important to consider co-viewing situations for a product of this nature," Anne explains. "When people play a CD-ROM together, their interactions help to structure stronger memories of the experience. This enhances the potential for meeting educational objectives."

For the creative team, the idea was to make the narrative and characters compelling enough to interest adults, but make the overall through-line of the story understandable and emotionally engaging for kids as well.

A Cool Core Interactive Concept

In essence, *Pyramid* is part of a childhood dream come true, a fascination for foreign times and places, and an interest in the great structures ancient peoples built to proclaim to their world and future times that they were there, living, breathing and going about their daily lives. It's also a phenomenally good idea for an interactive simulated environment—it taps into the very human mechanical fascination of how things get built. It's amazing to us that a 747 can fly, but we can sort of understand that our technology is capable of doing something like that. But a pyramid—4,000 plus years ago—when they didn't have cranes, bulldozers or cement mixers? When you throw in a good story and good characters on top of all of this, you've got a cool core interactive concept going here.

The Deconstruction

The creators of *Pyramid* wanted this to be an authentic and realistic Egyptian environment, however it does not take place in a specific Egyptian Kingdom. Roughly, the cultural, historical, visual, social and scientific elements that went into the piece came from about a 200-year time period about 4,000 years ago. Anne explains, "I sought to create an environment that was as authentic as possible for the product. Selecting a particular time period was a challenge, because it meant committing to the technology, art, trade routes, and such that existed during that window. Once we decided to go with the era of the Great Pyramid, there were very few concessions made."

Ancient Egypt was very much the center of the world, and all the surrounding countries of the middle east thought them so. "They were leaders in the making of paper from papyrus, and linen from flax," Anne adds. "So they had clothing, and with the words that could be written on paper, they had communication." The Egyptians also had the Nile, which was a major source of transportation for them. It was an open land where people from foreign countries were welcome to travel. "It was an exciting time," Anne further comments. "I had a huge resource of material to draw on."

The Universe

So the physical universe of *Pyramid* is a plot of land next to a river on which the player causes a huge stone structure to be erected during the course of the game. You can fly around the construction site as you advance through the levels, fly over the river, visit the quarry, the docks, the kiosks and the encampment. "These hot areas," Anne tells us, "have games or people in them whom you can pick up knowledge from, and in general you can further develop your own relationship with the place by interacting with what's there."

Additionally, the not so physical universe of the game is represented by the customs, culture, science, the Pharaoh-ship itself, as well as the story and characters that have been tightly woven into the play experience.

The Interaction and the Interface

The interface for *Pyramid* was designed to be very natural for kids. As Anne is quick to point out, "Our audience has a lot of media savvy. Time lapse, quick cuts from place to place, dissolves, wipes—all of these format cues are readily understood and accepted by the media fluent eight-year-old American child. Equally important, clicking and dragging is second nature to most members of our target audience. Nonetheless, I was careful to place clues and nudges that will make even a first-time gamer comfortable with the design."

Clicking, dragging, and picking up things—activities almost second nature for kids who play computer games—was the order of the day.

A Scarab's-Eye View

"From the beginning," says Roger, "we knew we wanted to have traditional game-play character interaction. We knew the Scarab character was going to handle inventory, as well as be the guide—and we specifically made this character part of the narrative." Roger also knew that he didn't want text anywhere in the main game playing area, consequently, the need for an animated changing cursor.

As previously pointed out, Roger also wanted the piece to feel very cinematic. To be able to fly around the construction site in "kidney-shaped flight patterns" was very key, as well as to transition down out of virtual flight (into hot areas) and still be moving into scrolling screens. "I knew very clearly," Roger adds, "that I wanted to merge a sort of photo-real, hyper-real miniature pyramid construction set with the animated foreground characters as a look for the piece." This vision was also particularly attractive to Anne, coming from a background in IMAX (large format) filmmaking, and knowing well the significance of high production values when it comes to learning materials.

Essentially, the way one mind-melds with "Pyramid" is through a changing animated cursor that lets you maneuver through virtual flight and click on hot spots. These hot spots start animated sequences featuring primary or secondary characters who give you information or get you through a puzzle or game. You can also use the cursor to pick up items to place in your inventory or get help from the saucy Scarab by offering her grain.

And Every Day People

In general, you move forward in *Pyramid* by being curious, by exploring, by being enticed by the cleverly written and designed characters. The rich environment also takes you out of your normal time and space and sets you down into a not-so-familiar land of gods and Pharaohs, priests and regents, boatmen and common laborers. They take you into their daily lives and let you see that, yes, they too lived. They had dreams. They loved, had fears, fun, made mistakes, and had honor too.

The whole "Pyramid" experience leaves you wondering what the folks four thousand years from now—looking back via their own virtual building simulations—will think about our own customs, rituals, justice, architecture (strip malls?), art, science, and jokes. Will they laugh or be appalled?

Story and Character

The basic arcs for the lead characters, the Pharaoh, Dendara, Venomar (the Regent) and the two gods Amen-Ra and Anubis, were pretty much set at the very beginning. "We knew that there would be a five-year-old Pharaoh who would age," Roger explains, "and that the beginning of the game would be his dream." This would set the ground rules for the piece.

Live from Ancient Egypt

It was decided that the gods of ancient Egypt would come alive for the users, and that they would have a character arc through the game, which was to get to a point where their Master Builder knowledge was sufficient enough to win the respect of the gods. At this point, a player would earn the right to enter the tomb for the first time (which is the reward for completing the seven levels successfully).

Excavating Your Own Past

The basic shape of the story was also known at the beginning. The player would start off as a turn-of-the-century (1907) archeologist, and they would be sent back in time—in the role of the Master Builder—to help build the pyramid. "We knew that the crisis of the piece," Roger adds, "would be the moment where someone, probably the Regent, had the ability to kill the Pharaoh. The climax of the piece would be his coronation, and the *denouement* would be the player, in a later year, being able to excavate the tomb."

The Begrudging Guide

It was also decided early on that the Scarab would be an antagonistic begrudging guide, and the player would start to earn her respect around levels 3 or 4. By level 6, the Scarab would feel so confident of the player's ability that she could be released from her earthly guide duties, and pass into the afterlife.

A Non-Randy Regent

There were also a lot of early discussions about how to handle the particulars of the regent. "Developing the Regent's character required real thought," explains Anne, "in the end, I decided that this character must be female. If there had been a male regent, then he would naturally have designs on Dendara. After all, she is next in line to the throne if something happened to the Pharaoh."

So it was decided that the regent would be female, evil, in charge of running the country, and that at some point she would make a move to get rid of the young Pharaoh. But it was also decided that she would have a point of view that was pretty well grounded. She thinks that irrigation projects, projects to feed the masses, social projects, were a little more relevant than building a tomb to a five-year-old god.

> **"When we started testing the early levels," Roger explains, "what was resonating extremely well with kids was the idea that there was a young person in jeopardy at the center of the game. What was working for the adults was that there was a political figure, the regent, who was at severe odds with her own sense of what's right and what's good. The critical mistake she makes, however, is that she thinks she can take the boy's life." It was this strong narrative, Roger found during testing, that compelled people to finish the game.**

Digging a Little Deeper

Pyramid also abounds with well-drawn, in-depth minor characters. "Having a lot of detailed secondary characters for the player to interact with," Anne tells us, "added significantly to the depth of the user experience—like the Captain of the barge, who sails up and down the river ferrying rocks to the construction site. He's done this for so long, that he falls in love with his rock, and you have to win the rock from him by playing a game of Senet. And he feels badly when you win, and take the rock away." So attention was taken to give the minor characters personalities, and valid motivations for when users interacted with them.

Anne took further pains to insure that the major and minor characters all had a different "take" on the Master Builder. For instance, the Scarab gives attitude because she doesn't want to be there, Dendara's helpful, and the foreman is skeptical about the Master Builder's real knowledge, but willing to reserve judgment till later. "You're involved with a number of characters," Anne explains, "and each of them feels differently about you. It all adds depth to the player's experience."

Playing Your Own Games

The games and puzzles created for *Pyramid* where part of the story too. Solving them propels you forward in your role as the Master Builder. "I tried to select content for the games," explains Anne, "that was appealing to different kinds of learners. I used mathematical elements, audio elements, mechanical elements. In each game we tried to bring in different kinds of things from the environment so that a person who was interested in the arts, or say physics, would be able to enjoy these subjects in a game."

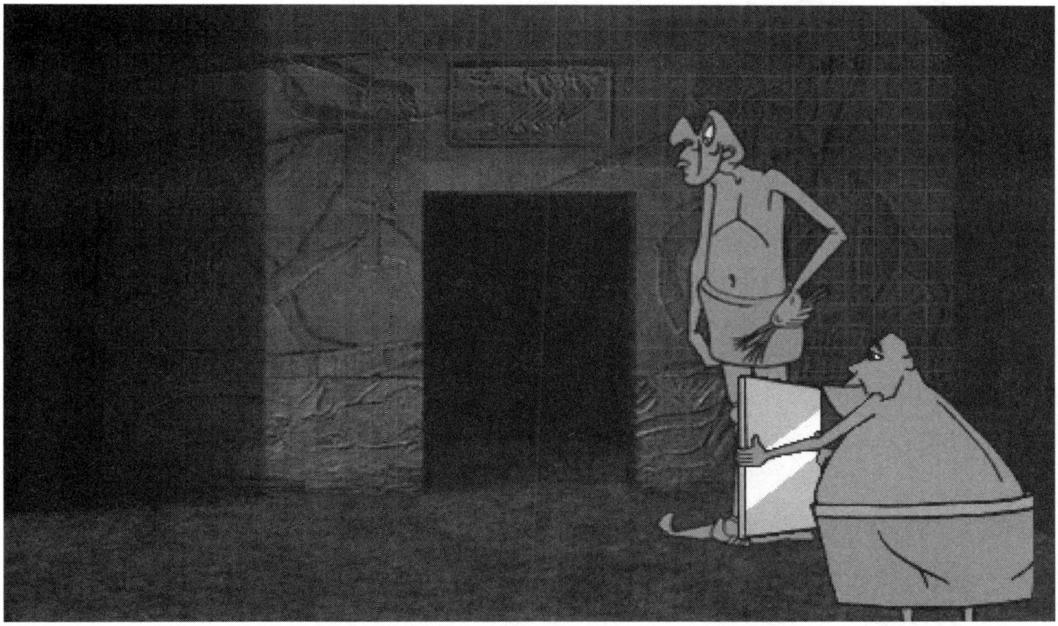

This concept is nicely illustrated in the game where the player has to light the inner chamber of the pyramid so the artists can paint the walls. The chamber is well within the body of the pyramid, and the only way the player can get light in there is to arrange a series of shiny metal surfaces that will take light from the outside and reflect it into the interior. It's all about ray reflection and physics. "And you can also enjoy the interactions and social dynamics of working with the artists," Anne adds, "you learn what paints they're using, where the material came from, and what they're painting, and why."

Structure and Design

The overall design for *Pyramid* took place in roughly three phases.

- **Phase One:** Roger produced an initial concept document that contained the idea of the game, building a pyramid over seven levels, with maybe 60% of the puzzles and 20% of the narrative worked out. Anne was then brought in to flesh out basic story points and plot beats. No plot specific or puzzle specific dialogue was created at this point.
- **Phase Two:** Roger, the production designer, producer, and lead artist, storyboarded every screen for the piece, about 150 in total.

- **Phase Three:** Anne was called back in and "married at the hip," as Roger recalls, to game designer Hal Jordy. Hal's task was to work out the specifics of the puzzle play and game elements, and to build the game design document, while Anne concentrated on the narrative, character, and dialogue work.

> **"It was an interesting experience for the two of them," Roger says. "Anne had never written a game before, and Hal had not worked from day one with a writer where his game interactions had to work for her too. It got me what I wanted though. A game design that was interwoven with a narrative."**

By Level Seven of the game, the pyramid is built and the Pharaoh is dead (or not dead, depending on how you played the game), and now it's time to roll up your sleeves and assist the morticians in embalming a body.

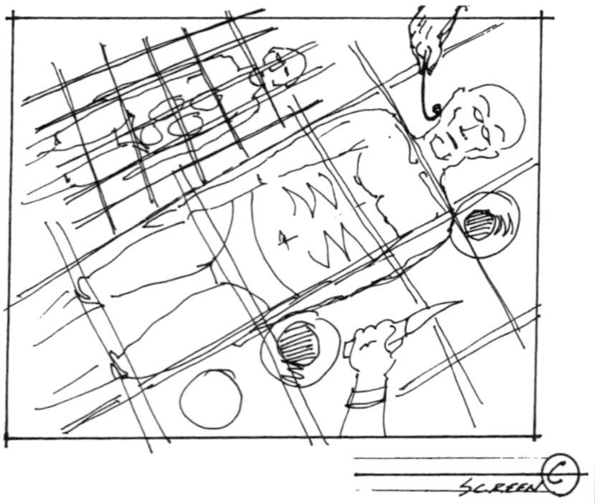

Scribbleboards to Storyboards

While creating the first short concept paper, Roger and his producer, Albert Reinhardt, sat down and literally scribbled out (diagrammed) all seven levels of the game, including many of the puzzles involved. The storyboard artists then took Roger's scribbles and turned them into more finished sketches that were used to inspire the final visualizations.

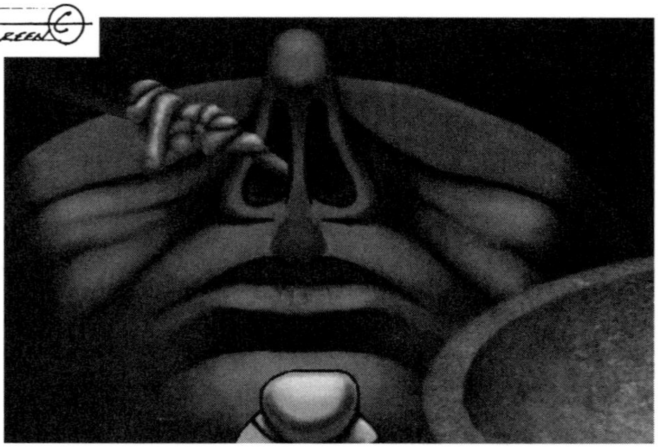

About Anne's Script

Anne's script for the "Embalming the Pharaoh's Body" section (see the sidebar for Script 9.1) starts with you in the Ghost Room, with Anubis presiding over your next task—a little mummy work. You then enter Level Seven through virtual flight, which allows you to zoom right up to the embalming temple entrance. You're standing just outside the embalming tent, looking in on the cadaver's feet.

> **Anne's script sort of looks like a film script, but not quite. Dialogue was added later on when the game document was produced, and instead of individual slug lines that tell you whether the scene is interior (INT) or exterior (EXT), Anne simply refers to screen letters and the type of screen that it is. For example, "B SM" means you're dealing with Screen B, and that Screen B is a scrolling menu.**

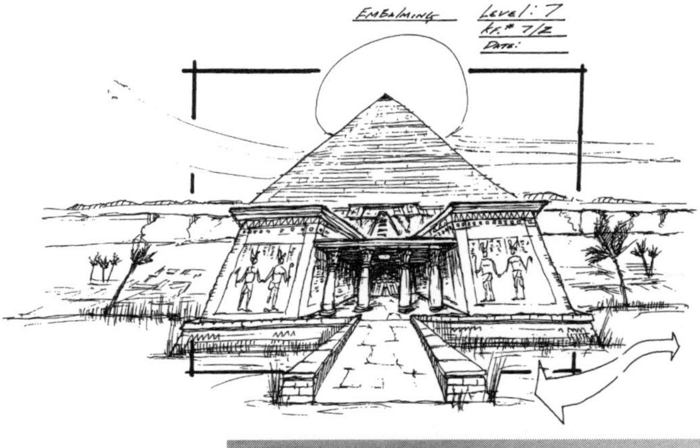

Before we get into the Game Document, go ahead and take a few minutes and read Anne's script (Script 9.1) for the "Embalming the Pharaoh's Body" section. To make things a bit more clear, here's a list of the abbreviations you'll be seeing:

- **SS**—Single Screen
- **SM**—Scrolling Menu
- **LM**—Linear Movie
- **ZM**—Zoomscape
- **MM**—Mouse Movie

Script 9.1

LEVEL 7

SCENE 7 / 1
INT / LM / GHOST ROOM

The seventh wall of the Ghost Room lights up. A richly illustrated page from the Book of the Dead is transposed here. Part of the page is missing. In the carving, we see ANUBIS presiding over the mummification procedure.

VIRTUAL FLIGHT - L7

LEVEL 7

SCENE 7 / 2
INT / GAME / EMBALMING THE PHARAOH'S BODY
A SS

We are outside the EMBALMERS WORKSHOP, located near the VALLEY TEMPLE. It is an enclosed tent. We are looking up from a low angle. The tarp door is pulled back, revealing some of the interior. The PHARAOH'S body is just inside the opening on a table. The Isis Glyph can be seen in a peripheral area of the screen. Flies buzz around the tent. In the immediate foreground is one of the tent poles. It is made of wood. A fly lands on the pole.

> LM
> All of a sudden, a huge dragonfly swoops in and ensnares the hapless fly.
>
> LM
> Our sack is tossed into the screen. It slides to a corner.

We may click on the entrance to the tent to go inside.

B SM

We are inside the EMBALMER'S WORKSHOP. The dead body of the PHARAOH is in the center of the room, on a tilted embalming table. We can SCROLL around to explore the WORKSHOP from a table-level vantage point. Potions, amulets and tools are set on an open cupboard to the side. A box containing four tall canopic jars has been placed near the PHARAOH'S body. After a few seconds, a LINEAR MOVIE begins.

If we did not save the PHARAOH from the poison in LEVEL 6, the PHARAOH is on the table and the following LINEAR MOVIE takes place:

LM
A PRIEST wearing an ornate golden collar enters the room. The PRIEST prays over a large mask of the jackal-headed god ANUBIS. He picks up the mask and places it over his head.

If we did save the PHARAOH from the poison in LEVEL 6, the dead body on the EMBALMING TABLE is VENOMAR'S. In this case, the following LINEAR MOVIE takes place:

LM
An ASSISTANT enters, takes the jackal-headed mask and exits. A moment later, this ASSISTANT returns accompanied by the PRIEST. The PRIEST is wearing the MASK.

We may SCROLL around the room and explore the mummification materials. We can click on the PRIEST, or objects of interest to us.

LM
If we click on the PRIEST, he explains that only a properly preserved body will be recognized by its owner's Ba, the spirit which will return to reside within it. It is our job to properly preserve the PHARAOH'S body.

An ASSISTANT enters the room.

There is a knife on the table. We may pick up the knife and begin the procedure. We can cut the body ourselves, or give the knife to the ASSISTANT or the PRIEST.

LM
If we make the cut ourselves, we are chased out of the room by the angered PRIEST.

LM
If we try to give the knife to the PRIEST, he tells us that it is

wrong to cut an Egyptian. He cannot.

LM
If we give the knife to the ASSISTANT, he makes the proper cut along the side of the body. After doing the messy job, he is chased out of the room by the PRIEST, cursing in Egyptian.

C SM

We see a somewhat jarring CLOSE SHOT of the deceased, from near the head and above. Fixed to the wall is an anatomical drawing of a human body. It shows the placement of the internal organs. If we pick up the tool which looks like a dentist's instrument, we CUT TO a close up of the PHARAOH'S HEAD (SCREEN F).

F SS

CLOSE UP of the PHARAOH'S head. From this SCREEN we may remove the PHARAOH'S brain. It takes several plunges into the nose, with accompanying SLURPING SOUND EFFECTS to properly remove the brain. We must dispose of the brain in the leavings bowl.

C SM

Return to the view of the body. The drawing of internal anatomy is on the wall. Hieroglyphic carvings on the walls help us to determine the correct jar for each organ. We must remove the PHARAOH'S important organs for preservation separately.

LM
After we have successfully extracted the brain, the PRIEST presents us with the first of the canopic jars. We must place each organ in its proper jar.

LM
The PRIEST tells us that one of the organs is very important. It houses the PHARAOH'S very soul. This organ must not be touched. We are to place the remaining four organs in the proper canopic jars.

If we choose to stand right next to the body, we can pick up a medical instrument that looks like little tongs.

We put our medical instrument over the wound. Our instrument goes inside. Organs become active when we are in their close proximity. When we click to grab the organ, we acquire it.

LM
If we touch the heart, a supernatural alarm (like a car alarm, but magical) sounds. Lights flash, we hear the angry voice of ANUBIS saying "Stop! Put that organ down and step away from the body!"

LM

If we try to place the wrong organ in the jar, the priest is horrified. We see his expression, hear his reaction and put the organ down on a smooth plate next to the tools. We must return to the surgery.

LM

If we try to put an organ in the wrong jar a second time, the PRIEST demands that we leave. We return to VIRTUAL FLIGHT.

LM

If we successfully place the correct organ in the first jar, the PRIEST acknowledges our success and brings a second canopic jar.

LM

If we correctly place the right organ in the second jar, the PRIEST thanks us and brings a third canopic jar.

LM

If we correctly place the right organ in the third jar, the PRIEST thanks us and brings the fourth and last canopic jar.

LM

If we put the proper organ in this last jar, the PRIEST is satisfied and grateful.

When the brain has been evacuated and the organs placed in their proper containers, the following LINEAR MOVIE is initiated:

D LM

We are looking at the body from a position near the head. The PRIEST packs the PHARAOH'S body with Natron (a salt mixture). On the inclined table, the body begins to drain.

We see the PHARAOH'S body from directly above. The PRIEST sets the water clock. We wait for about forty days. The time passes in seconds. We observe the drying of the body in time-lapse. Through a window in the WORKSHOP, we can watch the sun as it rises and sets.

E SM

The timer indicates the drying is done, and we are ready to complete the mummification procedure. Linen and resin have been prepared. Our directions are from the ancient Egyptian <u>Book of the Dead</u>.

The PRIEST directs us to place specific items of jewelry on the body, including the headpiece and pounded gold toe covers. We apply a first coat of resin, wrap the body with linen, then apply a second coat of resin to the outside of the mummy.

```
LM
When the resin has been applied, PRIESTS and PRIESTESSES arrive.
They place a gold mask on the mummy, and put the body inside an
elaborately decorated coffin.

LM
Our gloved hands enter the sides of the screen. We make a relevant
journal entry, with a sketch.
```

A SS

If we are mummifying VENOMAR:

The PRIEST removes the shawl from his head, and looks directly into the SCREEN.

It is the PHARAOH. He smiles wisely and gives his closing speech.

Breaking It Down and Building It Up

As you have seen, Anne broke the embalming story down into scenes and screens, describing the environment, and what the player could do in that environment. "And then I sat down with Hal," Anne explains, "and we negotiated what could actually be done in terms of gameplay—would we need two more screens to do this, or if somebody moved that object and put it there, would we need a new screen."

Hal then took Anne's script and broke it down into logic charts—all the possible permutations of what a player could do in the game as described by Anne. Hal also included areas in his logic charts for a synopsis of the set design, character description, dialogue, and cursor change. Once the script was broken down in this manner, Anne then went back in and added detailed characterization, and the dialogue for all the permutations of the game.

Anne tried to make all the dialogue with the secondary characters as progressively evolving as possible, in the sense that if you had an interaction with a particular character in an earlier level—in a game or in one of the kiosk areas—that past action would be reflected in a later experience with that same character.

The Gaming Document

The opening sequence of "Embalming the Pharaoh" (see Script 9.2—Gaming Document) starts off with a statement about the objective of the scene, elaborates on the ideal sequence of play, has some programming notes, elaborates on the reward sequence, and finishes off with character information.

Minor details add up to a rich interactive experience. Note how in the Character Information section "Assistant 1 is a nervous guy." This is a good example of the detailed characterization Anne managed to work into all of her minor characters. The "nervous guy" is nervous because he has to cut the Pharaoh open with the knife, and anybody who cuts the flesh of the Pharaoh is eternally cursed. Tough job, but somebody has to do it.

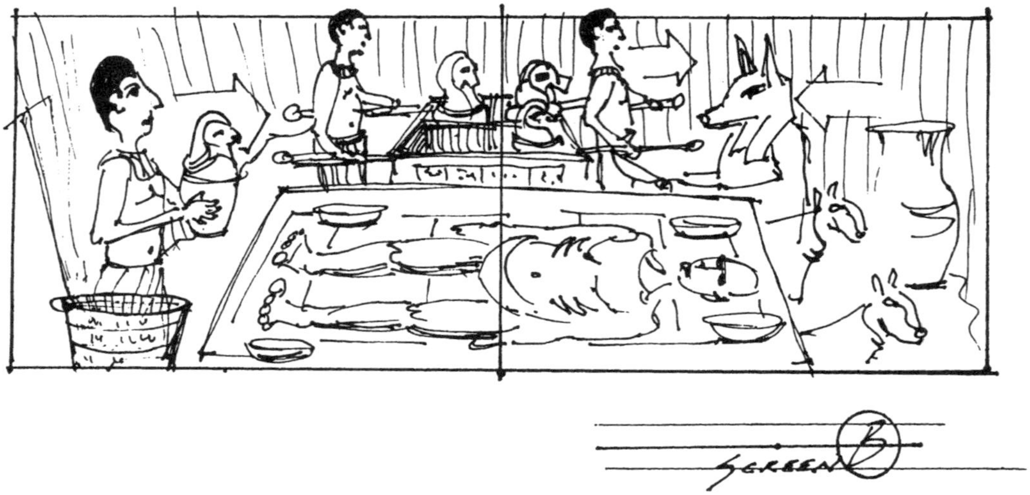

After the character information, we are then at SCREEN A1 (SS), which is pretty much the way Roger originally scribbled it out in his scribble boards. After the screen description, the "program conditions" are presented, stating the "if thans," and the "go tos" of anything hot in that particular screen. There are only four actions available for Screen A1, but this quickly changes once you enter the next screen, the embalming tent.

Script 9.2—Gaming Document

Scene 7/2 Embalming the Pharaoh

Objective: Embalm and mummify the Pharaoh.

Ideal Sequence of Play: Enter the workshop. Extract the brain from the body. Give the knife to the assistant to cut the Pharaoh. Place the major organs in the appropriate canopic jars and throw away the brain. Watch as the body is laid in natron. Cover the body in resin. Wrap the body in bandages. Cover the mummy in resin. Watch as the mummy is placed in the inner mummy case.

[Programming Note: Each time this game is played, the priest should bring the canopic jars in a different order, so we're forced to learn which organ goes with which jar, not just the order than the priest brings the jars to us.

[Programming Note: There should be flies buzzing around the rather rancid-smelling tent, if and when possible, in this embalming sequence.]

[Reminder: The Scarab went away in Level 6 and we now carry our inventory in our pack. We have to get hints about what to do from the other characters in the scene.]

Reward Sequence: Witness the completion of the mummification process.

Character Information:
Assistant 1 is a nervous guy. He calls us "Confident One". Assistant 2 is an Embalmer. He will help us with the embalming process. This Embalmer's background is in natural science in general, and biology in particular. The Embalmer character was the Physician treating the Foreman in the Encampment, Level 6. He is truly more knowledgeable about anatomy than the Priest. So as not to offend the Priest, the Embalmer whispers or speaks under **his** breath to us. In this game, we are Head Embalmer.
The Priest takes morbid pleasure in his job today. Even so, he has a heavy heart. The Priest calls us "Seeker of the Pharaoh's Dream" or "Dream Seeker".

Walk-through:

SCREEN A1 (SS) <X72BA001>
Just outside the Embalmer's Workshop. We are looking into the entrance. The Isis Glyph is to one side. There is a fly on the tent pole.

PROGRAM CONDITION:
As we enter the screen from Virtual Flight:

(LM) The Archeologists pack is tossed into the screen; it slides into the corner. A dragonfly swoops into the screen and eats a fly that has been sitting on the tent pole.

Available Actions:

Object/Area	Cursor	Result/Response
Isis Glyph	Nothing	Return to Virtual Flight.
Back Pack	Nothing	Opens our inventory.
Entrance to Temple	Nothing	Enter the Mortuary Temple

SCREEN B1, the embalmer's workshop (see Script 9.3—Gaming Document) is a scrolling menu with tons of interactive stuff for the player to do. The list of available actions goes on for three more pages than what is shown here. Once again, please note all the pithy dialogue these crazy characters have the option to say.

Script 9.3—Gaming Document

SCREEN B1 (SM) <X72BB001>
The Embalmer's Workshop. The body of the pharaoh is in the center of the room, on a tilted embalming table. We have a 360 degree view of the room in our scrolling menu. The player objective is to give the knife to the Assistant to make the incision in the body, remove the organs and brains (in Screens C2 and F), and place the brains in the leavings bowl.

PROGRAM CONDITION:
The first time we enter this screen from Screen A1:

IF THE PHARAOH IS ON THE TABLE (WE DIDN'T SAVE HIM)

(LM) A Priest wearing an ornate golden collar enters the room with an Assistant. The Priest prays over a large mask of the jackal-headed god Anubis. He picks up the mask and places it over his head. The screen transitions to the interactive state.

IF VENOMAR IS ON THE TABLE

(LM) The Assistant should enter and take the Jackal-headed mask, then the Priest and Assistant reenter together with the Priest already wearing the mask.

As we scroll around the workshop we see: a side table with potions, and tools; an open box containing four canopic jars; a water clock; a table near the body with knife, brain hooks, and tongs.

Available Actions:

Object/Area	**Cursor**	**Result/Response**
Right or Left edge of screen	Nothing	Scroll the image right or left respectively
Bottom of screen	Nothing	Return to area outside the Valley Temple where our back pack and the Isis Glyph are.
Table of ointments, etc.	Nothing	Transition to Screen H; closer look at table of ointments.
Canopic Jars	Nothing	Transition to one of Screens G1-5; closer look at the Canopic Jars. (Which screen depends on the state the box of jars is in—which jar the Priest is holding)
Body	Nothing	If the abdominal incision has NOT been made: transition to Screen C1. If the abdominal incision HAS been made: transition to Screen C2.
Leavings bowl	Bowl of brains	Deposit Brain in the leavings bowl. If we have already placed all of the other organs into canopic jars, we transition to Screen D.
Leavings bowl	Brain hook (w/ brains)	The brains are placed in the leavings bowl and the hook is now empty.
Leavings bowl	Brain hook	Places the brain hook in the leavings bowl.

Leavings bowl [Priest]	Any Organ (Stomach, Lungs, Intestine, Liver)	We place the organ in the leavings bowl. (LM) We are chased from the room as the Priest says: <D1> (Irritated:) Serpent of the desert! To which god shall I denounce you! </D> (He chases us out of the room. Then:)
		<D94> You who would throw away the Pharaoh's stomach. You call yourself an embalmer? Humph! </D> (OR...)
		<D95> You who would throw away the Pharaoh's lungs. You call yourself an embalmer? Humph! </D> (OR...)
		<D96> You who would throw away the Pharaoh's intestines. You call yourself an embalmer? Humph! </D> (OR...)
		<D97> You who would throw away the Pharaoh's liver. You call yourself an embalmer? Humph!
Water Clock	Nothing	<J419> Note goes into our journal about the use of a water clock.</J>
Assistant 1	Nothing	<D2> (Assistant 1 is uncomfort able about performing his job. Nervously:) In order to remove and preserve the Pharaoh's organs, a cut must be made. Unfortunately - - one who cuts the skin of an Egyptian - - is, is cursed!

SCREEN C1 is a closer view of the body (see Script 9.4—Gaming Document). If you pick up the brain hook and move it to the Pharaoh's body, you then transition to SCREEN F(SS).

Script 9.4—Gaming Document

SCREEN C1 (SM) <X72BC001>

Closer view of the body. There is a crude schematic of the internals of the human body fixed to the wall before us. The body is before us and somewhat below. The tools we need are on a tray beside the body.

Available Actions:

Object/Area	Cursor	Result/Response
Bottom of screen	Nothing	Return to Screen B1
Brain Hook	Nothing	We pick up the Hooking tool for the Brain and it becomes our cursor.
Pharaoh's Head	Brain Hook	Transition to Screen F, where we remove the Pharaoh's brains.
Bowl (for brains)	Nothing	We pick up the bowl for brains and it becomes our cursor.
Knife	Nothing	Picks up the knife to make it our cursor.
Body	Knife	(LM) We cut the Pharaoh's body. Transition to Screen B1 where we are chased out of the room to Screen A2. The option to reenter the room is barred. We have failed and must enter Virtual Flight and return to try again.
Tongs	Nothing	Picks up the Tongs and they become our cur sor. (Since we haven't yet made the inci sion on the body, there's nothing to click on with the Tongs.)

SCREEN F (see Script 9.5—Gaming Document) is a close-up of the Pharaoh's head, and if you click on the head, the hook goes up his nose (yuck!) "with a satisfying slurping sound" and extracts some brains. Please note in the game document Anne's dutiful attention to fully writing out the sound effects.

Script 9.5—Gaming Document

SCREEN F (SS) <X72BF001>
Close version of the Pharaoh's head where we remove the brains.

Available Actions:

Object/Area	Cursor	Result/Response
Bottom of Screen	Nothing	Return to screen C1.
Pharaoh's Head	Brain Hook (empty)	First-Fourth Click: (LM) The hook goes up the Pharaoh's nose with a satisfying slurping sound and we extract some brains so that our cursor is now a hook with brains) Fifth Click: (LM) We hear a dry scraping sound to indicate that the head is empty and the hook comes out empty.
Pharaoh's Head	Brain Hook (w/ brains)	First Click: (D70) (aston ished murmurs (but nothing comprehen sible) from the priest and assistants (we've made a mistake))) </D> (cont. in (D610))
Priest		<D610> Blundering baboon! </D> (cont. in (D611))
Assistant 2		<D611> (Watching from the sidelines, confused by the move:) Is he putting them back in? </D> (The hook comes out with brains still on it.)

Priest		Second Click: (LM) Transition to Screen B1 background: <D1> (Irritated:) Serpent of the desert! To which god shall I denounce you! </D> (He leads us out the door to Screen A2. We must enter Virtual Flight to return.)
Bowl (for brains)	Brain Hook (w/ brains)	We tap the brains into the bowl with a satisfying splat.
Bowl (for brains)	Brain Hook (without brains)	We put the brain hook into the bowl.
Bowl (for brains)	Nothing	We pick up the bowl for brains and it becomes our cursor.

Brain Dead and Dried Out

As you continue the game the brain gets thrown away because to the Egyptians it served no useful purpose. And the liver, intestines, lungs, and stomach get stored in the proper canopic jars. Once these tasks are completed, you have to pack the body with natron (a salt mixture) and wait 70 days for the body to dry out. You then wrap and resin the body, place it in an elaborately decorated coffin, and that's the end of your lovely day.

Music and Ambient Sound

The creative team wanted *Pyramid* to have a feature film narrative feel, and correspondingly, they wanted a very high-end music and sound design. So feature film composer, Randy Hale, was brought in to do a score which was historically driven from what was believed to be the music of the time.

> **"In motion pictures," Roger explains, "people will tell you that the score is about 33% of the impact of the movie—and in games, up to this point, music has been insignificant for the most part."**

Clueless in Cairo

"One thing about ancient Egypt," adds Anne, "is that we don't even know what the sound of their language was like. We have no one who can speak it—it's a dead language. And there's no written record of their musical notes, or what songs they played." However, there is documentation about their musical instruments—the rattles and harps played by the priests and priestesses. "So we created instrumentation samples that, at least to our ear anyway," Roger continues, "sounded like music in a style that research has lead us to believe existed then."

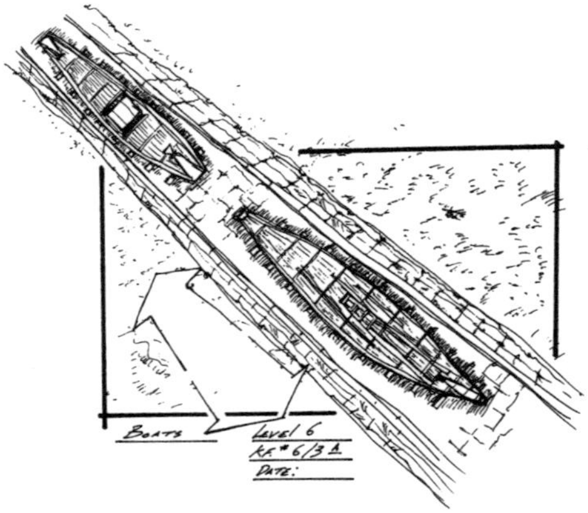

When writing the script, Anne was very conscious of when she wanted music, and the tone and pacing of the music, and she annotated this as part of her description of the scene or the environment. There was over 45 minutes of music score, with specific themes for each level and game. Most of the composing and instrumentation was created by sampling, but a small portion of the percussion sequences were recorded live.

Huffing and Puffing

One of the many interesting production features on *Pyramid* was that the sound effects and voice-overs for the animation were done on a traditional sound stage. QuickTime animation sequences were projected onto a large screen in front of which the actors performed their lines, as well as the sound effects associated with each character. "When the workers were pulling the blocks," Roger recalls, "the actors were grunting, and huffing and puffing away, just like the real thing."

Another critical element to the sound design was that when you were in virtual flight above the pyramid, and you neared an area that looked interesting, the sound would ramp up, letting the player know that they were over a region they could make a transition into. If the area was passed over, the sound would then ramp down.

Heard but Not Seen

A couple of the puzzles were specifically designed as sound puzzles. "The only way to find the blind astronomer who's lost in the marsh and being chased by a man-eating crocodile," explains Roger, "is by the proximity of his voice as you transition in and out of the reeds in the marsh." If the astronomer becomes lunch for the crock, you're never going to learn how to find true north; therefore, you can't build the pyramid—which is going to annoy Amen-Ra and Anubis greatly, and the prospect of your being entombed forever starts looking pretty good.

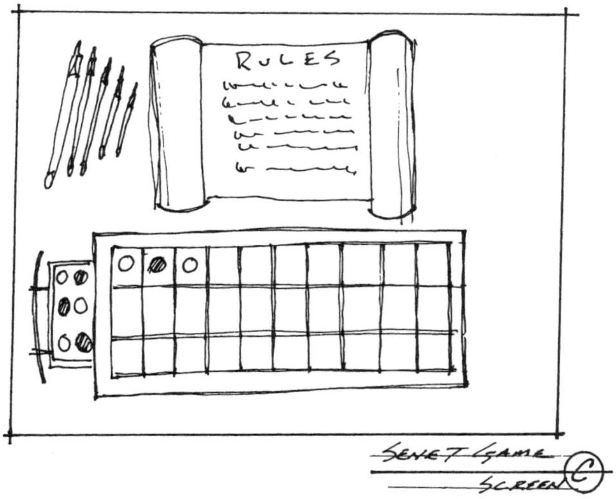

The Technology

The virtual flight sequences for *Pyramid* were absolutely essential for the feel that Roger wanted to create for the piece. Equally important was the look of these flight sequences, and for the creative team, the only way to obtain this look was to photograph an actual miniature set of the pyramid construction site.

> **"Digital 3-dimensional rendering and digital imaging, at least at this point in its technical life-cycle," explains Roger, "does not have the presence of a lit, photographed 3-dimensional object yet."**

Techno Tut

For *Pyramid* to succeed then, Roger wanted the virtual flight to feel exactly like the player took a helicopter four thousand years back in time, and piloted it around the site during the seven major levels of construction. "And the only way to get that," Roger adds, "is on some level doing it for real." However—and a big *however* here—before a green light could be given for construction and photography, which is a very expensive proposition, the virtual flight concept had to be tested.

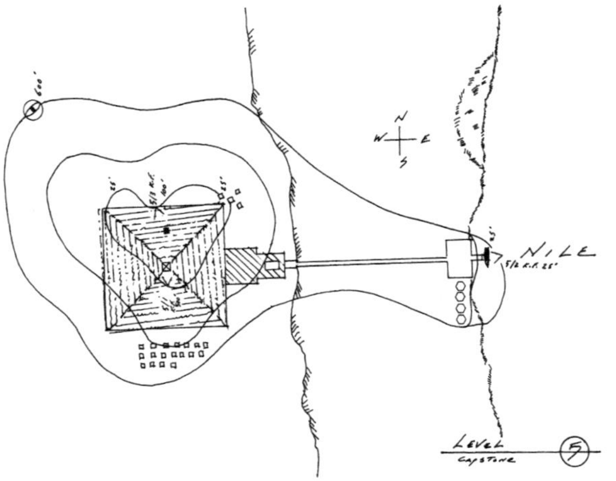

So a wire-framed digital model of the pyramid was built. The dimensions of the set, as well as the physical limitations of the gantry system that would fly the camera, were all coded into a computer. Lens tests were made too, and a lens size entered into the program. The chosen flight paths were "flown" and digitally photographed, and the digital frames were then exported into the virtual flight engine that would be part of the game.

Smooth Transitions

At this point, a prototype was created where the transitioning between flight levels was checked, as well as the interface that the player would use to "pilot" the virtual flight sequences. The creative team was happy with what they saw. And the upshot of all of this? They didn't have to do a single retake on over ten weeks worth of photographing the actual model set.

In the initial concept phase, the virtual flight paths were envisioned as being concentric circles around the pyramid, with the tightest circles being the highest flight paths. As the creative team moved forward with the production, these initial virtual flight concepts radically changed—the circular flight paths

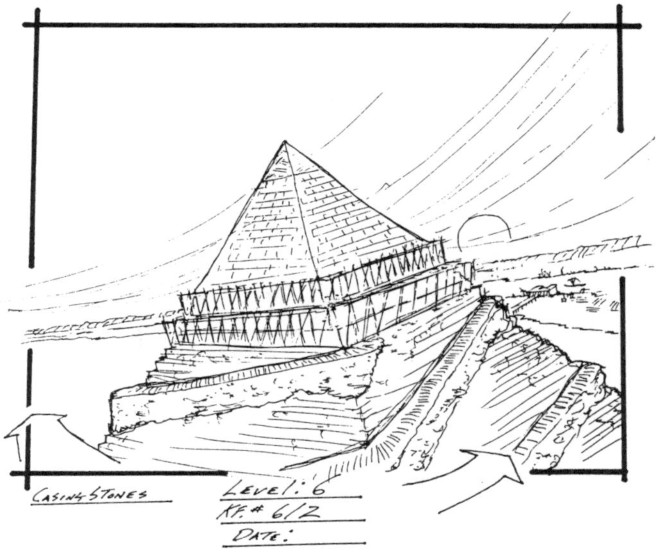

became kidney shaped, the farthest-out paths became the highest in terms of altitude, and the virtual flight engine, as it turned out, was flexible enough for smooth transitions from flight ring to flight ring.

And Happy Landings

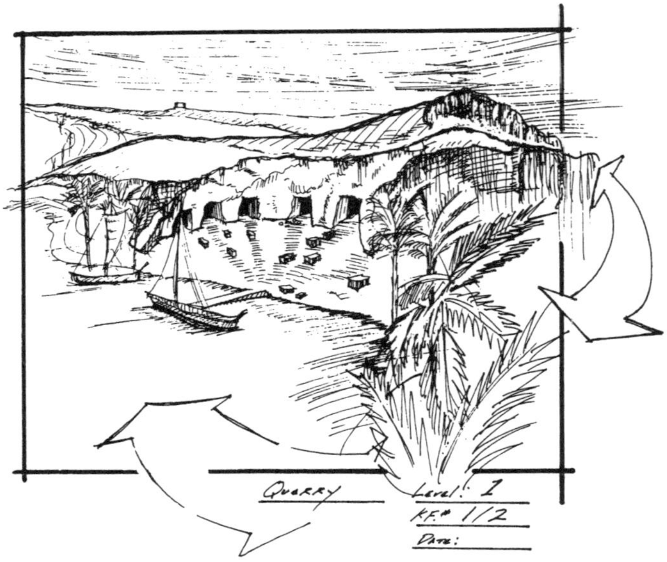

Level One features a long kidney shaped flight pattern that whips out past the construction site, over the desert, and then swoops down by the river, right in front of the quarry site. Level Six's flight patterns, more phallic than kidney, concern themselves with the pyramid and the dock area. At this point in the game, the sides of the pyramid are being smoothed down, and the funerary boats are being hauled up on the ramp.

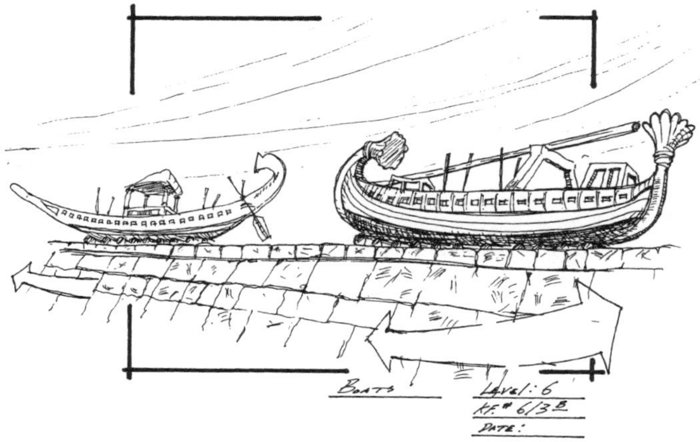
BOATS
LEVEL: 6
KF.# 6/3B
DATE:

CHAPTER 10

Wing Commander IV—The Price of Freedom

"SMART QUOTE"

"The shaping of the story on *Wing Commander III* was more performance driven. On *Wing Commander IV* it was less performance and more a matter of choices that were story and character driven."

Terry Borst—co-writer, *Wing Commander IV*

Our mission in this chapter is to unravel an interactive space adventure movie/game set in the future and built around a flight simulation experience. *Wing Commander IV—The Price of Freedom* stars such Hollywood notables as Mark Hamill, Malcolm McDowell and John Ryhes-Davies. Wing IV is the latest installment of the Wing Commander series produced by ORIGIN System, Inc. Chris Roberts is the original creator, designer, producer and director of the series, and he repeated all of these roles for Wing IV. Terry Borst and Frank De Palma wrote the screenplay for *Wing Commander III,* and were brought back to repeat their magic for Wing IV.

Co-writer Frank Borst feels that: "Audiences are already growing wary of pushing buttons to kill enemies, and the dramatic interactive dialogue sequences at the end of "Wing Commander IV"—where choices are offered and made in the heat of an emotionally charged human confrontation—present just a glimpse of where interactive movies can go in the future."

All screenshots from "Wing Commander IV—The Price of Freedom" © Origin Systems, Inc. 1996 and provided courtesy of Origin Systems.

Jet Jocks

Terry Borst and Frank De Palma are long-time partners in the writing and directing of film, television, and interactive projects. Together they have written the highly rated TV movie *Midnight Run Around* and the feature film *Private War,* both directed by Frank. Additionally, they have also developed screenplays for studios and independent producers and performed unaccredited rewrites on several produced films.

Terry has also published fiction and poetry in a variety of literary magazines and anthologies. Frank's other directorial credits include episodes of NBC's *Earth 2,* ABC's *Land of the Lost,* and the syndicated *Tales from the Darkside.*

Terry says that "the most exciting aspect of helping to create 'chapters' III and IV of the Wing Commander series was the feeling of doing groundbreaking work in a genre that is just beginning to define itself. Working in interactive fiction is a little bit like working in the earliest days of film or television—nobody knows what this thing is going to be just yet, but there's a feeling it might be a genre that opens up entirely new dimensions of thought, emotion and experience."

Frank confesses that he knew nothing about the interactive world and had never played a computer game when he was asked to co-write *Wing Commander III.* "I quickly became fascinated by the task of writing a story that was almost as wide as it was long." Terry and Frank are both members of the Writers Guild of America, west.

(See Appendix C for a complete list of credits).

A Mission Briefing

Before we race off into the unknown here—for those of you who haven't seen *Wing Commander III* or *IV*—I'm going to briefly explain what their interfaces are like so the discussions in the rest of this chapter don't lose you completely.

A more detailed discussion of Wing IV's interface does appear in The Deconstruction section of this chapter, so you can read on for an appetizer, or do the deconstruction, get the full meal, and come back here later. In this best of all possible interactive worlds, the choice is yours.

Methods of Interaction

First off, in *Wing Commander IV,* the player has an on-screen alter ego called Colonel Christopher Blair, played by actor Mark Hamill, and at numerous points in the game, the player has control of where Blair goes, who he talks to, and what he says. Otherwise, *Wing Commander IV* (like *Wing Commander III*) has basically three ways of presenting material to the user:

- **Midgames:** These are short films that segue the story in and out of scenes. Midgames cannot be interacted with by the player.

- **A Starship Environment:** Here's where you, the player, may direct your alter ego, Christopher Blair, to explore various rooms within a starship. You may also direct him to speak with characters who happen to be in these rooms. If Blair speaks with somebody, then a short movie plays. This movie can either play straight through without user interactive, or it may have an interactive branch possibility. If it has an interactive branch, the movie will pause at the branching and "thought blurbs" will appear on the top and bottom of the screen. If you move your cursor to one of these blurbs, you'll hear Blair's voice speaking the lines that are on the screen.

> In theory, hearing Blair's voice-over gives you the sense that you are in Blair's head, listening to him musing on the two branching possibilities that he's confronted with. You can then choose one of the offered avenues, and the movie branches in that direction.

- **A Flight Simulation Environment:** The cockpit of a space fighter that you have total control over.

The Plot Synopsis

"You're headed for the big litter box in the sky!" you taunt, as you pitch your Arrow fighter ten degrees right to get the Kilrathi warship in your crosshairs.

"The Confed ape dares to attack?!" growls back the Kilrathi pilot, taking evasive action, very much the big kitty on steroids.

No, no—hold it. Wrong story.

We're dealing with *Wing Commander IV* in this deconstruction, the sinister Kilrathi, dreaded cat-like enemy of the human race, got to meet their collective feline makers in *Wing Commander III* (that's if you won the game), so they're no longer a threat to children, mothers, lollipops and apple pie.

Hurrah!

Kilrathi No More

In *Wing Commander III,* mankind vanquished the nasty Kilrathi, thus allowing the entire galaxy to lay down its collective arms after a decade or more of struggle, and get back to living a life of peace and tranquillity again.

For Colonel Christopher Blair, "the heart of the tiger" and hero of the Kilrathi war during *Wing Commander I, II,* and *III,* this is a dream come true. Peace and tranquillity. He has lived most of his adult life in the cockpit of a fighter and now it's time to kick back and go bowling.

Home on the Range

So when *Wing Commander IV* opens, we quickly find Christopher Blair on Nephele II, working a modest farm that is nothing more than a lot of rocks and heat. Terry Borst and Frank De Palma's script describes Blair as "looking a little out of place with his feet on dry land rather than on the deck of a carrier." But Blair is not a happy ex-wing commander, he "sighs in frustration and surveys the half-acre of vegetation that surrounds him. It's hard to tell if he's proud of what he's done or sorry he ever started it."

But Colonel Blair doesn't get much of a chance to ponder these morbid thoughts. He soon gets a telecom message from Major Todd Marshall, call sign Maniac, a former wing mate he flew with throughout the Kilrathi war. "What's this, not home?" taunts Maniac, in his usual sarcastic style, "maybe you're down at the feed store chewing the fat with the local yokels? (going serious) Meet me at the Nephele II star port. I'll be in the canteen. We got to talk. It's important."

Blair stares at the blank message screen totally surprised, Maniac was the last person he ever expected to see again.

A Certain Lack of Social Graces

So Blair meets Maniac in the canteen—Maniac's there ahead of time, leaning against the bar and pulling his usual crude number, "scratching his butt as he talks to an ATTRACTIVE WOMAN." A moment later the woman of course slaps him in the face, and leaves, and Blair, taking it all in, knows that some things in this universe never change.

Blair and Maniac chat for a bit—Manic talks about flying, Blair about farming, and then finally Blair gets down to business, "So what's the 'important' matter you wanted to discuss?"

Is It Drafty in Here?

"Colonel Christopher Blair of the Confederation Space Force Reserves," Maniac blithely replies, "it is my duty to inform you that you are being recalled to active military service."

Blair's mouth drops.

"Why they want to put an aging earthworm back in the cockpit is beyond me," Maniac continues.

Terry and Frank write, "The shock in Blair's eyes is slowly replaced by 'The Glint,' The Gameface, the look of a man who's deprived himself of a certain pleasure for far too long."

Blair quickly asks "why is this happening?" and Maniac shrugs back, "you think they tell me anything?"

Suit Up and Show Up

Blair then thinks about all of this for a total of two nanoseconds, then stands and says, "OK, let's go."

And so our hero gets the "call" to action, and off he goes.

Colonel Blair soon learns that it's his old boss, Admiral Tolwyn, who's called him back to active duty. The Border Worlds appear to be waging some sort of guerrilla war against the Confederation, but nobody can figure out exactly why.

> **Tolwyn gives Blair the classic call to action: "Not only will you assist me in solving this mystery by being my eyes and ears, your very presence in the Border Worlds will be a potent message to all the galaxy."**

A Tailhook Reunion

So Blair, along with Maniac, is assigned to the TCS Lexington, a carrier of the Concordia-class, commanded by Captain Eisen, Blair's former commanding officer aboard the Victory. Besides having Maniac around for laughs and excitement, Blair is also reunited with another former wingman, 1st Lieutenant Winston Chang—call sign Vagabond.

The Lexington "jumps" for the Border Worlds and so begins the first of fourteen acts or "series" of *Wing Commander IV* (see the game flow chart shown here). Within each series there are anywhere from two to four "mission sequences" the player must fly.

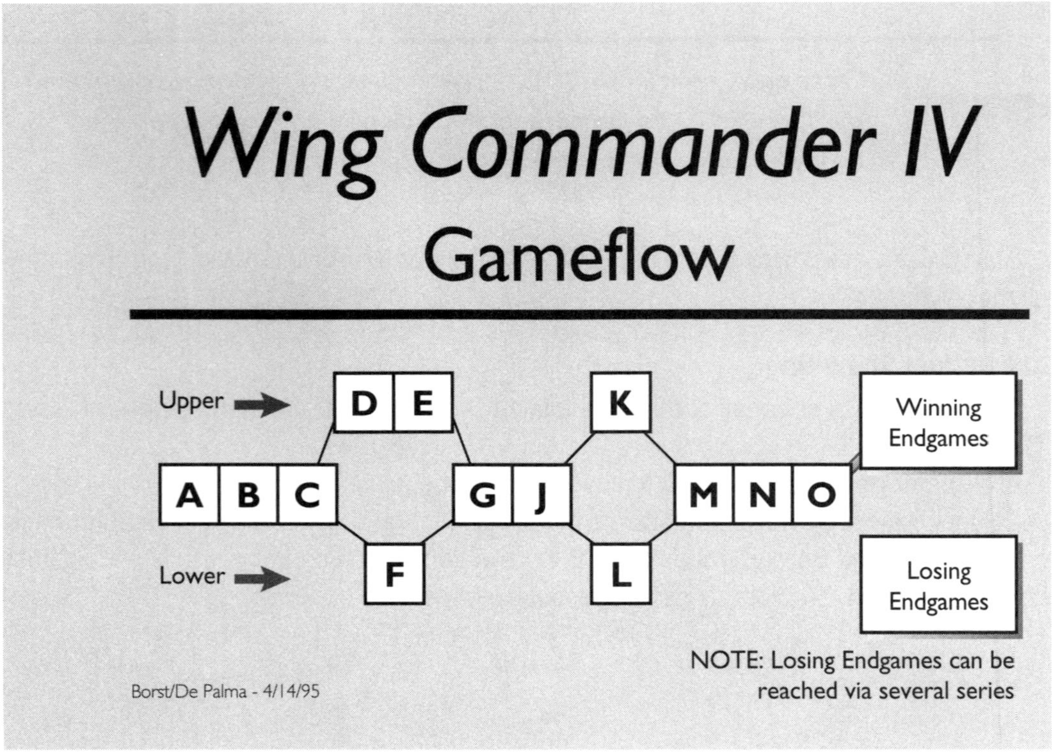

A Big Bad Odor

Once in the Border Worlds, Colonel Blair soon discovers that something stinks big-time. The missions Blair and his men are forced to fly somehow don't "seem right," and mysterious sleek fighters with no insignia, "like nothing we've ever seen before in the Wing Commander universe," are provoking the Confederation to declare war on the Border Worlds. And Blair isn't certain these fighters are even from the Border Worlds.

To further complicate matters, tensions aboard the Lexington are running high because Captain Eisen is suddenly, and for no apparent reason, relieved of his command.

Blair's comfortable Confederation universe—where things were once all black and white when fighting the Kilrathi—doesn't seem to be making all that much sense anymore, and he's not certain what to do about it.

A Duo of Devious Defectors

And then to his utter amazement, he is suddenly summoned to the briefing room where the new Captain of the Lexington gives him orders to track down and kill, if necessary, Captain Eisen and Maniac who, surprise-surprise, have just stolen a shuttle and are defecting to the Border Worlds militia with valuable intelligence information.

Maniac and Eisen defecting? What kind of bull is this?

Colonel Blair, obeying his commanding officer, dutifully mounts his mission and flies his fighter to intercept Maniac and Captain Eisen in their stolen shuttle.

Blair Must Decide

When he is within firing distance, Blair must then decide whether to fire on Eisen and Maniac—or go with them. Can he? Does he? The choice is yours.

Colonel Christopher Blair is suddenly faced with one of the biggest decisions of his entire military career. He has fought for the Confederation for most of his adult life, and now he must decide whether to switch allegiances.

If you choose "yes," Blair joins the side of the Border Worlds, and flies his fighter onto the Intrepid, an old Border Worlds destroyer. The Intrepid has recently taken some serious damage fighting the Confederation forces, and has also lost her Captain when the bridge was destroyed.

Flying Economy Class

Through the course of events, Blair is soon made Captain of the Intrepid, and besides having to fly missions, he (and you, the player) must now make executive command decisions that will determine the fate of the Intrepid, her fighter pilots, and the game.

Ultimately, in fighting the Confederation forces that have been sent to the Border Worlds, Blair uncovers information to expose a very large RAT within the Confederation administration who is instigating all of this unpleasantness and not necessarily for their own personal gain, but because, as Franks puts it, "the villain is a man who believes deeply that what he's doing is right—it just happens to be terribly unhealthy for a lot of innocent people."

Winning the Grand Game

Blair's mission is then to get to Earth and convince the Assembly that his information is correct, as the Border Worlds are innocent of any wrong-doing, and a declaration of war should not be instituted. So Blair takes the Intrepid and heads for Earth, running the gauntlet of Confederation forces guarding the home world.

In a grand showdown on the Assembly floor, worthy of the best Hollywood trial movies, Blair verbally plays cat-and-mouse with his nemesis, and depending on how clever and resourceful he is (how resourceful *you* are, actually) you either win the grand game, or—face a firing squad. Good luck.

The Concept Backstory

"The essential challenge in *Wing Commander IV* was that in *Wing Commander III,* all the bad guys, the Kilrathi, got killed off," explains Terry. "Because we—Chris Roberts and everybody else–honestly thought *Wing Commander III* was the end," Frank quickly adds.

They thought it was a trilogy. In number three, they wrapped it up, because nothing was supposed to come after it. So how can you continue the Wing Commander universe if you don't have any villains to shoot down? Easy. Come up with another set of baddies. It's a big galaxy out there, and somebody or something's got to be up to no good.

The Enemy Within

"When we started off," Frank says, "Chris Roberts had some story ideas, and Terry and I came up with a bunch of two-line ideas, and then we just started discussing them." In these initial conversations, other alien-type races as antagonists were considered, but quickly dropped. "I think one of the interests in *Wing Commander IV* for Chris," Terry explains, "was let's see if we can do a story without aliens. And if you think about it, with things like *Star Wars,* the ultimate struggle is humanity vs. humanity." "Exactly," Frank adds, "the age old struggle we all deal with constantly—the dark side of our nature."

Blame It on the Border

"The Border Worlds were something that always existed in the Wing Commander universe," Frank further explains, "Chris had this idea of doing something along the lines of the American Revolution where the outer colonies wanted to break away from the confederation. Terry and I brought Vietnam into it and gave it the twist of having the villain come from WITHIN Confed—the side you, as the player, are originally on. This villain is trying to make the Border Worlds the bad guys and essentially start a war where there is none."

Chris Roberts also came up with the idea about two characters fighting for your soul, which eventually turned into the characters Hawk and Panther, who you meet when Blair eventually defects to the Border Worlds. "The woman [Panther] keeps trying to get you to do the human thing," says Frank, "while the guy tries to get you to go for weapons."

Because Wing IV didn't go the alien nemesis route, Frank and Terry felt it forced them to come up with a good story—a story that had more depth to it instead of just bashing another alien race. "Wing IV doesn't revel in bloodshed either," Frank says, "we spent hours discussing this—if the enemy is from within, and you're fighting the Border Worlds, then you're potentially killing other human beings."

Stringing Out the Story Line

So after Chris, Frank and Terry's initial discussions, the story line for Wing IV became the following:

- Because of the decade long war with the Kilrathi, the human race had organized itself into a very efficient military industrial complex, with most human worlds pretty much under martial law.
- As far as some of the human leaders were concerned, this wasn't a bad setup to maintain even though the war was over.
- So the antagonist in Wing IV is a certain rotten core of the Confederation that's turned more fascist, and wants to rule everybody in sight with an iron fist.
- "And our hero," says Terry, "suddenly realizes, after having worn the Confederation uniform for his entire adult life, that he may be on the wrong side."

Now that's a pretty good story.

> **Once the story line was decided on, Terry and Frank quickly fleshed it out into a full fledged outline, almost treatment really, including extensive notes on the flight sim missions.**

Melding Mission and Game

Now, digression for a second here: When Terry and Frank were originally hired to write the script for Wing III, all of the flight missions had already been decided on, and some of them were actually being coded when they came on board. So their task for Wing III was to construct a story line around the mission sequences, sort of like hanging meat on a skeleton.

In Wing IV, however, as they were in at the get-go, Terry and Frank were responsible for scripting the missions directly into the plot. "The player's still having conversations with people," Frank explains, "still wandering around a ship and discovering things, still going out and flying missions. But it's all much more organic now, because the missions have more to do with each other, and they have more to do with what you're talking about with people on the ship."

> **"There's definitely a greater integration of story and game element," Terry says, "the story influences the missions. If you didn't do a certain something a little while back, it can come back and get you right while you're flying. Also, midway through a mission things can happen that change the objective of the mission, offering the player a choice."**

Hanging with the Hackers

Once Terry and Frank completed their first draft of the outline/treatment, with mission ideas sketched in, they then went and brainstormed with the programmers at Origin in Austin. And the programmers were really into it, they wanted to try new things and make the flight sims more interesting for the player. Frank explains, "We spent many hours in a room with the programmers and game designers knocking around ideas. You'd think you had a really great idea that would make a thrilling mission, only to have somebody else point out glaring holes in the logic, or that it was done somewhere else."

> **"It's tough," Terry comments, "coming up with fresh new missions, especially after Wing III, and all the other flight sims out there on the market."**

Pausing for Photo-Ops

A good example of how the missions were integrated into the plot is when, in "Series B" (see the game flow chart earlier in this chapter), Colonel Blair is given the task of getting back a scientist who'd supposedly been kidnapped by the Border Worlds.

"There're three missions involved with this concept," explains Frank, "and the dramatic scenes before and after each of the missions involves the extraction of this scientist." The first mission of this series is a re-con mission, where you're firing laser cameras instead of laser cannons. "Something unusual for the Wing Commander universe," Terry adds, "you're taking pictures instead of firing a gun." If the reconnaissance mission is successful and you obtained enough information to pinpoint the scientist, then the second and third mission of the series is fairly easy. If you didn't get enough information, then they're much harder.

Learning to Fly a Desk

In addition to having plot integrated missions, Wing IV also allows the player to make some big overall interactive decisions. In other words, the player gets put into a managerial-type role. "Which proved to be an interesting problem to solve from a writing standpoint," recalls Frank.

> **"The player has to make decisions that affect the story in a big way," says Frank. "In Wing III you were always just taking orders. And the story shifted or changed on how well you shot down the bad guys while you were flying. In Wing IV, major branches of the story are based on the player making command decisions."**

"I think the concept was," adds Terry, "that testing on Wing III showed that basically most players got pretty good at flying at a certain point, so branching based on performance was moot."

Dealing with Dilemmas

So Frank and Terry made these major branches dependent on some very thought provoking, moral/philosophical/tactical issues. For example, the player's first big choice comes when they get the chance to defect to the Border Worlds. You can see this choice quite graphically on Wing IV's game flow chart (reproduced earlier in this chapter). During "Series C" you are given the choice to defect, or not to defect, and then whatever your choice, you move on to series "D" or "F," respectively.

Another big decision point comes when the player has to decide whether to help out a group of people on a world who are being slaughtered by the bad guys ("Series K" path), or go pick up some badly needed weaponry ("Series L" path) that will ultimately help you reach your goal of returning to Earth to face the Assembly with your knowledge that the Border Worlds are innocent.

> **"And there are prices to pay," warns Frank, "based on these decisions that are not all black and white to the player to start with." Sounds just like life, huh?**

Cue the Courtroom Closing

Beside plot related missions and further empowerment of players with significant command decision, the creators really wanted to expand beyond the flight sim arcade action at every turn possible, hence the dramatic "trial" ending. Words, not guns, are the way out of this pickle.

> **"Our model for the ending," says Terry, "ended up being the scene in "A Few Good Men" where Tom Cruise and Jack Nicholson confront each other during the final trial scene."**

Writing the scene for Terry and Frank was a challenge. It's a conversation where you constantly have to make choices, and, you have to make enough of the right ones in order to win the game.

Dueling with Words

Here's the setup: You, as Colonel Blair, have fought your way back to Earth, and now you're standing in the great Assembly hall confronting your nemesis, who just so happens to turn out to be none other than Admiral Tolwyn himself. So Mark Hamill and Malcolm McDowell are on the screen, facing off, dueling with words.

> **Tolwyn is sophisticated, powerful and slippery of tongue, and you, as Blair, probably have only about 60 seconds to get everybody's attention—before they call in the guards to haul you off to the firing squad.**

Thought Blurb Badinage

At each conversation branch, the movie pauses, and thought blurbs come up on the top and bottom of the screen, suggesting possible approaches to continue the battle of words and wits. As Terry and Frank cleverly worked it out (see the sidebar for Script 10.1), they set the conversations up into such modes, or headings, as "sidestep the taunt," "fight fire with fire," "question," or "attack," "bring up devious weapons," or "bring up devious methods," etc.

> **Guile and cunning then are the watch words the player, a.k.a. Colonel Blair, needs to lock and load when coming into this home stretch confrontation.**

A point system was worked out so that when you get to the end of the scene, the Assembly votes on whether to declare war on the Border Worlds or not, and how they vote will depend on how successful you were in convincing them of your case.

Scoring Some Positive Points

As the script implies, when the thought blurbs come on, it's not entirely clear to the player which direction will produce a positive game point—all choices are valid. So a naturally aggressive player will make aggressive choices, and win some points, but probably in the end will lose the scene, and the game. Conversely, a cautious player will make cautious choices, winning some points, and also probably losing in the end. The player has to figure out how to make the right combination of aggressive and cautious choices, at the right time.

Tricky.

The creators of the piece seem to have taken the high road in pushing the envelope in interactive storytelling for the flight sim genre. Terry Borst and Frank De Palma were charged by Chris Roberts to integrate story and character arc into the overall design of the game. Missions were not just missions to tout flying abilities this time around. Missions were very much part of the dramatic action, with many choices to be made while flying in the cockpit.

Script 10.1

O-368

MIDGAME: WASHINGTON, D.C.. SKYLINE (352-02)

Blair's Black Lance fighter buzzes the Capitol Building on its way towards a landing...

DISSOLVE TO:

MIDGAME: ASSEMBLY FLOOR (353-02)

TOLWYN WRAPS UP HIS SPEECH...

TOLWYN
...yes, formal Declaration of War is a terrible thing. It should not be undertaken unless all other options have been exhausted.
(beat)
I'm afraid those options have indeed been exhausted...

AS TOLWYN CONTINUES, A WEARY BUT DETERMINED COLONEL BLAIR QUIETLY ENTERS THE REAR OF THE HALL...

ASSEMBLY FLOOR (354-02)

TOLWYN
...We did not fight the Kilrathi for decades only to allow an infection to hollow us out from the inside. If there is a cancer among us, let us cut it out. You must vote yes on this Declaration —

MURMURS OF "HERE, HERE" AND "AYE" COURSE THROUGH THE ASSEMBLY...

BLAIR MUST <u>CHOOSE</u>...

SPECIAL NOTE: Throughout the rest of this scene, choices will be presented in left and right columns. Like <u>all</u> choices presented in the <u>entire</u> script, the onscreen cues for these choices should <u>never</u> be consistent. In other words, Left Column choices should sometimes be at the top of the screen and sometimes at the bottom.

SPECIAL NOTE: A "point system" has been devised for "scoring" Blair in this confrontation...

O-369

To step forward and be heard {+1 pt.}:

BLAIR
(shouts)
There is a cancer that needs to be cut out!

THE ASSEMBLY REACTS. HEADS TURN. THERE'S A COLLECTIVE GASP AS BLAIR MOVES FORWARD.

BLAIR
But it is not on the frontiers of our galaxy. It's right here before you.

TOLWYN COVERS HIS SURPRISE WITH A COLD SMILE. HE ADDRESSES THE ASSEMBLY.

TOLWYN
Ahh, Colonel... The hero of the Kilrathi war ... who has betrayed the Confederation and now fights for the Border Worlds.

AS THE ASSEMBLY REACTS TO THIS NEWS, PALADIN STANDS.

PALADIN
Seize that man!

To hang back and see how things proceed {-1 pt.}:

TOLWYN SHAKES HANDS WITH PALADIN AND OTHER SENATORS. HE TURNS AND SPOTS BLAIR. HE COVERS HIS SURPRISE WITH A NARROW GAZE AND A STEELY TONE IN HIS VOICE.

TOLWYN
Seize that man!

A PAIR OF ASSEMBLY GUARDS SWOOP DOWN ON BLAIR AND GRAB HIM.

TOLWYN ADDRESSES THE ASSEMBLY, REGRET MIXED WITH DISGUST.

TOLWYN
May I present to you the hero of the past war ... who has forsaken us, and now fights for the Border Worlds.

A PAIR OF ASSEMBLY GUARDS SWOOP DOWN ON BLAIR AND GRAB HIM.

BLAIR STRUGGLES WITH THE GUARDS AS TOLWYN'S SMILE WIDENS.

BLAIR MUST <u>CHOOSE</u>...

0-370

To state his case {+1 pt.}:

BLAIR
I fight as I always have – on the side of peace and honor.

(to Paladin)
Please, hear me out.

Go to "Paladin looks at Blair" below.

To attack Tolwyn {-1 pt.}

BLAIR
Admiral Tolwyn is lying to all of you.

(to Paladin)
Please, hear me out.

CONDITION: IF Blair's score = 0 or more: Go to "Paladin looks at Blair" below.

IF Blair's score = less than 0, CONTINUE with:

PALADIN
Remove this turncoat from the premises. We shall now take the vote.

AS THE GUARDS USHER BLAIR AWAY, TOLWYN SMILES WITH SATISFACTION, LOOKING UP TO THE ELECTRONIC "TOTEBOARD" TABULATING THE VOTES.

OVERWHELMINGLY, THE VOTE IS "YES"...

Go to Losing Endgame 2, Parts B & D only.

PALADIN LOOKS AT BLAIR, THINKING...

THEY TOO, HAVE A LONG HISTORY BETWEEN THEM.

PALADIN
Let him speak.

THE GUARDS RELEASE BLAIR WHO LOCKS EYES WITH TOLWYN.

BLAIR
What price freedom, Admiral?
(to Assembly)
I've come here to tell you the truth; the truth about what's really been happening on the outer fringes of civilization –

TOLWYN
Colonel... You insult me as well as everyone here. Do you really believe this body to be ignorant?

BLAIR MUST CHOOSE...

O-371

To sidestep the taunt {+1 pt.}:

BLAIR
No, Admiral. No one here is ignorant — least of all you. I simply seek to shine a new light on events.

THE SENATORS REACT POSITIVELY.

To fight fire with fire {-1 pt.}:

BLAIR
No. I'm saying the Assembly has been duped by a charade — an elaborate charade perpetrated by you, sir, who requires their ignorance in order to carry out a personal agenda.

THE SENATORS GRUMBLE WITH QUESTIONS.

BLAIR
The Border Worlds have fallen victim to a plot which — if allowed to proceed — will make all of humanity a victim.

TOLWYN
Ahh, there is strange logic in that...

TOLWYN SHARES HIS AMUSEMENT WITH THE ASSEMBLY.

TOLWYN
Tell us more, Colonel.

BLAIR MUST CHOOSE...

To question Tolwyn {+1 pt.}:

BLAIR
Admiral, do you believe in the concepts of law and order?

TOLWYN
Of course... I've devoted my life to them.

(to Assembly)

Haven't we all?

To attack Tolwyn {-1 pt.}:

BLAIR
Do you deny, Admiral, having anything to do with the troubles on the frontier?

TOLWYN
Only in my attempts to end the troubles. To maintain law and order.

BLAIR
And you believe these concepts to be the foundation of a strong society?

TOLWYN
Indeed. Without law and order... we are lost.

O-372

BLAIR TURNS TO THE ASSEMBLY.

BLAIR
'Law and order.' Control. Maintaining the status quo. That's what this is about.
(beat)
Harmony among men is a secondary issue.

TOLWYN
Harmony is maintained <u>through</u> control.

BLAIR MUST <u>CHOOSE</u>...

To question Tolwyn {+4 pts.}:

BLAIR
Was it 'harmony' that made me – as a Confed pilot – party to the theft of a Border Worlds laboratory and the outright abduction of a Border Worlds bioconvergence chemist?

TOLWYN
How <u>you</u> interpret operations, Colonel, is of no consequence. Your job, as a soldier, is to carry out orders – <u>without</u> question.

To attack Tolwyn {-4 pts.}:

BLAIR
Control at what cost, Admiral?

TOLWYN
I am a warrior – as you once were, Colonel. I do what is necessary for victory – without question.

BLAIR
'Without question'?
(to Assembly)
Have any of you questioned the Admiral about his Black Lance forces?

A RIPPLE OF SURPRISE ROLLS THROUGH THE ASSEMBLY. PALADIN LEANS FORWARD.

PALADIN
(to Tolwyn)
What is this 'Black Lance'
he speaks of?

The Deconstruction

In *Wing Commander IV,* humankind seems to have unlimited energy at its fingertips. Punch a button and you "jump" to the far side of the galaxy. Press the trigger on your fighter's joystick, and you annihilate anything in your cross-hairs with lethal doses of missiles or energy. Space ships are huge, and fairly common, dwarfing skyscrapers by miles. It's *Star Wars, Star Trek,* and some of the grand old space operas of the pulp science fiction days like E.E. Doc Smith's *The Lensmen* series all rolled into one.

Joseph Campbell would probably call "Wing Commander IV" a perfect place for a hero's journey—it's a universe in conflict, a place of seemingly constant war, where men fight hostile alien creatures, and then, becoming victors, fight themselves. When you think about it, it's not exactly a pretty place to spend time in.

The Universe

Geographically, *Wing Commander IV* lets you travel to many star systems, including the Border Worlds, as well as eventually to Earth itself. And you do all this commuting in the first part of the game via the Confederation carrier Lexington and, in the latter part of the game, by the Border Worlds destroyer-converted-to-carrier Intrepid.

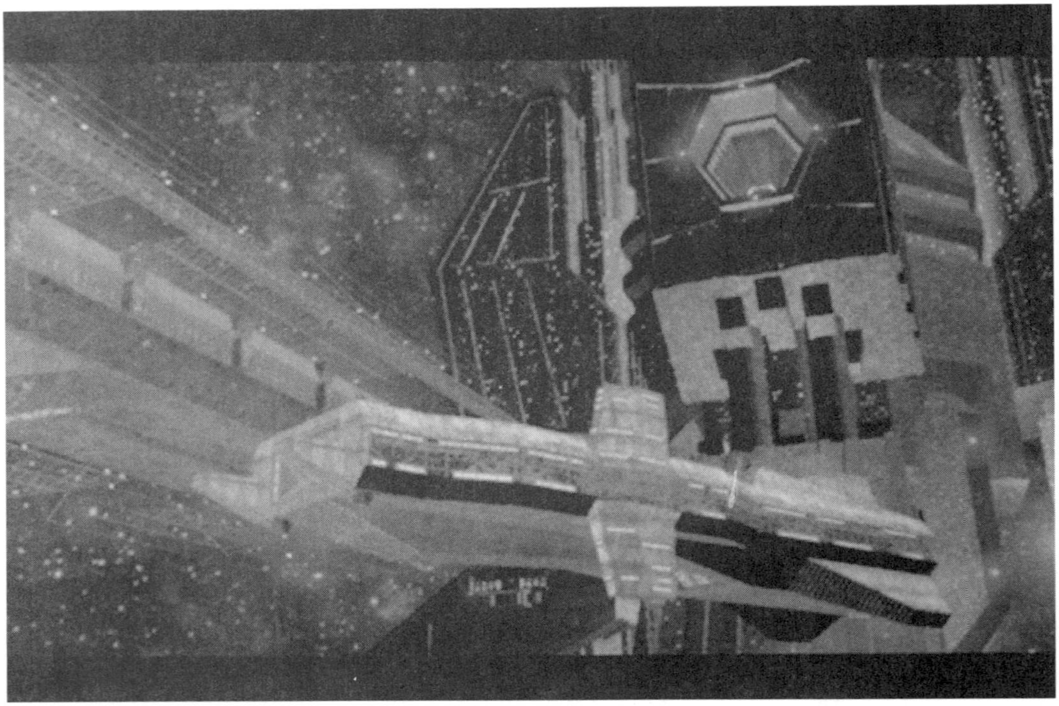

While Heading for the Border Worlds

At the start of the game, when you are heading out to the Border Worlds (and if you're not flying a mission), the player, as Colonel Christopher Blair (Mark Hamill) may wander the Lexington—exploring and talking to people at will. The player has five areas within the ship to explore:

- The flight deck
- Flight control
- The briefing room
- The officer's lounge
- Captain Eisen's cabin

And when you're flying a mission, you have the choice of numerous fighter space craft to pick from.

Cruising around the Intrepid

Later in the game, when you have defected to the Border Worlds, you may also wander the Intrepid freely. However, as the ship is heavily damaged, your choices are limited to:

- The launch deck and hangar bay

- The control bay
- The combat information center and chart room
- A storage hold
- A galley and upper galley

On the Intrepid you have your choice of numerous fighter craft too.

"Initially," Terry adds, "when we started writing Wing IV, we were planning on having the player moving around several ships during the story, as well as working from a ground base. Due to production reasons, the environment collapsed to some degree into just two ships—the Lexington and the Intrepid."

Or Taking a Movie Break

To further flesh out this ship and fighter universe, the creators have come up with film-like scene segues called Midgames. Frank and Terry define Midgames as: "Cinematic sequences that are triggered by a wide variety of events. These are like short movies a player simply watches."

These Midgames have the capacity of taking the user out of the confines of the interactive areas of the game, giving a broader sense of the Wing Commander universe at large.

The Interface

When Terry and Frank were brought on board to write *Wing Commander III,* the player interfaced with the program through the use of a joystick and mouse control. For *Wing Commander IV,* it stayed pretty much the same.

When aboard the carrier's Lexington or Intrepid, the player has the ability to move from room to room, clicking on doors, going up and down elevators. If people are in the room you just entered, you have the choice to click on them and interact, or not.

Being Colonel Blair

The player relates to the Wing Commander world through the point-of-view (POV) of Colonel Christopher Blair. When wandering around any of the ships, or involved in a Midgame, the player is for all practical purposes riding on Blair's shoulders—you literally see him on the screen, and you see and hear what he sees and hears.

As you have seen before, if you are in a sequence where you can make choices and direct the dramatic flow, the game pauses, the on-screen character Blair is talking to looks directly at you, and "thought blurbs" appear at the top and bottom of the screen. These blurbs represent the inner musings of Colonel Blair. They tell you what he is thinking about the particular situation at hand. When you place the cursor on one of these blurbs, you actually hear Mark Hamill speak his thoughts. It's then up to you to decide how Blair is to direct the rest of the conversation.

Morale Boosters

Many of these "thought blurb" conversations are programmed to a morale counter. That is, the character Blair is talking to will have his or her morale go up or down according to the answer you direct Blair to give. A character's morale will later determine how well he flies when they are on a mission with you—if their morale is down, they fly badly, potentially putting you in danger. If their morale is good, the mission is potentially easier to complete.

As Terry and Frank point out, "Wing Commander IV" has a lot less conversations, or choices, that directly affect morale than "Wing Commander III." "It was felt that the whole morale business," Terry explains, "was much to subtle in terms of tangible effect on the game."

"When we had a player make a choice in Wing IV," adds Frank, "we wanted that choice to count right away, really affect the flow of the story immediately, so that they could feel and experience the outcome of their decision. We cut down on morale-type conversation and went for branches with more tangible impact."

Sliding into the Cockpit

When the player actually flies a mission, the on-screen persona of Christopher Blair disappears (you see Mark Hamill slide into the cockpit of his fighter) and then the game becomes first person point-of-view. During the flight sequences, video images of different characters appear on the control board, asking you questions or giving you advice. You communicate back by clicking on predetermined message panels on your "com." You can send back "affirmative," "negative," "break and attack," etc. And of course you have complete control of your fighter via your joystick, and other controls.

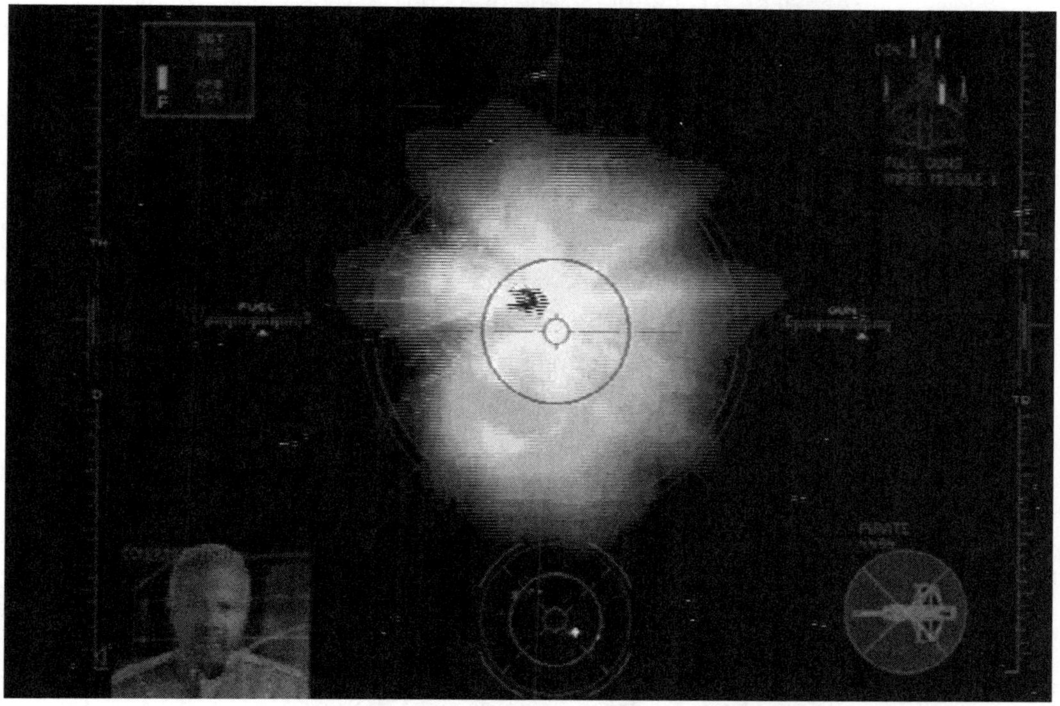

The Interactivity

Once the story line was determined, and a structure fleshed out, "our big decision beats where there for us," explains Terry, "to defect or not to defect [Series C], to go for weapons or to help the people on a planet [Series J]—so obviously we had interactivity at those points."

Going Out on a Limb

The decision to make a particular scene interactive or not was determined as Frank and Terry worked the script segments out on index cards (see the later sections in this chapter on The Writing Method and Turning It into a Script for more information on the index card method). "Many of the scenes seemed to offer some potential for interactivity," Terry continues, "but we had to be careful page-wise, because every one page scene you branch at the end, adds at least half a page to it. That's fifty percent more, and those half pages add up quickly."

> **"Not every scene really works in terms of interactivity," Frank points out. "We were always looking for valid choices, and valid branching. There wasn't a rule which said, Ok, every five minutes there'll be a clickable scene or a choice to be made. We didn't really need to worry about it, because in a way, the player is always making choices."**

Deciding 'Til You Drop

In *Wing Commander VI* you are interacting at least once a minute. For example, you have to decide where to move in the ship, and if you see somebody, you have to decide if you want to talk to them or not.

To further increase the game's overall interactiveness, Terry and Frank added a character called Pliers, the head mechanic on the Intrepid. Pliers is constantly working on new gadgets for your fighter that'll give you an extra edge, like a cloaking device, or a new missile, etc., and he's always coming up to you and asking if you want his "new" something or another added to your ship.

> **Working with Pliers, Frank says, "will affect the outcome of your next mission—which you don't know anything about at that point—and you have to flat out decide right then and there to let Pliers go ahead and add it to your fighter, or not." And it isn't automatic that every time he offers you something that you should take it. "Because this stuff," Frank warns, "can screw you up too."**

Bossing Your Way Around

As you have seen, in addition to adding the Pliers character to boost up interactive choices, once Colonel Blair defects to the Border Worlds, and becomes Captain of the Intrepid, you must now make command decisions in terms of how and where to direct the Intrepid's resources.

"We wanted to empower the player," explains Frank, "In Wing III you were an employee. You were given missions, and you had to go out and fly them. In Wing IV you still fly missions, but at a certain point you also become the boss. You have to choose the missions for everybody."

"And writing-wise," adds Terry, "this created all kinds of interactive challenges. We honestly didn't know if we could pull it off." Terry and Frank set things up so that when Blair takes over the Intrepid, there is a Border World Admiral—Admiral Wilford—who basically feeds Blair information, and potential courses of action for the Intrepid to take. You and Blair then have a menu of mission options to choose from.

Playing Stick and Throttle Games

Besides interacting with characters and story line, the player, as in Wing III, also has a variety of fighter craft to choose from and wing men to fly with. And of course, once you're in the cockpit of your fighter, you're in total, absolute control. You can't get more interactive then in a flight sim.

Character Development

Wing Commander IV has about a dozen speaking roles, with maybe half of them being what you would call main characters. Colonel Blair of course has top billing in the sense that he's the player's alter ego, and is therefore always around.

Wanted: a couple of game characters with a few good epiphanies. Is this dreaming, or what? Is it possible to "character arc" flight sim characters? How can you possibly make a die-hard shoot 'em up gamer give a Kilrathi's butt about whether characters live or die?

Flatlining the Headliner

Wing Commander IV is somewhat comparable to a big Hollywood action movie, and according to the genre, the headliner (Blair, in our case) doesn't really change in a significant way. "He's a reluctant hero at the beginning," explains Frank, "who gets pulled into a situation, meets obstacles, has setbacks, and continues the battle until he wins. The difference here [from a movie], I guess, is the interactivity. If the player doesn't do everything correct, he can end up dead."

So on the surface you'd expect that Blair's character-arc is going to be pretty much Hollywood-action predictable. Right? However, when you think about it, and when you actually manipulate Blair through his paces—interacting with other characters, making decisions that affect the story line—the details of how you and Blair arc to a conclusion are so subtly rich, that you actually have a much deeper main character experience than you'd get from a Hollywood action movie. At least I think so anyway.

Panther and Hawk

As Frank further points out, "in the last third of Wing IV or so, there's a battle for Blair's and the player's soul. Two characters, Panther and Hawk, a woman and man respectively, become very important to you. At critical branching points, they are usually there giving you advice—one supporting one choice, the other character supporting the other choice. And either choice is valid—it can lead to winning, or loosing." Whatever direction you decide to go in, you are going to make one of them (Panther or Hawk) happy, and the other angry.

> **In a very real sense, Panther always represents a higher morale ground—though, in a time of war, this is sometimes not necessarily the best ground to take. Hawk, as his call sign implies, represents a more pragmatic—perhaps harder—but definitely longer view of things. Either point of view is valid.**

Pick a Fate

Terry and Frank have written the script such that if you are successful in the end trial sequence (Series O), then one of two possible ending Midgames (movie sequences) will play. Which one plays depends on whether you sided with Hawk or Panther the most during the game.

If you chose to go more towards Panther's point-of-view, taking a higher morale ground in your decision making, and you win the trial and the game, then you and Panther end up together as mere flight instructors, teaching—"newbies" how to fly. Blair gets asked, "but you could of had anything you wanted." And in response, Colonel Blair just smiles and shrugs. In other words saying "I'm exactly where I want to be—thank you very much."

If you chose time and time again to go the more pragmatic Hawkian point-of-view, and win the game—then the last scene has Blair, now a general, giving orders for Hawk to unleash the Black Lance fighters to help put down a rebellion on some unsuspecting planet. In essence, you have traded places with your nemesis. You have inadvertently chosen power and control as a way of living your life. A valid choice for some, I suppose.

Arcing the Character Afterall

So there is very much a character arc for the main character, and without a doubt the player controls that arc. "And it's what you want," Terry says, "that's the idea with it being interactive. It's supposed to reflect on you. Maybe you'll learn a little about yourself by the end of the game."

> **"Maybe we're over thinking it," adds Frank, "but being the writers we can't help but do that. Whether or not the player is conscious of this kind of stuff, that's what is going on. The player is being forced to make decisions that go far beyond just 'do I go in this door, or that one.'"**

An Itch That You Catscratch

Frank and Terry also effectively used other secondary characters to help thicken the dramatic experiences. Catscratch, for instance, is the archetypal rookie pilot, Blair's protégé, who changes through the course of the game. The war hardens him, makes him more sure of himself, and he even gets a love interest.

Maniac is more or less there for comic relief, Shakespeare's fool in a sense, though he does have a serious moment or two, right before he defects. Script 10.2 shows this nicely (see the sidebar).

Tolwyn of course is the antagonist, "He's a good guy initially," explains Terry, "and becomes more ambiguous and changes course with the story, but he's changing in the sense of you seeing him in a new light."

Script 10.2

C-82

OFFICERS' LOUNGE - MANIAC (78-C3)

CONDITION: This REQUIRED scene available ONLY IF Blair chose "to obey orders" in Scene 74-C3.

MANIAC PUSHES A GLASS BLAIR'S WAY.

MANIAC
Compliments of the Maniac.

BLAIR
What'd I do, win the lottery?

MANIAC
(distracted)
Hmm?
(beat)
You can buy one for me ... next time.

BLAIR
So how did it go with the biochemist?

MANIAC
(beat)
I struck out, Colonel. Big time.

MANIAC KEEPS LOOKING OFF, CLEARLY PREOCCUPIED.BLAIR IS PUZZLED BY THIS RARE DISPLAY OF HONESTY.

BLAIR
Well, like you always say — there're other nuggets in the asteroid belt.

MANIAC
Yeah... I hope you're right...

HE STANDS UP.

MANIAC
Did you like being on the farm, Colonel?

```
                    BLAIR
          It had its moments.
MANIAC CONSIDERS THIS, NODS.

                                        C-83

                    MANIAC
          Someday...
                    (beat)
          I just remembered something I have
          to do.

                    BLAIR
          Okay. See you 'round.

MANIAC EXITS.
```

The Writing Method

Once the story line was determined, Frank and Terry did an eighty-page outline and went to Austin to work with the programmers on the missions. After that, writing the script began in earnest. As Frank succinctly puts it: "We didn't have a lot of time to screw around."

"Our process for everything that we work on together," explains Terry, "is a very traditional method of writing and structuring things—we use 3x5 index cards." And Frank continues: "It works beautifully for us, I wouldn't know how to do it otherwise."

It's in the Cards

Each scene is sketched on one card, though a big scene can be on more than one card. "The cards allow us to talk out each other's problems on a per scene basis," says Terry, "*that* won't work because of *this,* or because of *that.* Working out the structure this way allows us great freedom in the actual writing of the script."

> **Eventually, over two hundred and eighty index cards where used for structuring "Wing Commander IV." According to Frank, a normal linear feature film script usually has fifty cards, tops.**

The cards were broken down into 14 acts or series, labeled A through O, with the final series containing the Endgames (see the game flow chart earlier in this chapter). "The cards stretched from my dining room, across the living room floor to the fireplace," says Frank, "It was huge, but they were the only way we could see the whole picture." Terry adds: "We could lay them on the floor and literally walk around our story—around act I or act II—and see the structure. There are software programs that keep track of all of this stuff, but it's not the same thing."

Shuffling the Deck

Once the cards were done, and *Wing Commander IV* had its overall structure, Frank and Terry then knew—scene for scene—what was going to happen. At that point, they each took a section of cards, went their separate ways, and started writing the script for the cards in their possession. They never saw each other for weeks during this period. "There was no need," explains Terry, "eventually we'd trade off passes, reviewing what we each wrote, and then ultimately, we'd need to be in the same room together, to go over every single line and fight over commas."

> **Because of the nature of the interactivity—wandering through the various environments, clicking on people you see, playing scenes with or without branching—the index cards where a big help to Terry and Frank in working it all out.**

"We can sort of guide the player," Frank says, "figuring if they enter a room and see two people, they'll click on the closest person. But maybe not, maybe they won't click on anybody. Writing this stuff gets to be a real interesting exercise because you can't necessarily make these scenes build on each other in the normal sense."

Dealing a New Hand

Terry points out: "You have no guarantee that a conversation has already taken place, so that you can refer to it within the current conversation." Frank interrupts: "Exactly, and this is where the cards really help. We were discovering new ways of laying them out on the floor, shifting them around, seeing where a scene was really required, making it impossible for a player to leave that room without talking to a certain person, which we tried to do in an artful way."

Color Me Required

Terry and Frank also color coded the cards. They used different color ink if the scene was to be a required scene, a slider, an optional scene, a mission, or a midgame. (For more on how each of these scene types work and where the cards take you, read on!)

> **So imagine, all of those two hundred and eighty-odd color-coded cards laid out on the floor, with two grown guys crawling around, shifting some here, moving a few there, pretending they're flying space ships. Weird, huh?**

Turning It into a Script

Before we take a look at the script—and to give you a better idea of what you'll be seeing—here's an overview of the different types of scenes Frank and Terry devised to keep the game moving and to maximize the interactivity:

- **Midgames:** These are short movies the player watches (and cannot interrupt). Midgames transition you in and out of scenes (see the sidebar for Script 10.3).

Script 10.3

C-55

Series C: After heading to the Masa System, Captain Eisen is relieved of command, and soon Blair must make the biggest decision of his life, weighing the bonds of personal loyalty against his sworn duty to the Confederation.

MIDGAME: LEXINGTON FLIGHT DECK (54-C1)

A SHUTTLE LANDS...

BLAIR JOINS A GRIM EISEN ON THE FLIGHT DECK.

BLAIR
What's up?

```
                              EISEN
                    Got company.

CAPTAIN HUGH PAULSEN, MID-40S, STEPS OUT OF THE SHUTTLE. HE STANDS RAMROD
STRAIGHT, SNAPS OFF A SALUTE.

                              PAULSEN
                    Captain Hugh Paulsen, attached to
                    the Third Fleet, with orders from
                    Regional Command.

                              EISEN
                    Welcome aboard, Captain. Must be
                    important orders for you to have
                    personally carried them so far.

                              PAULSEN
                    All Confederation orders are impor-
                    tant, Captain. The Lexington is to
                    head immediately to the Masa system
                    where we'll rendezvous with the
                    Third Fleet.

EISEN RAISES AN EYEBROW.

                              EISEN
                    I'll inform my helm. You'll be
                    filling me in on Confed's plans?

                              PAULSEN
                    We have much to discuss...
                         (glancing at Blair)
                    ...in private, Captain.
```

Please note, that in the finished script segments shown here, Frank and Terry put all the general notes to the programmers in italics.

- **Required Scenes:** These are scenes a player has to take part in sooner or later in order for the game to move forward. If a scene is not labeled optional or sliding, it is required. "Most of the scenes in the script," explains Frank, "are in this category." For example, at a certain point in the game, Captain Paulsen has relieved Captain Eisen of his command and is giving orders. Paulsen sends Colonel Blair on his second mission of Series C, and, as the script indicates (see the sidebar for Script 10.4), Blair finds that his usual pick of Wingman has thinned out—new men loyal to Paulsen are being transferred in, while men loyal to Blair and Eisen are disappearing.

Terry and Frank kept all spoken dialogue scenes to about one full page in length, though sometimes they'd go over a page, but not by much. In cinematic terms, one page of dialogue takes about one minute to play on the screen if there are no interruptions.

Script 10.4

C-69

BRIEFING C2 - PAULSEN - BRIEFING ROOM (66-C2)

PAULSEN
Exemplary work on the spacelab, Colonel.

BLAIR
Thank you, sir.

PAULSEN
Rescuing it and the biochemist will be of tremendous benefit to Confed's plans.
(beat)
Now to the business at hand: Predictably, the Border Worlds Union brazenly defies Confed's air-space edict. We approach one such outlaw convoy now. Military ships that have invaded Confed territory, and maneuver with no Confed escort. They have ignored orders to turn back, and have even taken potshots at Confed's forces.
(beat)
They are a grave threat, and their presence can no longer be tolerated. We shall issue one more warning. If they refuse to cooperate,

```
                    you are to enforce the
                    interdiction, Colonel.
                              (beat)
                    By any means necessary...
                    Dismissed.
```

WINGMAN SELECTION NOTE: Blair finds that the flight roster has been thinned out even more. X+Y% of his usual "Red-shirt wingmen" are unavailable due to "transfers" and disciplinary actions.

- **Missions:** These are gaming sequences where the player is in the cockpit of a fighter. Usually, if you fail in a mission, you are not sent into a losing endgame but are allowed to continue with the series. That is, of course, if you don't get shot down—remember, that possibility is always there throughout the game. After you fly a mission, you are then debriefed (see the following sections, starting with On a Mission, for an in-depth discussion of how Frank and Terry prepared the mission scripts).

> **When you look at the paths Terry and Frank offer in the script, it's not always obvious which dialogue path will have what effect. Clearly the Wing Commander universe isn't all black and white. And as Frank comments on branching dialogue: "Both choices are always valid choices, they just tend to steer the scene and potentially the story in different directions."**

- **Optional Scenes:** These are dramatic scenes the player may or may not choose to take part in. The player does *not* have to talk to everybody they see. Optional scenes, however, are only available during the mission sequence in which they appear. Once you take off on a mission, these optional scenes are history, and the player has to play a new game to see them (see the section entitled: Clicking on Catscratch and the sidebar for Script 10.6).
- **Sliding Scenes:** These scenes are a special case of the optional scenes. Once again, the player has the option to take part in these scenes or not—if they choose not to, and the player flies a mission, these scenes are still available. They "slide," in other words. Once the final mission of a series is flown however, these scenes are no longer available.

While reading through the following sections and the scripts, it's also important to remember that in *Wing Commander IV,* you are—for the most part—either:

- Sitting on Mark Hamill's shoulder (aboard either the Lexington or the Intrepid) guiding him from room to room and—if you like—instructing him to talk to whoever happens to be there
- Or, in the cockpit of a fighter—with a first-person point-of-view—trying to survive a mission

On a Mission

When developing the mission ideas, Terry and Frank were constantly confronted with the problem of: Well, if you lose a mission, does that automatically put you on one of the losing endgame tracks? The answer to this question is actually fairly simple if you remember that the flight missions are organically grown from the story line.

When you think about it, certain missions, if not completed successfully, would obviously prevent the story from moving forward. For example, if you "don't" get the space lab back in Mission C1, you're screwed as the space lab is a critical story element later on in the game. Failure in Mission C1 means you can't continue. You have to go to the losing endgame without passing "go" and collecting the two hundred bucks.

In the case of Mission C2, you're flying out to teach a Border Worlds' convoy a lesson. Success or failure in this mission is not so critical for forward movement in the story.

And Back at the Base

After you come back from mission C2—win or lose—you get out of your fighter on the flight deck, and you're free to go four places on the ship:

- Flight control
- The briefing room
- The officer's lounge
- Eisen's cabin

The first place you encounter interactivity (or forward motion in the story) is in the officer's lounge. Here, you get the opportunity to chit-chat with Catscratch (see the sidebar for Script 10.5).

If you enter the officer's lounge, and see Catscratch there—again, you do *not* have to talk to him. You can have Blair turn right around and go to another room. However, and this is a big however, no matter where you wander in the ship from then on—to Eisen's cabin, to the flight deck, etc.—you will meet nobody, and nothing will happen other than moving Blair from place to place. To get the story going, you have to go back to the officer's lounge, and talk with Catscratch.

Intuitively, this freedom to wander the ship endlessly would seem to create a large dead spot in the forward motion of the story/game. Not to worry, Frank and Terry point out, most gamers rush into a room, and when they encounter somebody they can talk to, they click on and have a chat.

Script 10.5

C-74

OFFICERS' LOUNGE - CATSCRATCH (72-C3)

CATSCRATCH, HIS BROWS KNITTED, HUNCHES OVER A CUP OF COFFEE. THIS IS NOT THE CATSCRATCH WE'RE USED TO SEEING...

CATSCRATCH
Can I ask you something, Colonel?

BLAIR
What's up, partner?

CATSCRATCH
Attacking that convoy...
(hesitates)
Is ... is this the way wars start?

BLAIR
Wars are like bombs — the fuse gets lit before you actually hear the bang. Sometimes the fuse is pretty long.

CATSCRATCH
(beat)
Did you know I was from the Border Worlds, sir?

BLAIR
Figured you were Terran-born, if anything.

CATSCRATCH
Terran-educated. But my parents were third generation Border Worlders.
(beat)
Guess I'm just having some problems with these missions. On whether they're right.

Catscratch's morale UP:	*Catscratch's morale DOWN:*
BLAIR (nods) Can't say I like being kept in the dark, either. Hard to make a decision without all the data. (thinks) Captain Paulsen's not going to help. Maybe Eisen's holding out on me. Think maybe I'll talk to him again.	BLAIR If you start second-guessing every mission you fly, you're not going to last long out there. (beat) Besides, you signed on to fly for Confed. An oath of loyalty should still count for something.

Clicking on Catscratch

So moving on: You go to the officer's lounge, click on Catscratch, and he starts talking about how these missions don't seem right. As the script indicates, the conversation branches and you have the choice to boost his morale or to lower it.

If you boost Catscratch's morale, you then have the option to wander into Eisen's cabin and have a talk with him about what is really going on, or you can go back to flight control and have a talk with Maniac (for both of these conversations, see the sidebar for Script 10.6).

If you talk with Maniac, an announcement suddenly blares from the PA system kicking everybody out of Flight Control who doesn't have a security clearance, because a shuttle is coming in with VIP on board. Maniac then says: "Let's go get a drink." You have the choice to disobey orders—stay on the Flight Deck and see who's coming in—or you can go get a drink with Maniac.

Script 10.6

C-75

EISEN'S CABIN - EISEN (OPTIONAL) (73-C3)

CONDITION: Scene available ONLY after Scene 72-C3 has played AND ONLY IF Blair said he would talk to Eisen in that scene.

EISEN MAKES NOTES AT HIS DESK. HE STOPS, LOOKS AT BLAIR.

EISEN
I'll be shipping out soon. I'd like to make sure we don't make it too big a deal.

BLAIR NODS IN UNDERSTANDING, SITS OPPOSITE EISEN.

BLAIR
(beat)
Lately, some of the men aren't so sure of the missions they're flying for Confed.

EISEN
No?
(beat; thoughtful)
During the war with the Kilrathi, things were easy. Loyalty to Confed required little commitment – because what were the alternatives? Now? With the war over? Second-guessing is easy.

BLAIR
Never thought I'd see the day where I'd be shooting down my own kind.

EISEN

Humans will always vie for power. The Confederation may be less than perfect. But don't forget it was the driving force behind our victory. It succeeded in uniting humanity in a way no institution ever had before.

C-76

BLAIR

That's our ultimate duty, isn't it?

EISEN

Yes...

(long beat)

The difficulty is in knowing how best to execute it.

BLAIR STANDS UP.

BLAIR

Well, sir...

HE SALUTES. EISEN EXTENDS HIS HAND. THEY SHAKE WARMLY.

EISEN

I sincerely wish you a long and happy life, Colonel. It's been a pleasure and an honor commanding you.

C-77

FLIGHT CONTROL - MANIAC (74-C3)

CONDITION: This REQUIRED scene available ONLY after Scene 72-C3 has played.

BLAIR SEES A REDSHIRT WALKING AWAY FROM MANIAC.

MANIAC

Same to you, buddy.

MANIAC LOOKS AT BLAIR, SHAKES HIS HEAD.

MANIAC

Some of these guys... Not exactly friendly...

BLAIR
What about that bioconvergence chemist? Friendly? Or friendly fire?

MANIAC LOOKS AT THE GROUND AND RUBS HIS CHEEK.

MANIAC
Uhh—

AN ANNOUNCEMENT RINGS THROUGHOUT THE SHIP:

NAISMITH (V.O.)
Attention: All personnel without Level 5 security clearance clear the Flight Deck immediately. There will be no unauthorized access to the Flight Deck until further notice.

MANIAC
Pretty soon we'll have to get hall passes to visit the latrine... Wonder who's coming aboard.

BLAIR SHRUGS.

MANIAC
Well, since we're not wanted around here, I'm gonna have myself a libation up in the lounge. You comin'?

BLAIR THINKS A BEAT AND DECIDES...

C-78

To disobey orders:

BLAIR
Think I might stick around.

MANIAC
Paulsen doesn't look like he cuts a guy much slack. I'll be sure to visit you in the brig.

BLAIR
Maybe I'll get lucky and they'll be bringing another biochemist on board.

MANIAC WINCES...

MANIAC
Suit yourself.
...AND EXITS.
Go to Scene 75-C3. (No other options will be available.)

To obey orders:

BLAIR
Sure.

MANIAC
Why don't I meet you up there? I just remembered I was supposed to drop by Eisen's cabin. Guess the old man wants to tell his best pilot au revoir.

MANIAC EXITS...

BLAIR
Fine. But I get first dibs on any biochemists sittin' by themselves.
Go to Scene 78-C3. (No other options will be available.)

The Good, the Bad, and the Ugly

If you choose to disobey orders, you end up hiding on the Flight Deck, hoping for a chance to see who's coming in. This decision further branches into you finding a good or bad hiding spot. If it's a good spot (see the sidebar for Script 10.7), you get to see the bad guy Seether disembark from the shuttle. If it's a bad spot, Paulsen spots you, chews you out, and you miss who's getting out of the shuttle.

Script 10.7

C-79

FLIGHT DECK (75-C3)

CONDITION: This scene available ONLY IF Blair chose "to disobey orders" in Scene 74-C3. Scene triggered when Blair moves to Flight Deck.

A SHUTTLE HAS JUST LANDED. LEXINGTON FLIGHT PERSONNEL SCURRY TO MEET IT.SECURITY MEN MOVE ABOUT.

BLAIR SPOTS A STACK OF METAL DRUMS...

HE MOVES QUICKLY TO THE DRUMS, CROUCHES DOWN BEHIND THEM, AND WATCHES AS...

SEETHER EXITS THE SHUTTLE... THERE SEEMS TO BE A LOT OF IMPORTANCE ATTACHED TO HIS ARRIVAL.

BUT SEETHER? HIS ICY EYES MAKE HIM INSTANTLY RECOGNIZABLE TO BLAIR: THE THROAT-GRABBER BACK AT THE NEPHELE CANTEEN.

CAPTAIN PAULSEN HURRIES TO GREET SEETHER.

PAULSEN
(worried)
This is certainly unexpected—

SEETHER
Things haven't been progressing as anticipated...

TOGETHER, THEY MOVE AWAY OUT OF HEARING RANGE...

Upon completion of this midgame, Blair will find himself on the flight deck. Go to Scene 79-C3.

Somehow It All Works Out

As Terry and Frank explain, they had a lot of branching in their first draft script, but ultimately, for production reasons, a lot of it was eliminated, or simplified.

Think you can create an interactive script from all those possibilities—scribbled on all those note cards?

APPENDIX A

A Proposal and Demo Script

This appendix contains the proposal and a demo script (see the sidebar at the end of this appendix) for a game called *deusX: Ghost in the Machine* that Jeff Sullivan and Bruce Onder put together. In the proposal, the various sections break down as follows:

- **The Story**—defines the universe, the genre—science fiction—and explains a little about the mysteries and dangers the player will face. It also tells you how the user will interface with this world—through the telepresence transmitter (TP). In essence, this section sets the stage and the stakes, and it does so with an attitude of entertainment—not English Literature.
- **The World**—defines in detail the five component environments of the universe outlined in the Story section. Each environment is radically different—ranging from an anthropologist's apartment on Earth to an alien space craft circling a sun in a distant galaxy. Different environments give you contrasting visuals and sounds as well as the story rational to create highly divergent interactives and puzzles. For example, the alien ship environment may operate entirely differently than the apartment environment on Earth.
- **The Characters**—describes each character in a couple of terse sentences.
- **The Backstory**—presents the major questions—plot puzzles—associated with each environment.
- **The Look and Sound**—takes great care to point out what the game will look and sound like, and how it will employ state-of-the-art graphics and special effects.
- **The Interface**—explains how the user will navigate through the different worlds, how objects will be manipulated, and how inventory will be handled.

"deusX: Ghost in the Machine" is an environmental mystery game, with minimal character interaction. The user navigates through contrasting environments, solving puzzles along the way.

deusX: Ghost in the Machine

The following sections are the text of the proposal Jeff Sullivan and Bruce Onder created for *deusX: Ghost in the Machine.*

The Story

After a prolonged period of silence, you are invited to pay a visit to your brother, a research scientist currently stationed on the Red Nova Illsun Research Outpost (RNI), a small research facility located on a moon in the Lyra Ra system, the closest system to the star Lyra Osiris, a recently discovered nova.

Of course, a jaunt across the galaxy is no easy matter, even in your day and age. So in order to save time and money, you travel to RNI using a telepresence (TP) transmitter, which looks like a jumpsuit dangling from hundreds of electrodes. You strap in, press a button, and presto—your mind is transmitted electronically across trillions of miles of empty space, where it is digitally programmed into a telepresence drone, a humaniform robot that lets you walk and talk with the scientists at the station.

There's only one problem.

Nobody's home.

Okay, we lied. There's another problem.

Somebody's rigged your drone so that you can't disconnect. This means that you can't go home, unless you figure out where everybody went, who trapped you here, and why.

Did we mention the third problem?

Somebody's trying to kill you. More specifically, the drone housing your consciousness. But if your drone is destroyed, you're pretty sure your consciousness won't fare better.

But hey, this is life in the future.

The World

The world of *deusX: Ghost in the Machine* takes place in the future, on Earth and across the galaxy, where a dying sun is expected to give its last gasp, and an alien complex gives the first proof of extraterrestrial life—all in a complex web of deceit that only humans can weave.

The Apartment

This is where the player lives. The player is an archeologist, just back from an extensive project in Antarctica.

This is where the player gets video mail from Ric, the player's brother. Ric is one of the research scientists on Red Nova Illsun, the scientific outpost overseeing the last days of Lyra Osiris.

Ric invites his sibling to pay a visit to the station to share in the news of something spectacular. Ric has programmed one to the station's telepresence droids, reserving it for the player.

Red Nova Illsun Research Station

Red Nova Illsun is a research station on a moon that orbits planet Lyra, the only planet in the Lyra Ra system.

When the player arrives, he notices two things.

First, the second TP drone is not in its dock. Somebody's using it.

Second, nobody's here. That means...

...what does it mean?

The player navigates through the station, collecting clues about the recent events on the RNI base.

Eventually, the player stumbles across the entrance to the Creator Complex, an alien space station submerged beneath the moon's surface.

The first aliens ever encountered in the history of mankind!

The Creator Complex

Only, nobody's home here, either.

Well, that's not exactly true. The second TP drone is down here, and it seems intent on causing trouble for the player.

There's also an alien here, but it isn't of the race that created this station. It's a T'Carath, wounded by the rogue TP drone and holed up in a secret room, with access to all the functions of this alien complex.

The question is, is this alien friend or foe?

Another question: If the scientists aren't here, and they aren't in their own station, then where are they?

The player collects more clues, including research findings left behind by the scientists as they explored this spectacular discovery. The player also finds some pieces of a very alien-looking device (The Key).

Eventually, the player discovers two possible paths to find the scientists: a sleek, dangerous-looking pod in the space bay, and a weird teleportation chamber.

But where do they lead?

The T'Carath Mother Ship

The shuttle pod takes the player on a wild ride through space, to the pod's mother ship. This is the T'Carath's ship.

Here, the player can find out more about the T'Carath, but some of the information is misleading.

For instance, the T'Carath are peace-loving traders, but if you looked aboard this ship, you would find dozens of sleek, black missiles.

In reality, these missiles are terraforming rockets, used by this particular T'Carath to seed dead planets and make them live.

But the player might make other assumptions.

Planet Lyra Ra 1

The teleportation chamber beams the player to the surface of Lyra Ra 1.

Lyra's a desert planet, baked by Lyra Ra and its sibling, the nova Lyra Osiris. Harsh sands blow across the surface of this world. Two blazing suns scorch the ground and anything that dares to travel on it.

The player beams down to a station in the middle of this wasteland.

The Creators have built a city around the station. An astounding feat of engineering, but once again, deserted and dead.

Deserted, except for the scientists who are being held captive here. One of the scientists is the bad guy. It's just a question of which one.

The player encounters Ric in the city, being held in a field of molecular disruption. Whenever Ric moves, his molecules are perturbed by an unknown force, his body exploding and reforming at the slightest twitch.

Then the player discovers the hostage camp, and a TP interface like the one in the apartment.

It's at this point that Ric steps forward. As the bad guy.

It seems that he was the first to unravel the mysteries of what the Creator Complex is. What it does. And what it's worth.

The Creator Complex, he explains, controls a machine that's buried in the heart of Lyra Osiris, the red nova. The machine uses the energy of the sun to create a warp in space. In fact, the Creators had placed a network of gateways throughout the known universe, and provided these shortcuts to the rest of the universe.

Ric was working on the Creator technology when he stumbled across two vital bits of information:

The first is that the Creators had perfected a language translator that was able to learn any of a million languages, translate instantly, and bridge forever the communications gap between the various civilizations.

The second was that one of those civilizations was knocking on the door, asking to be let in.

Ric talked with the leaders of this race, and struck a bargain with them. In exchange for letting them into our galaxy, Ric would be granted the rule of Earth, and swear fealty to them for all time.

But Ric needed his sibling here, in order to decrypt the final codes in The Key that will let him open a gateway to another galaxy. And let out a horde of conquering warriors who will finally be able to expand beyond the confines of their own technological limits.

The story has two main conclusions: One is upbeat, and ends with the player defeating his own brother and sealing the hordes away forever. The other ends with Ric getting the upper hand, and yanking the knowledge he needs from the player's trapped mind.

Which one plays out depends on the player's skill in fitting together the pieces of the mystery. And putting the resulting big picture to good use.

The Characters

RIC DYLAN, the player's brother and the associate astrophysicist on the project. He is in charge of running experiments, collecting data, and performing preliminary data analysis.

CARL TREMIERE, the project manager and astronomer. He provides insight in studying the nova, and compiles periodic reports for the federation.

MIRANDA CARLISLE, the lead scientist on the project, an astrophysicist and computer scientist.

WARREN GREYS, a computer scientist and engineer. He's responsible for keeping the research station operating at peak efficiency.

The Backstory

The mystery of *deusX: Ghost in the Machine* has several layers. Although the answers are not presented here, these are some of the questions that form the mystery:

The Scientists

Where are the missing scientists?

What happened to them?

Who's behind their disappearance?

How can they be rescued?

Who is operating the rogue TP drone?

The Creator Complex

What is its purpose?

Who created the complex?

What are the creators like?

Where are the creators now?

The T'Carath

What is it doing?

Why is it injured?

Is it a friend or a foe?

The Look and Sound

deusX: Ghost in the Machine will be presented in 16-bit color, 3D rendered graphics. Through careful choice of color palettes, we can create photo-realistic imagery.

Extreme care and attention to detail will be taken with the modeling of the scenes to be rendered. *deusX: Ghost in the Machine* will clearly demonstrate its visual excellence when compared to the current CD-ROM titles available.

Characters, for the most part, will be displayed through carefully-controlled means such as small video screens. Toward the end of the game, several characters will be shown in full perspective, shot against a bluescreen and chromakeyed into the 3D world.

The visuals in *deusX: Ghost in the Machine* will also be state of the art, including such digital effects as morphing, distorting, and ray-tracing, as well as a collection of cinematic transitions and effects, such as wipes, fades, dissolves, mattes, chromakeys, color filters, embossing, and more. Video editing and effects tools currently available provide capabilities comparable to high-end television editing systems and effects houses at a fraction of the price.

The ability to move the imagery of *deusX: Ghost in the Machine* into and out of digital video gives us a powerful collection of tools to paint the often surreal and bizarre concepts of the piece.

deusX: Ghost in the Machine will employ a high-quality stereo soundtrack and Q-sound stereo surround sound effects to enhance the atmosphere of the story.

The Interface

The key word for the *deusX: Ghost in the Machine* interface is elegant. It's deceptively simple—about as close as you can come to an interface-less interface.

The entire screen is filled with the player's POV in a first-person-perspective view of the game world.

Movement

Navigation is accomplished in *deusX: Ghost in the Machine* by moving the cursor to an extreme edge of the screen. At the edge, the cursor will change to indicate if and what kind of movement is possible in that direction. If movement is possible forward, a forward-pointing arrow will appear when you move the cursor to the top of the screen. If you can turn to the right, then a 90-degree turning arrow will appear when you move the cursor to the right side of the screen. (If you can only look forward and backward in a particular area, then the cursor will change into a 180-degree turning arrow when you move it to either side of the screen.)

Movement into or through an object in the environment (e.g., doorways, ladders, holes, elevators, etc.) is accomplished by clicking on the item. If it's a ladder, you'll go up it. (If the ladder goes in both directions, the cursor will turn to an upward-pointing hand when the cursor is over the top half, and a downward-pointing hand when the cursor is over the bottom half.) If you click on a doorway, you'll go through it. If you click on a boat, you'll get into it.

Object Manipulation

To manipulate objects in the game world, you click on them.

For on/off objects—like buttons, switches, simple levers, and so on—clicking on the object toggles its state (from on to off, up to down, etc.).

For continuous objects—like throttles, slider switches, and more complex levers—the cursor will change to a grasping hand as long as the mouse button is held down. Moving the mouse will result in corresponding changes to the object's setting.

For radial objects—like dials, steering wheels, and valves—the cursor will change into a curled hand. A small red arrow around the hand will indicate whether clicking will turn the object clockwise or counter-clockwise. Generally, holding down the shift key while clicking will rotate the object counter-clockwise, while normal clicking will rotate it clockwise. Some objects will turn in one direction only.

Clicking on doors, drawers, boxes, etc. opens them, if they're not locked.

Many objects in *deusX: Ghost in the Machine* are shown at a lower level of detail than is required to inspect or operate them. When you click on one of these objects, you will zoom in for a more detailed view. From this detailed view, you can then manipulate the object directly. For example, the player might encounter a computer. Clicking on the computer will zoom you into a full-screen representation of the computer with keys, dials, a screen, etc. You can then click on the keys and switches of the computer and examine its display screen. When you're done with the close-up view of an object, simply click outside of the object, and your view will pull out to the full scene.

Inventory

The notion of inventory in *deusX: Ghost in the Machine* is greatly simplified. There is no collection of objects that must be carried around until their use is clear. Virtually all of the "stuff" the player needs to carry from place to place is information.

A Sample of the Scripter's Art

The demo script Jeff and Bruce prepared (see the following sidebar) shows just how rich and complex an interactive multimedia game environment can get—and this is just a sample.

> The demo script breaks the game environments down into individual architectural units and describes their look in great detail. The "Red Nova Illsun Research Outpost" (RNI) is broken down into the "Bay," "Upper Deck Hallway," the "Elevator," etc., and within each architectural unit, a scene takes place. The sound of the environment and the various moves and interactions that the player can make are also well scripted out.

Demo Script

RNI-BAY—TELEPRESENCE DRONE BAY

This chamber is roughly 4 meters square. A sliding door leads out to the upper deck hallway. The door has an inch-wide, charcoal-gray, ceramic-like frame.

On the left-hand side of the frame is a green button, which, when pressed, will open the door. clicking on the door will have the same effect. (The door opens swiftly, with a SOFT WHOOSHING sound that betrays its highly efficient electro-pneumatic mechanism.)

There is also a red button on the right-hand side of the door that will "lock" the door, keeping anyone on the other side from being able to open it (unless they have a higher security clearance).

The TP drone dock dominates the player's view of the north wall. The dock is a cross between a cordless telephone cradle and a coffin built for two: The black-painted metallic dock is rectangular, and houses a pair of vaguely humanoid-shaped mold/frame/clamp constructions where the drones are secured when not in use.

Electrode connections at the head and lower-back sections of the molds plug into the drones when they're docked. Conduits running from these connection areas to bulges in the framework molding indicate that substantial machinery must be hooked up to them. Indicator lights and cryptically-labeled meters surround the molds.

ATMOSPHERIC: A LOW HUM is constantly present around the dock, which fades as you move away from it.

The player's journey through the telepresence suit interface ends with the "takeover" of drone #1's memory. The player's first move will be to detach from the drone bay and take a step out into the chamber.

If the player is at all observant, he will notice that drone #2 is missing.

As the player steps away from his recess, he will receive another v-mail message from Ric:

RIC
Hey, glad to see you made it!
Sorry, but if I didn't greet you
in person that means I'm actually
doing work around here.

(laughs)
Hey, listen, ask any of the others
for directions to my quarters, and
I'll meet you there.

(checks watch)
I'd better get back to work.
Miranda really counts every second.
See you soon, kid.

RNI-UPP—UPPER DECK HALLWAY

The upper deck of the RNI is 3 meters wide and 4 meters high, fairly bare, with metallic floors textured for greater traction, walls of white plastic-like tile, and a ceiling comprised of interlocking hexagonal modules that emit soft white light.

There is a small, two-man (or one drone) elevator set into one end of the mid level Hallway. A green call button will summon the car and open the doors.

There are four vidscreens set into the walls, two on each side. The vidscreens allow an operator to press a button corresponding to the four scientists or the two drones.

Pressing any of the four buttons for the scientists rings a SOFT CHIME throughout the base. The button for that scientist lights on all vidscreens, until the button is pressed again, turning the page off.

No scientist answers the page.

Trying to page drone #2 gets this response:

FEMALE SYNTHETIC VOICE
Telepresence drone #2 is currently
offline, and not answering pages.
Please try again later.

Trying to contact drone #1 (the player) produces a paging icon on the player's TP interface screen. Pressing the vidscreen button again turns off the page. Clicking on the TP interface paging icon "answers" the page, turning off the vidscreen button and sending a video signal to the vidscreen.

RNI-ELE-ELEVATOR

Standing inside the elevator, one can see buttons for upper and lower level decks, as well as a vidscreen like those seen on the mid level deck.

Only one of the buttons works at a time. If one is on the upper level, then only the lower level button works. The doors are always open on whatever floor it is parked on.

The vidscreen works exactly like the others, and gives the same results as the others, too.

RNI-LOW-LOWER DECK HALLWAY

The lower deck hallway is the same width and height as the upper deck hallway. The layout is different, because the lower deck opens upon a different type of rooms.

But the vidscreens are set into the walls at regular intervals, and they work just like the ones upstairs.

RNI-AIR-AIRLOCK DOOR

The airlock door is controlled by the RNI computer system. The door itself is made of a super-strong alloy and has three sliding layers to prevent atmosphere leaks.

The hallway terminates in an irising airlock-type door (much like a camera shutter). Black and yellow lettering on the door reads:

RESTRICTED AREA

Cleared Personnel Only

FTC 0178.96.B.1

To the left of the airlock is a small control panel with red and green status lights.

If the player clicks on the airlock door, there is an ELECTRONIC BEEP, and the green light starts blinking.

MALE SYNTHETIC VOICE
Scanning...

After two seconds, there is a BUZZ, the green light goes out, the red light starts blinking.

MALE SYNTHETIC VOICE
Clearance code verified.

The airlock irises open with a <u>SHARP METALLIC RASP,</u> revealing the decontamination chamber. The red light stays on.

MALE SYNTHETIC VOICE
Good evening, Professor Dylan.

<u>RNI-DEC—DECONTAMINATION CHAMBER</u>

This chamber has been outfitted with a collection of sprayers, scanners, and projectors so it looks like a robot's car wash.

A cylindrical, central compartment rotates so the single opening allows access to both the lower deck hallway (RNI-LOW) and the mine shaft (RNI-MIN).

<u>ATMOSPHERIC: The sound of many pieces of equipment powering up or shutting down is always heard in the background in this room.</u>

The cylinder rotates so that the opening of the inner cylinder is sealed against the closed portion of the outer cylinder (no matter which room you come from, the cylinder is always rotated to the same sealing location).

The entire room is bathed in red light, while a <u>LOW BUZZING</u> fills the air.

The red light and <u>BUZZ</u> shut off with the <u>CLANK</u> of a major transformer shutting down, and a sharp <u>HISSING</u> fills the room. The view dissolves into a cloudy, hazy image (simulating the injection of a milky gas into the chamber).

The cloud vanishes quickly as <u>POWERFUL EXHAUST FANS</u> clear the air.

Then a robotic arm extends from the wall and passes a green laser-scanner across the player's viewscreen, scanning every inch of the TP drone.

Finally, the male synthetic voice common to RNI hallway 2 announces:

MALE SYNTHETIC VOICE
Decontamination process completed. You may proceed.

The inner cylinder rotates so the opening is aligned with the opening of the room opposite the one the player just came from.

<u>RNI-MIN—MINE SHAFT</u>

One of the areas of research RNI is charged with is the study of the geological composition of the moon. To that end, a short mine shaft was dug with the aid of lasers and TP drones.

Of course, one of the results of digging the mine shaft was the discovery of the Creator complex. The mine shaft ends with an opening onto a large alien-hewn chamber beneath the moon's surface.

A collection of viewing, sensing, and less-recognizable equipment is situated around the entrance to the alien chamber.

Something is visible on the floor several meters below—a symbol of alien origin.

If the player descends into the Creator complex, the following sequence occurs:

A message appears on the TP interface:

WARNING: VIRUS DETECTED!

ATTEMPTING TO PURGE...

Then, there is a RENDING SOUND, and the inner frame of the TP interface expands to fill the frame (causing the TP interface controls to disappear) in a psychedelic feather-zoom effect.

Following the effect comes a WET SNAP and the screen FADES TO WHITE

NOTE: From here on, the TP interface is gone, and once again, we have the full screen for the player's POV.

Slowly, the scene fades back in. However, all traces of the user interface are gone. The player is locked inside the drone.

APPENDIX B

The Classics, Some Contacts, and a Contract

This appendix is a bit of a catchall, but it contains (and I think you'll agree once you check it out) a veritable mother lode of great stuff. There are a variety of things to inspire you, some lists of people and places with which to share your concepts and ideas, and a bit of sound contractual guidance (and the paperwork to back it up) once you've become a true player in the world of interactive multimedia. So, read on, reach out, and write yourself into a sweetheart deal.

A Few Good Reads

The Alexandria Quartet:
Justine
Mountolive
Balthazar
Clea
by Lawrence Durrell
Dutton & Company

Art & Physics: Parallel Vision in Space, Time & Light
by Leonard Shlain
Quill
William Morrow, 1991

Eighty Fairy Tales
by Hans Christian Andersen
The Pantheon Fairy Tale and Folklore Library
Pantheon Books, 1976

The Elements of Screenwriting: A Guide for Film and Television Writing
by Irwin R. Blacker
Collier Books
MacMillan Publishing Company, 1986

The First Love Stories: From Isis and Osiris to Tristan and Iseult
by Diane Wolkstein
Harper Perennial, 1991

The Hero with a Thousand Faces
by Joseph Campbell
Bollingen Series XVII
Princeton University Press, 1973

Magister Ludi (Or the Glass Bead Game)
by Hermann Hesse
Translated from the German *Das Glasperlenspiel*
by Richard and Clara Winston
Bantam Books, 1969

Possession
by A.S. Byatt
Vintage International
Vintage Books, New York, 1990

The Writer's Journey: Mythic Structure for Storytellers & Screenwriters
by Christopher Vogler
Michael Wiese Productions, 1992

Zen in the Art of Writing: Essays on Creativity
by Ray Bradbury
Joshua Odel Editions
Capra Press, 1990

Who's Who and How to Reach Them

InterActive Agency (Public Relations)
Tony Winders
Email: tony@iagency.com
Alan Wallace
Email: awall@iagency.com
630 S. Masselin Avenue
Los Angeles, CA 90036-5763
Tel: 213-932-8368
Fax: 213-932-0043

Interactive Media Festival
448 Bryant Street
San Francisco, CA 94107
Tel: 415-357-0100

The Interactive Multimedia Sourcebook
Templin Bogen Associates
507 Howard Street, Suite 200
San Francisco, CA 94105
Tel: 415-281-3637
Fax: 415-281-3630
Email: TBA1994@aol.com

The Multimedia Directory
Jon Samsel & Clancy Fort
The Carronade Group
ISBN-1-885452-04-7
Tel: 213-935-7600

The Penga Group (Producers)
3622 20th Street
San Francisco, CA 94110
Tel: 415-824-9661
Fax: 415-206-0399
Email: penga@hooked.net

S.O.S., Inc. (Distribution Consultants)
Joey Tamer
100 Driftwood #1
Marina de Rey, California 90292
Tel: 310-306-1814
Fax: 310-306-4861
Email: joeytamer@aol.com

Walker & Associates (Marketing Consultants)
Becki Walker
310-821-5898

Writers Guild of America, east
555 West 57th Street
New York, NY 10019
Tel: 212-767-7800

Writers Guild of America, west
7000 W. Third Street
Los Angeles, CA 90048-4329
Tel: 213-951-4000
Web: http://www.wga.org

The WGA Website and Interactive Program Contract

The Writers Guild of America, west's website at http://www.wga.org features excerpts from *The Journal* (the Guild's monthly magazine), current press releases, membership information, registration of scripts and treatment information, library and publication information, and special goodies called Cyber Glitz—fun, insider stuff from the Hollywood entertainment industry that'll keep you coming back for more. Additionally, the site will be linked with numerous writer-related and resource sites of interests. So check it out.

The following two pieces of paper may be very useful when you enter the deal-making stages of your interactive career. The first is a description of the Writers Guild of America, west Interactive Program Contract—what it is, how it works, and who it benefits. The second item—the "Letter of Adherence"—is the actual contract.

The Writers Guild of America, west Interactive Program Contract documents are reproduced here simply to give you some idea of the things you should be looking at and considering when you're ready to go to contract. For more information—and the official scoop on WGA membership and contracts—check out the WGA, west website at http://www.wga.org or write to either of the two addresses provided in the "Who's Who and How to Reach Them" section of this appendix.

The Interactive Program Contract . . .

WHAT IT IS:

The Interactive Program Contract covers writing and/or designing interactive digital programs produced for disc, cartridge-based platforms and on-line services.* Writing for interactive television is covered by the WGA Agreement and is not eligible for the Interactive Program Contract.

**(Excluding certain news format reporting and other text-only on-line journalistic writing.)*

HOW IT WORKS:

Using the contract is simple. Producers specify their name, address, financial structure, the title of the project, and the amount of money which will be paid to the writer(s) for their services--the writer's "gross compensation."

By signing the contract, producers agree to make standard pension and health contributions equal to twelve and one-half percent (12 1/2%) of the writer's gross compensation. For example, if the writer is paid $20,000 for a project, the producer will contribute 12 1/2% of that amount ($2,500), on behalf of the writer to the Writer's Guild Pension Plan and Health Fund (6% and 6 1/2% respectively).

After the Interactive Program Contract has been completed, please send to: Department of Industry Alliances, WGAw, 7000 West Third Street, Los Angeles, California 90048.

The Pension & Health form, along with appropriate contributions, should be sent to: Producer-WGA Pension Plan, 1015 North Hollywood Way, Burbank, California, 91505.

WHO IT BENEFITS:

Writers and designers of interactive programs earn contributions on their behalf to the Guild's pension and health funds. The Producer-Writers Guild of American Pension Plan and Writers Guild-Industry Health Fund are among the most comprehensive pension and health plans in the entertainment industry.

By using the Interactive Program Contract, non-Guild writers may become eligible for membership to the WGA. Units for Interactive Programs are currently interpreted on a case-by-case basis.

Producers using the Interactive Program Contract gain access to the most skilled and experienced writing talent in the entertainment community.

For Questions:

Department of Industry Alliances

In Southern California:
Lori Lieberman or Kay Schaber
7000 West Third Street, Los Angeles, California 90048
Telephone: (213) 782-4511 Fax: (213) 782-4807

In Northern California:
Susan Gerakaris
1222 Quail Circle, San Jose, California 95120
Telephone: (408) 323-1898 Fax: (408) 323-1897

■ INTERACTIVE PROGRAM CONTRACT ■

Letter of Adherence ■ Single Production Only

Company ______________________ **Phone: ( )** __________

Street Address: ______________________

City: __________ **State:** __________ **Zip:** __________

Financial Structure

Corporation:	☐	*Partnership**	☐	*10% or more owner:*	☐
*Joint Venture**	☐	*Sole Owner:*	☐	*DBA:*	☐

If Corporation, name of state in which corporation is registered: __________

If Corporation, name of officers and principal owners: __________

____

****List names of Partners or Joint Venturers:*** __________

____

TITLE OF PRODUCTION: ______________________

COMPENSATION: *(Writing and/or Designing Services):* __________

LENGTH OF PROGRAM *(In Minutes):* __________

WRITER(S) EMPLOYED UNDER THIS CONTRACT

Name: __________ **SS#** __________

Name: __________ **SS#** __________

On behalf of the writer(s) employed on the above-named Interactive Program, the undersigned Interactive Program Producer hereby agrees to make contributions to the Producer-Writers Guild of America Pension Plan ("Plan") and the Writers Guild Industry Health Fund ("Fund") as set forth in Article 17 of the 1995 Writers Guild of America Theatrical and Television Basic Agreement ("the 1995 WGA MBA"), by reference incorporated herein and available on request. Producer agrees to be bound by the terms and conditions of the Plan Agreement and the Fund's Trust Agreement. No other terms of the 1995 WGA MBA shall apply to the employment of such writer(s).

Currently, the contribution rates set forth in Article 17 are six percent (6%) of gross compensation for writing services to the Plan and six and one-half percent (6.5%) of gross compensation for writing services to the Fund.

Accepted and Agreed:

______________________ ______________________
(Company) ***(Print Name and Title)***

By: ______________________ ______________________
(Signature) ***(Date)***

WRITERS GUILD OF AMERICA, WEST, INC. on behalf of itself and its affiliate, WRITERS GUILD OF AMERICA, EAST, INC.

By: ______________________

—For Office Use Only—

Accepted this __ day of __________, 19__, Producer-Writers Guild of America Pension Plan and Writers Guild Industry Health Fund. By: __________ ***Title:*** __________

•Return completed form to•

Department of Industry Alliances
Writers Guild of America, west, Inc.
7000 West Third Street
Los Angeles, California 90048

•For Questions•

SO CALIF: *Lori Lieberman, Kay Schaber*
Phone: (213) 782-4511 Fax: (213) 782-4807
NORTHERN CALIF: *Susan Gerakaris*
Phone: (408) 323-1898 Fax: (408) 323-1897

APPENDIX C

The Credits

As promised, here are the credits—a listing of all those who worked to create the interactive multimedia titles deconstructed in Chapters 8, 9, and 10 of this book. If you're one of those people (like me) who sits in the movie theater, long after the final dramatic scene, and watches a seemingly endless list of names and titles go by, I'm sure you'll appreciate what this appendix has to offer.

Psychic Detective

Cast	
Laina Pozok	BEATA POZNIAK
Eric Fox	KEVIN BREZNAHAN
Sylvia Bourget	MARCIA PIZZO
Max Mirage/Lexi Golitsyn	JARION MONROE
Monica Pozok	ZACHARY BARTON
Madam Tikunov	SHARON LOCKWOOD
Moki Valdez	LUIS OROPEZA
Sergei Nosenko	ERIC BEAVERS
Vladimir Pozok	ROB NILSSON
Bouncer	STEVEN A. JONES
Chad Bitalski	WILLIAM HALL
Jeanine, the Miragequester	ALLISON CHASE
Bobby, the Bar Patron	MATT MENGARELLI
Officer Griggs	RALPH PEDUTO
Officer O'Brien	TONY HANEY
Exotic Dancer	MEAGHAN GANNETT
Pawnshop Owner	DAVID E. KAZANJIAN
Skateboard Kid	DARRIN LEE ROE
Bag Lady	ADELE PROOM
Anna Slaznowicz	MONICA BABER
Cleaner	MICHAEL HALTON
Cleaner's Partner	ROSS MARTINEAU
Courier	J. STEPHEN COYLE
Delivery Man	ROBERT ERNST
Bag Man	BEN GARDNER
Male Reporter	PAUL GHIRINGHELLI

Female Reporter	MEGAN DODDS
Drunk Inmate	SCOTT BEACH
Miragequester	ALYSOUN QUINBY
Karelian Woman	MICHELLE McHALL
Mansion Guests	EILEEN FINN, HOLLY LADDIA, LEROY KOPP III, MARY MACKEY, BLAKE TORNEY
Waiters	GREG CALA, RON KAELL
Arabian Sheik	DENNIS POPPOLARDO
Hong Kong Businessman	PETER SOE
Macho Woman	KRISTEN KUEHN
Trio of Musicians	PETER DIVONO, ROBERT GARVER, NORBERT STACHEL
Brick Guests	ERIN CAMPION, KATHLEEN DUNNE, PAULA EDWARDS, LYGIA SERRA, JULIE TAYLOR, MICHAEL CRATE, SCOTT McCLAIN, RON ROGGE, CHIP WASSON, JON SCAMAN
Little Lexi	OLIVER KANE
Eric's Father	DAVID ROSENTHAL
Little Eric	IAN CONKLIN
Little Laina	AMBER JOY SMITH
Lexi's Mom	BRONWYN SMITH
Anna's Little Brother	DAVID BILLS
Eric's Mom	KATHLEEN TURCO-LYON
Little Monica	ALICIA JAMARILLO
Little Anna	MEGAN DOHERTY-BAKER
Man with Pocket Watch	SCOTT DEVENNEY
Laina's Mother	JEANNE PETERS
Customer	DIANE WASHINGTON-SHEPARD
Dog Walker	BOB SIBILIA
Old Man	SHELDON TROMBERG
Parking Attendant	DON ROSENBERG
Stranger	JOE PEER
Kid Scaring Moki	RYAN ASHFORD
Lounge Audience	JAMES COTTON, KAREN JENNINGS-BAUER, BILL JONES, RAMONA SCOTT, JERRY MARK

Pedestrians	CAROL HODGES, LISA SARRAIL, KEN STEIMETZ, EDDIE JESSE, JOHNETTA SHEARER, WESLEY WATKINS, ED HANSON, BECKY ROY, WILLIAM BOYD
Jailer	BRIAN DANKER
Jogger	JENNIFER OKABE
People Staring	GARY PETTINGER, ELAINE THOMAS
Miragequesters	COLIN ANDREWS, STEVE BAKUNAS, MICHAEL BELLINO, DAN BELZER, DENA BIKERSTAFFE
Myki the Dog	MYKONOS PHELAN-McKEE

Production Crew

Director	JOHN SANBORN
Writer	MICHAEL KAPLAN
Producers	DON HOWE, SALLY BENTLEY
Assistant Director	MICHAEL KITCHENS
Director of Photography	SKIP SWEENEY
Camera Assistant	HRAFNHILDUR GUNNARSDOTTIR
Lighting Director	DARRELL FLOWERS
Production Manager	KELLY COURTNEY
Script Supervisor	MINDY RODMAN
Production Coordinator	EILEEN McKEE
2nd AD	PAUL LOWE
2nd 2nd AD	CURT BUTZ
Key Grip	JAMES CHILDERS, HUE FREEMAN
Best Boy	PAUL MEISE
Grip	JOE VICTORIA, BRUCE THOMPSON
Utility	PHIL STOCKTON, MICHAEL KNIGHT, JOEL BACH, PAUL SCHERMAN
Grip Truck Drivers	LUKE HOCK, JIMMY STEWART, BRUCE JONES
VTR	MIA LOR HOULBERG
Sound	STEVE BALLIET
Boom Operator	REED MAIDENBERG
Locations Manager	LAURIE NOLL
SF Casting	NANCY HAYES CASTING
LA Casting	NICOLE ARBUSTO & HELEN JOY DICKSON
Background Casting	WESLEY WATKINS

Production Design	STERLING STORM
Set Decorator	BILL McGIRR
Set Dressing	KIM NIES, SUZY SKAGGS
Make-Up Artist	STEVE ANDERSON
Hair Stylist	PAMELA HARRIS
Makeup Assistant	RICHARD BATTLE, MARIANNA DEFINA
Prop Master	CRAIG PATTERSON
Wardrobe Mistress	CAROLYN TYLER
Property Assistants	SCOTT BARRETT, DEAN ZINGUS, LIZ CAMPANA,
Art Assistants	WENDI LYND, SUE CHAN
Wardrobe Assistants	KATHLEEN BLAKE, STEPHANIE SCHNEIDER, CASANDRA CARPENTER, ESMERELDA KENT, ASHLEY GIBBS
Weapons & Effects	BILL CURTAIN
Pyrotechnics	T. HUNTER McCANN
Still Photographer	MELISSA MULLIN
Production Assistants	MARY MATHAISELL, JOEL BACH, GUY COUSSEMENT, DOUG KIEFFER, DARIUS MILNE, CHEYENNE MILNE, DEBORAH PHELAN, PETER WEST, SHERRY RUSSELL, BRUCE READY, VAN KINDEL, DIANNE CHILD
Production Accountant	SUE LONG
Craft Service	JENNIFER LONG
Stage Facility	STUDIO (COLOSSAL)
Stage Managers	TIM LLOYD, RUBEN O'MALLEY, MICHAEL HARDWICK
Set Construction	SCENE II
On-Set Construction	DEAN ZINGUS
Art Assistant	SEAN HENNESSEY
Russian Translator	LENA PISELSKAIA
Motorhome Drivers	MARK FRAIZER, JERRY WINSTON, ROSIE MALLEY
Talent Wrangler	STACY HOLMES
Welfare	RENIE GUIMOND, DONNELL BARNES
Security	C&F MOTION PICTURE SECURITY
Logo Design	MICHAEL BRUNSFELD

Storyboard Artist	TOM HOLLOWAY
Video Equipment	VIDEO FREE AMERICA
Caterer	ZOCALO
Neon Art	AARGON NEON
Collector Fabrication	JAMES BELVINS
Limousine	COURTESY-A CHAUFFEURED LIMOUSINE
Black Diamond Vortex Art	ANDREW GUEVARA
Miragequest Signs	LANDMARK SIGNS
Photo Prints	SKYLAB
Photo Blow Ups	BLOW UP LAB
Hotel Accomodations	HOTEL PRESCOTT
Motorhome Rental	SWIFT-LESLIE
Prop Autos	ATLAS AUTO RENTAL
Production Truck	RANAHAN RENTS
Automobile Rental	BAY AREA RENTAL
Travel Agent	VALLE TRAVEL SERVICE
Walkies	BRICKLEY
Special Thanks	SAN FRANCISCO STATE UNIVERSITY SCHOOL OF CREATIVE ARTS, CITY OF SAN FRANCISCO, BOB PUTZ OF THE SFPD, PORT OF SAN FRANCISCO, CITY OF BERKELEY, SGT. BUD STONE OF THE BERKELEY POLICE, CITY OF OAKLAND, ALAMEDA COUNTY SHERIFF'S DEPARTMENT, JOHN BOTT OF S.F. HERBST THEATRE, DUNSMUIR HOUSE AND GARDENS, DAVIES, THOMAS, CONDIOTTI GRIP & LIGHTING, FALORE CHRYSLER, SARAH CAHILL, SUSAN HOFFMAN, LESLIE SIMMONS

Post Production

Video Footage produced by	(COLOSSAL) PICTURES in association with ELECTRONIC ARTS PRODUCTIONS, INC.
Post Facility	VIDEO FREE AMERICA
Special Thanks	SUE MARCOUX
Editors	HRAFNHILDUR GUNNARSDOTTIR, STEVE JENSEN, LEDA MALIGA

Technical Support	SKIP SWEENEY, LARRY REPP
Post Production Supervisors	SHAWN CUDDY, SALLY BENTLEY
Authoring	JOHN SANBORN
Composer	PAT GLEESON
Sound Designer	JEFF ROTH
Mixed at	FOCUSED AUDIO, SAN FRANCISCO ©1995 Focused Audio. All Rights Reserved
Additional Sound Design	AL NELSON
GUI/Interface Art	JIM COLLINS/SMOKE AND MIRRORS
For Electronic Arts	
Executive Producer	JIM SIMMONS
Assistant Producer	RIC NEIL
Software Engineers	TIM LEARMONT, RANDY MOSS
Director of Development	KEITH McCURDY
Project Managers	LUCY BRADSHAW, STEPHEN BARRY, IRENE LEE
Technical Director	COLIN McLAUGHLAN
Business/Legal Affairs	CAROL T. CONTES
Business Affairs Coordinator	SHERI BURGOS-SARKIS
Digital Audio Engineers	KEN FELTON, MARC FARLY, JIM SPROUL, DON VECA, PHIL BURKE
Video Colorist & Compression	FREDERIQUE GUETTE
Additional Code & Graphics Processing	LAURENT BENES, CHARLES CAFRELLI, KEN DYKE, MARGART FOLEY, ERIC KORNBLUM, JEFF LITZ, PHILLIPE TARBOURIECH
Product Manager	LISA HIGGINS
Documentation	VALERIE E. HANSCOM
Package Art Direction	NANCY FONG
Artist's Photo	ROSALIND DELLIGATTI
Special Thanks to	TIM BRENGLE, JEFF GLAZIER, JOHN WILLIAMS

Pyramid: Challenge of the Pharaoh's Dream

Production/Design

Executive Producer/Creator/ Supervising Designer	ROGER HOLZBERG
Producer/Co-Creator	ALBERT REINHARDT
Line Producer	VERNA HARVEY
Writer	ANNE MARIE CASAVANT-CHANEY
Game Designer	HAL JORDY III
Associate Producer/Dialogue & Journal Editor	ALBERT BRAUN
Production Coordinator	GIL GORDON
Egyptologist	ALESSANDRA CAROPRESI
Mac Wizard	BEN HARPER
Production Assistants	MICHAEL FOX, JASON JACKSON, DAVID FOX
Interns	MATT MAHONEY, SUE HILLEBRAND
Quality Assurance	JEFF LORENTZEN
Special Thanks	TODD WADE, STEVE CRANE, CAMILLA CALAMANDREI, STEVE CALVER

Art

Art Director/Lead Artist	PAM SPERTUS
Visual Concept Designer	TOM WALSH
Character Designer/Lead Animator	SEAN JONES
2nd.Artist	DAVID PALMER
2nd.Animator	TIM DECKER
3D Artist	LEE CRIM
Assistant Animators	SIDDARTHA OLMEDA, TOM KLEIN

Music and Sound

Composer/Audio Director/ Sound Designer	RANDY HALE
Sound Designer	HAMILTON ALTSTATT, GARY MORAN
Audio Technology	MARK PAGE, DAVE ATHERTON

Technical

Technical Director / Lead Programmer	ARI SCHINDLER
Tools Programmer/GameProgrammer	TIM CROWDER
Game Scripter/Database Programmer	TYLOR HAGERMAN
Game Programmer	MICHAEL KANTNER
Additional Tools Programmer	MALAY JALUNDHWALA

Dream Quest Images

Visual Effects Supervisor	MIKE SHEA
Visual Effects Producer	DAVID McCULLOUGH
Digital Technical Director	ROB BURTON
Visual Effects Stage Supervisor	KEVIN FITZGERALD
Visual Effects Gaffer	SCOTT BEATTIE
Visual Effects Grip	RICK JOHNSON
Visual Effects Stage Crew	CRAIG MOORE, HOLGER FATH
3-D Animator	GENEVIEVE YEE
Compositors	BRIAN LEACH, STEVEN YAMAMOTO, AMY PFAFFINGER
Data Management	MARK DAWSON
Digital Illustrator	CHARLES CARPENTER
Model Supervison	DAVE GOLDBERG
Model Coordinator	WARREN FARINA
Model Builders	RAY CAVALLUZZI, CURT ENGLEMANN, JOHN HESS, RAMON JUNCAL, ADAM LOVELL, JAMES McGEACHY, TONY MOFFETT, WENDY POWELL, JAMES SMITH, MATSUNE SUZUKI, SCOTT THOMPSON
Model Production Assistant	JEFFERY GRANT
Visual Effects Editor	JEFF BEATTIE
Electronics Technicians	JOSEPH HAGEY, FEDERIC STERN
Camera Rig Machinist	REZA KASRAVI
Production Assistants	ROBERT CAMPOS, JASON LUX, STEVEN PIMENTAL, CHRISTOPHER TURNER
Creative Consultant	HOYT YEATMAN
DQI President, Film Group	KEITH SHARTLE
DQI Vice President, Film Group	DENNIS HOFFMAN

McGraw-Hill Home Interactive Production/Design Team

Executive Producer	PHILIP BOUCHARD
Director of Creative Development	DR. CHERYL WEINER
Director of Technology & Production	BRYAN WATERS
Multimedia Production Director	ERIK HOLSINGER
MHHI Quality Assurance	FRED KEACH, STEVE WHITE, ANDREW STESS, MIKE GIACONA, MARKO OSBORNE
Special Thanks	FRANK CATALANO

Wing Commander IV—The Price of Freedom

Game Development

Executive Producer	CHRIS ROBERTS
Game Producers	MARK DAY, DALLAS SNELL
Associate Producers	DAVID DOWNING, ADAM FOSHKO
Game Director	ANTHONY MORONE
Lead Programmer	FRANK ROAN
Programmer, Gameflow Coordinator	JASON HUGHES
Additional Programming	PETER SHELUS
Movie Compression & Playback	JASON YENAWINE
Programming Intern	DANIEL YEE

Design

Mission Design & Implementation	BEN POTTER, JEFF SHELTON, SCOTT SHELTON
Original Story Concept	CHRIS DOUGLAS
Additional Data Implementation	CHUCK KARPIAK, STEVE POWERS, CHARLES HARTIGAN

Audio

Audio Coordinator	MARTIN GALWAY
Original Score	GEORGE OLDZIEY
Interactive Sound Design	MARTIN GALWAY, STRETCH WILLIAMS
Interactive Music	GEORGE OLDZIEY

Music Recording	MARTIN GALWAY, GEORGE OLDZIEY, STRETCH WILLIAMS
Musicians	PAUL BAKER (SAXOPHONE), STRETCH WILLIAMS (GUITAR)
Spaceflight Dialogue Editor	MARTIN GALWAY, JAY MAHAVIER, STRETCH WILLIAMS

Art

Production Designer	CHRIS DOUGLAS
Art Director	JEFFREY "JC" COMBS
3-D Animators	RODNEY BRUNET, JEFFREY "JC" COMBS, CHRIS DOUGLAS, MARK LEON, DEAN McCALL, SEAN MURPHY, CHRIS OLIVIA, BETH FOSTER PUGH, PAULINE SAAB, MARK VEARRIER
Additional 3D Animators	JENNIFER AYERS, PAUL STEED
RealSpace 3D Modellers	DEAN McCALL, BRENNAN PRIEST
Additional Artists	JEFF HARRIS, DAMON WALDRIP
3-D Software provided by	ALIAS RESEARCH
Graphics Hardware provided by	SILICON GRAPHICS

Product Support

QA Project Leader	ANTHONY L. SOMMERS
Assistant Project Leaders	J. ALLEN BRACK, TODD WACHHAUS
QA Team	CINCO BARNES, NATHAN BATISTE, JOHN DARSNEK, CHRISTOPHER D. ERRETT, KENNY HOTT, KEVIN MELTON, MYQUE OUELLETTE, KENT RAFFRAY, CARLUS WESLEY
Hardware Lab Tech	BRETT J. BONNER
Translations Liason	ANDY BRUNCKE
Product Support Supervisor	MARIE WILLIAMS
Hardware Lab Supervisor	BRIAN WACHHAUS
Director of Studio Services	KAY GILMORE

Administrative

Finance	MIKE GRAJEDA, DOMINIQUE IYER
Executive Assistant	MADELEINE FOX

Resource Coordinator	WESTON GIUNTA
Network Administrators	DAVE REEVES, MARK RIZZO
Senior Technician	RICK McNEELEY
Unix Administrator	CHRISTOPHER ALEXANDER NORTH-KEYS
Director of Development Services	SEAN KELLEY
Director of Marketing	JENNIE EVANS
Product Manager	GALEN SVANAS
Assistant Product Manager	PATRICK BRADSHAW
Media Relations	DAVID SWOFFORD, TERESA POTTS, RICHARD STEINBERG
Unit Publicist	MICHAELS & WOLFE, INC.
Travel Coordination	MADELEINE FOX, BARRINGTON SMITH
Subtitles	MADELEINE FOX, ANA MORENO, JORG NEUMANN

Translation

Translations Manager	KIRSTEN VAUGHAN
German Translation	FRANK DIETZ, STEFAN KOLO, JORG NEUMANN
German Documentation	ANJA RUMBARGER
German Testing	JORG NEUMANN, KAI LEBERT, STEPHAN LIPS, ROMAN TRAYCEY
German Dubbing Studio	FFS GMBH, MUNICH
French Translations	PETER BERT, DOMINIQUE POUMEYROL-JUMEAU
French Documentation	ISABELLE RICE
French Testing	JEAN-LUC CHABRIER, LEMUEL HAHAM, DIDIER JUMEAU, DANIEL TAILLEFER
French Dubbing Studio	STUDIO LINCOLN, PARIS

Game Materials

Writing	TUESDAY FRASE, MELISSA TYLER
Additional Fiction	WILLIAM R. FORSTCHEN, BEN OHLANDER
Packaging	TREY HERMANN
Poster Art	SAM YEATES
Promotional Materials	JENNIFER DAVIS
Advertising	AL CARNLEY

Documentation	JOHN BOWIE, CATHERINE CANTIERI
Editing	DAVID LADYMAN

Film Production

Executive Producer/Director	CHRIS ROBERTS
Producer	MARK DAY
Associate Producer	ADAM FOSHKO
Co-Producer	DONNA BURKONS
Screenplay	TERRY BORST, FRANK De PALMA
Line Producer	MARYANN FABIAN
Casting Director	MIKE FENTON
Assistant Casting Director	JULIE ASHTON-BARSON
Casting Assistant	RACHEL DAVIES
1st Assistant Director	HARRY JARVIS
2nd Assistant Director	TIA ARDRAN
2nd 2nd Assistant Director	JOHN BRATTON
Production Coordinator	JAMES A. CAPP
Assistant Production Coordinator	RAY COBO
Set Production Assistants	WENDY PALMER, ANDREA NETZE
Production Assistants	SHAUN O'BANION, GARY SIMS, ORION WALKER
Assistant to Mr. Hamill	TRACEE SABATO
Assistant to Mr. Roberts	BARRINGTON SMITH
Mark Hamill's Stand-in	EMIDIO ANTONIO
Director of Photography	ERIC GOLDSTEIN
1st Camera Assistant	TOM RYAN
2nd Camera Assistant	TONY NAGY
Additional 2nd Camera Assistant	DAISY SMITH
Loader	AMY ABRAMS
Gaffer/General Foreman	JOEY BROWN
Best Boy/Chief Lighting Technician	COREY BIBB
Best Boy Grip/2nd Company Grip	SANDY BLOOM
Key Grip/1st Company Grip	BILLY BOSSON
Dolly Grip/Crab Dolly Grip	MICHAEL FLANINGAM
Grips	LIZ BOLDEN, MARC POLANSKI, ROBERT REID, KEVIN BALL
Apprentice Grip	ERIK WOLFORD

Electrical Lighting Technicians	URIEL URIBE, ANTHONY GUZMAN, ANDREW GLOVER, NGOLI NYIRENDA, DOUGLAS BLAGG, JOHN MASSARO, THOMA REAVIS, DAISUKE MIYAKE, DON CHONG, ERIC KRAMER
Ultimatte Operator	BOB KERTESZ
Tap Operator	GREG NOYES
Still Photographer	JOEL SUSSMAN
Sound Mixer	WALT MARTIN
Boom Operator	BILL RATCLIFF
Script Supervisor	KATE LEWIS
Storyboard Artists	MARC BAIRD, ALEX HILL
Production Designers	CHERIE BAKER, CHRIS DOUGLAS
Computer Graphics Art Director	JEFFREY "JC" COMBS
Art Department Coordinator	ANN GISELLE-SPIEGLER
Set Designers	CHRIS GORAK, JAMES O'DONNELL, BRYAN LANE
Model Builder	ROBIN SCHNEIDER
Set Decorator	CARRIE PERZAN
Leadman	RICHARD D. WRIGHT
Set Dresser	JOHN GREVERA, JAMES DEAN, ARA DARAKJIAN
On-Set Dresser	TOM WAISANEN
Costume Designer	KAREN MANN
Costumer	KRISTEN SAINTS
Wardrobe Supervisor	CAROL QUIROZ
Set Costumer	JOEL BERLIN
Costumer	DANA LOATS, ANITA BROWN, TAMMY SURBER
Costume Intern	JOYA FLORES, STACI RIESENBECK, PAULETTE URIS
Key Hair	LANA SHARPE
Assistant Hair	GLORIA PONCE
Hair Stylist	SHASTIE SHARPE
Key Makeup	BILL MYER
Assistant Make-up	KIM MINER
Kilrathi: Melek	CHRIS BERGSCHNEIDER
Kilrathi Suit Technician #1	JEFF FARLEY
Kilrathi Suit Technician #2	JO ANN BLOOMFIELD

Kilrathi Puppeteer	BUD McGREW
Kilrathi Puppeteer Assistant	MIKE NEWMAN
Kilrathi Prosthetics	OBSCURE ARTIFACTS, INC
Property Master	MARK ANDERSON
Assistant Property	LORI A. NOYES
Special Effects	STUDIO ART & TECHNOLOGY
Stunt Coordinator	ROCKY CAPELLA
Construction Coordinator	MIKE CLARK
Assistant Construction Coordinator	JENNY AYALA
General Foreman	KEITH COX
Construction Foreman	WADE ROBINSON
Welder/Construction	MICHAEL J. COHEN
Standby	STEVE DEGROODT
Prop Maker	MORGAN FLAHERTY
Carpenters/Prop Makers	PAUL T. CONTRERAS, MARTIN DUNCAN, GORDAN E. HOLMES II, TYLER DUPUY, RAY BARON, MAX K. BOZEMAN, SEAN A. DUGGAN, DAVID NUTE, STEVEN DOSS, SCOTT MILLER, ROBERT A.MASINI, DAVID WHEELER, TIMOTHY WALSH, MARTIN DUNCAN, TIMOTHY GRUSE, FRANK PALAZZO, CASEY WHEELER, KARL KOEB, DAVID CAMPBELL, GREGORY CAMPBELL, THOMAS WAGES, REX CASSANO, RONNIE MONTGOMERY
Lead Scenic/Head Painter	DAVE ROBINSON
Scenic Artists	CHRIS KELLY, PAUL MANCHESTER, LUZ
Head Decorator	CHRIS KELLY
Decorators	STEVE DEGROODT, LUZ
Painters/Decorators	BRIAN LYNK, PETER GEORGE, FRANK OLIVERI, GARY MARK, GUILLERMO TELLO, MICK RITCHASON, MARTIN ORTIZ, JAIME CASILLAS
Laborers	CESAR AYALA, RICK FINE, JUAN RAVE, DANIEL R. PARKER, JASON GREENWOOD, DAVID KITCHEN, DENNIS WINTERS, RUBEN DELGADO, APRIL DUNCAN
2nd Unit Directors	MARK DAY, ADAM FOSHKO

2nd Unit Consultant	JIM ROSENTHAL
2nd Unit Video Assistant	DAN DEVANEY
2nd Unit Video Intern	CHUCK HATIGAN
2nd Unit 1st Utility	DAVID WEINREB
2nd Unit 2nd Utility	JENNIFER LEAR
2nd Unit 1st Assistant Director	LOUIS MILITO
2nd Unit 2nd Assistant Director	BRETT BOYDSTUN
2nd Unit Script Supervisor	JUDITH SAUNDERS
2nd Unit Set Production Assistant	CURTIS MYER, CAROL GRONNER
2nd Unit Gaffer	REGINALD F. LAKE
2nd Unit Best Boy Electrician	SHERMAN FULTON
2nd Unit Electrician	VAN JOHNSON
2nd Unit Key Grip	IRV KATZ
2nd Unit Best Boy Grip	DAVE BODEN
2nd Unit Grips	MARK COMBS, JIM NIEUWENHUIS
2nd Unit Sound	WOLF SEEBERG
Medics	CHRISTINA HERSHEY, SUZANNE KUNKEL, JUSTIN BIRCHFIEL
Craft Service	JULIE ILES
Sound Stages provided by	REN MAR STUDIOS, HOLLYWOOD, CALIFORNIA, USA
Monitors Provided by	SONY CORPORATION OF AMERICA
Keyboards Provided by	KINESIS CORPORATION OF BOTHELL, WASHINGTON
Cantina Shoes Provided by	DEJA SHOES, THE ENVIRONMENTAL FOOTWEAR CO.
Eyewear Provided by	KATA EYEWEAR OF CULVER CITY, CALIFORNIA
Arriflex 535 Cameras Provided by	OTTO NEMENZ INTERNATIONAL, INC.
Special Thanks to	TRAGER MANUFACTURING COMPANY;AT&T; THE USS LEXINGTON MUSEUM OF CORPUS CHRISTI, TEXAS; VF-201 “HUNTERS” OF NAS DALLAS, TEXAS; 924TH FIGHTER WING “OUT-LAWS” OF BERGSTROM AFB, AUSTIN TEXAS; EA PRODUCTIONS

Business Office

Production Accountant	LAURIE WOKEN
Assistant Production Accountant	JULIE La PRATH
Business/Legal Affairs	CAROL CONTES, LESLIE ABEL

Post Production

Post-Production Director	PHIL GESSERT
Visual Effects Supervisor	STEVE MOORE
Visual Effects Coordinator	JEFFERY "JC" COMBS
Post-Production Coordinator	DAVID DOWNING
Avid Editor	PHIL GESSERT
Assistant Editor	JAY MAHAVIER
Post-Production Assistant	JIM CAPP
Video Processing Facility	EA MEDIA LAB
Video Processing & Digitization	JENI DAY
Video Technician	MICHAEL MOORE
Digital Compositing and On Line	WESTERN IMAGES, INC
Facility Producer	TODD LINDO
Technical Director	JERRY CASTRO
Telecine Colorists	JIM BARRETT, GARY COATES
D1 Online Editors	GREG GILMORE, MARK SORENSEN
Compositing Artist	ORIN GREEN
Rotoscoping Artists	DANIELLE CICCARELLI, ALI LAVENTHOL
Visual Effects	POST LOGIC, INC
Post Logic Producer	LESLIE SORRENTINO
Visual Effects Compositor	ROBBY VIGNATO
Telecine Colorist	MIKE EAVES
Telecine Assistant	MARIO BARRERA
D1 Online Editor	BOB BLUE
D1 Assistants	KO MARUYAMA, SHANE HARRIS
Digital Non-Linear Editing System	AVID TECHNOLOGY, TEXTSOUND
Film to Tape Transfers by	DELUXE VIDEO
Director of Film Audio Post-Production	MURRAY ALLEN
Dubbing Mixers	TONY BERKELEY, KEN FELTON
Dialogue Editing	TONY BERKELEY, KEN FELTON
Foley Editing	TONY BERKELEY, KEN FELTON

Music Editing	TONY BERKELEY, KEN FELTON
Supervising Sound Effects Editor	TONY BERKELEY
Sound Effects Editors	KEN FELTON, MARC FARLY
Sound Designers	TONY BERKELEY, MARC FARLY, KEN FELTON
Special Kilrathi Vocal Effects	TOM SEUFERT
Foley & ADR Services provided by	POST SOUND CORP.
ADR Mixer	JOHN REINER C.A.S.
Foley Mixer	RICHARD DUARTE
Foley Artists	MARGIE O'MALLEY, MARNIE MOORE
Foley Editor	DAVE NELSON

Cast

Col. Christopher Blair	MARK HAMILL
Admiral Tolwyn	MALCOLM McDOWELL
Maj. James/Paladin/Taggart	JOHN RHYS-DAVIES
Capt. William Eisen	JASON BERNARD
Maj. Todd/Maniac/Marshall	TOM WILSON
Seether	ROBERT RUSLER
2nd Lt.Troy/Catscratch/Carter	MARK DACASCOS
1st Lt. Velina Sosa	HOLLY GAGNIER
Lt. Winston/Vagabond/Chang	FRANCOIS CHAU
Col. Jacob/Hawk/Manley	CHRIS MULKEY
Col. Tamara/Panther/Farnsworth	ELIZABETH BARONES
Lt. Col. Gash Dekker	JEREMY ROBERTS
Chief Tech Robert/Pliers/Sykes	RICHARD RIEHLE
Vice-Admiral Daniel Wolford	PETER JASON
Captain Hugh Paulsen	JOHN SPENCER
2nd Lt. Drew Naismith	WILLIAMS YOUMANS
Dr. Brody	JESSICA TUCK
Voice of Melek	BARRY DENNEN
News Anchor	BARBARA NIVEN
Confed Redshirt #1	RICHARD GARON
Confed Redshirt #2	CHRIS CONRAD
Confed Redshirt #3	CASPER Van DIEN
Confed Redshirt #4	SUZANNE IRCHA
Telamon Female Comm Officer	KIRSTEN MOORE
Telamon Citizen	JOEL POLIS

Telamon Doctor	MICHAEL CAVANAUGH
Canteen Bartender	DYLAN BRUNO
Canteen Vet	PETER MARQUARDT
Canteen Man	DEAN TARROLLY
Border Worlds Pilot #1	MAURICIO MENDOZA
Border Worlds Pilot #2	LESTER BARRIE
Border Worlds Pilot #3	WALT GOGGINS
Vesuvius Helmsman	AARON KUHR
Vesuvius Comm. Officer	WANDA ACUNA
Transport Pilot	JANE A. ROGERS
Senator #1	DEAN SOMMERS
Senator #2	ED BERNARD
Senator #3	ROGER MERCURIO
Senator #4	SHIRLEE REED
Shuttle Pilot	DYLAN HAGGERTY
Confed Marine	DERIK HIXON
Border Worlds Lt.	CARL BANKS
Bluepoint Traffic Control	TODD COVERT
Helmsperson	BEVERLEY CASTALDO
Circle V Comm Specialist	SAXON TRAINER
B.W.S. Carrier Officer #1	ALLEN CUTLER
B.W.S. Carrier Officer #2	JOE FISKE
Confed Pilot	MICHAEL WACHTEL
Vagabond Double	PETER LAI
Com Base Guard #1	TIM MERIDITH
Com Base Guard #2	DAN BELL
Com Base Guard #3	SCOTT McELROY
Towlyn Double	RANDY HALL
Convoy Comm. Officer	MORGAN ENGLUND
Pirate	TODD KIMSEY
Melek	CHRIS BERGSCHNEIDER
Generic Cap #1	CHARLES ESTEN
Generic Cap #2	MICHAEL HAPLIN
Generic Cap #3	COOKIE CAROSELLA
Generic Cap #4	JEFFREY ARBAUGH
Slapping Woman	KIRSTEN MARYOTT

APPENDIX D

What's on the CD

The CD included in this book contains a demo version of *StoryLine Pro*—a nifty piece of software written by John Truby, America's most popular story coach. As a bonus, this demo version also contains the *StoryLine Pro* Fantasy genre software add-on that shows you how to construct a successful fantasy story.

The following sections describe in detail how to install and use this educational and enjoyable software.

> **The "StoryLine Pro" demo runs on Windows 95, 3.1 and the Mac. The last section in this appendix gives you step-by-step installation instructions for all three systems.**

Writing Like a Pro

StoryLine Pro can definitely give you a legup in your quest for the perfect interactive script. However, there are three points you should keep in mind as you work with the evaluation copy we've provided:

- *StoryLine Pro* is NOT an interactive formatting program (that is, it won't do things like give you a bunch of boxes to write stuff in that connect with other boxes to show branching possibilities.
- The examples in *StoryLine Pro* are for film, television, novels, and short stories. There are no interactive examples. But the program is extremely useful in helping you develop story, and other key features of multimedia scriptwriting.
- This demo is the full version of *StoryLine Pro*, but it is still only an evaluation copy. You won't be able to save or print out in this version. To do that you'll have to get the "real" thing via the 1-800 number at the end of this appendix. But this version will give you complete access to all *StoryLine Pro* screens and let you see for yourself first-hand how to plan and layer your story.

> **"StoryLine Pro," according to John Truby, "is an idea processor that coaches the user in how to write a great story. It works for writers of every ability, from beginning to advanced. It shows the user the potential in his idea, and then ties together the hundreds of elements needed for a successful story. The result is true creativity at a high level."**

A Very Personal Trainer

In brief, *StoryLine Pro* works not by telling you what to write, but rather by acting as a personal story coach as you write. For example, the software gently prompts you to work through the key 22 building blocks of your story. Or it can help you compare your hero with all your other characters, or show you if your plot points are building sufficiently in the middle of your piece. And best of all (in my opinion), the program has 29 different story examples (including *Star Wars* and Joseph Conrad's *Heart of Darkness*) to show you how the masters solved similar problems. After all, John Truby points out, "you learn best by example."

The program has a ton of other features that'll take more than a few uses to discover, so I suggest you load in the demo and just go for it.

Getting Started

Once you've installed the demo using the instructions in the last section, choose Premise Pad from the View menu, and then New Story. You must start a new story or nothing will happen. Type in a simple title and premise, then click on Load. Your screens are now loaded, and you can choose any of the writing steps listed on the Main Menu.

I'll pause here for a couple of tips for Windows users. In your version, when you run your cursor over the top menu bar, the drop-down menus appear without your clicking on them. This is okay. Your machine is not going haywire. Also, if you don't find a close button in the upper left-hand corner of your screen, look for a Back button. Clicking Back will take you to the previous screen.

My personal suggestion at this point is to go back to the View menu and click on First Draft. On the screen you now have a bunch of boxes where you can fill in a scene-by-scene account of your story. You can think of these boxes as index cards, and once you write something in them, the program will be perfectly happy to shuffle and reshuffle (use Edit menu) them in any order your heart desires.

But don't write anything yet! Go to the Examples menu, click on Film and choose Star Wars. Presto, like sleight-of-hand magic, a scene-by-scene breakdown of *Star Wars* is laid out before your startled eyes—68 scenes in all. Go ahead, start reading, the entire film is there. Cool, huh? I would then suggest trying some of the other features of *StoryLine Pro*, plugging in the *Star Wars* story example. May the force be with you.

And remember, Help menus abound. Screen-specific help is available from the pull-down menu. Program Help provides context-sensitive advice on whatever part of the program you're currently in. Definitions defines the parameters of the information you are about to give the program. On-line Analyst offers tips and reminders as you fill in these boxes. And Index lets you choose the category for which you need assistance. Refer to these menus anytime you feel lost.

Fantasy Coach of Your Dreams

The Fantasy genre software add-on, John Truby says, "helps you master the all-important three-part fantasy sequence that determines the success of any fantasy story, construct a unique fantasy world that your audience will adore, and matches it to the growth of your hero." The Fantasy add-on is automatically installed when you install the *StoryLine Pro* demo. To activate it, go to the View menu, click on Genre (at the very bottom) and choose Fantasy. The program will do a little 2-step dance for a moment, and then you're all set. By activating the Fantasy add-on you've now added three more film examples specific to the genre (see the bottom of the Examples list).

To get a detailed skinny on how to create your perfect fantasy, click on Genre and/or Charts on the top bar menu, extreme right-hand side. I suggest you click on Charts first, and read through the various headings offered under Fantasy (these headings tell you how to write the genre). Once you've got a handle on the topic, you can then click on Genre, and start filling in the various "maps" that come under the Fantasy heading. Another cool thing about the Fantasy add-on is that if you go to the 22 Steps feature (View, Structure), you'll find the story beats germane to fantasy lined up with your 22 key steps necessary for a good story.

Interactive Writing

StoryLine Pro has a number of features that can help you write a great interactive story. According to John Truby, "a good interactive story must combine choice (the horizontal line) with subsequent events (the vertical line)."

The Vertical Line

To help you figure out your vertical line—the events that happen to your hero as the story moves along—choose the 22 Steps feature by clicking on View and choosing Structure. These 22 steps are key stages found in any good story. As John says, "They're what make a story dramatic, and give the user an emotionally satisfying experience." All you have to do is fill in the boxes, and your event sequence (the story you're trying to write) should be pretty well fleshed out.

You can also tackle the vertical line by working on your characters first. Pull down the View menu, click on Central Casting, and then click on Cast. With these screens you can start giving names to your characters, developing their resumes, determining their relationship to your hero (e.g., whether they're an opponent or ally, etc.). Click on View/ Conflict and you get into their deeper psychological motivations—psychological and moral needs, etc. All of this is important stuff to figure out if you want compelling, well-developed characters. And again, there's no free lunch here. The program is not going to write any of it for you, it's only pointing out that you need these elements for a good story.

The Horizontal Line

The horizontal line—the choices available to you the user—can be fleshed out by using the Action Tracks and Visual Tracks (View menu, Texture). The Action Tracks show you all the threads of the story tapestry at once. The vertical line of the story is on the left, while across the top you can track what every character is doing at any point in time. Visual Tracks, like Action Tracks, help you break the story down into threads, but now you're concentrating on the visuals. If you want to use a recurring visual motif that's always associated with a particular character, mood, or pending action, Visual Tracks is where you can do it.

How Do I Install It?

Windows Users

1. If you're using Windows 3.1, click on the File menu of your Windows Program Manager and choose Run. If you're using Windows 95, click the Start button, then click the Run button.

2. Type: your CD-ROM drive:\slwdemo\instdemo
   For example: D:\slwdemo\instdemo
3. Click OK.
4. You will see a box called Select Destination Drive. Click OK if you want to install on your C drive. Otherwise, you can change the name of the drive in the bottom window. Do not change the name of the directory from \SLW.
5. A box will appear called Select Program Manager Group. Click OK.
6. Installation is complete. Double-click on the StoryLine Pro Demo icon, and go to the section Getting Started in this Appendix.

Mac Users

1. Open the SLP Mac Demo folder on the CD-ROM. Double Click on the StoryLine Pro Demo Installer icon.
2. Read the installation notes on your screen, then click on Install.
3. Select your hard drive from the pop-up box at the top of the screen. Do not change the name of the StoryLine Pro folder highlighted below the box. Click on Install.
4. When installation is complete, click on the Quit button.
   (For users of system 7.5.2 or above, the installation of "StoryLine Pro" is done. Proceed directly to step 6).
   (For users of system 7.5.1 or below, you must install the Apple Shared Library Manager. See step 5).
5. Open the ASLM Installer older fro the CD-ROM. Double-click on the Installer icon. Click on the Install button. After this process is complete, you must restart your machine.
6. To start the demo, open the StoryLine Pro folder and double-click on the "StoryLine Pro" Demo icon. Proceed to the Getting Started section of this Appendix.

How to Order?

StoryLine Pro costs about $299. Additional genre add-ons are about $99.

Inside the United States call 1-800-33Truby (1-800-338-7829)
Outside the United States call 310-575-3050

For questions about *StoryLine Pro*:
Mac users call 213-223-9652
Windows users call 818-861-6003

For loading and installation problems only, call Sybex technical support at 1-800-227-2346.

INDEX

Note to the Reader: First level entries are in **bold**. Page numbers in **bold** indicate the principal discussion of a topic or the definition of a term. Page numbers in *italic* indicate illustrations.

Numbers

A

B

C

D

E

F

G

H

I

O

P

Q

R

S

Y

Z

About This CD

The CD-ROM enclosed with this book includes an evaluation copy of *StoryLine Pro* and its *Fantasy* module. Windows and Macintosh versions of the software are included on the disk. See Appendix D for a more complete description of the software and for installation instructions. The software is copyrighted by Truby's Writers Studio in Los Angeles, California.

For *StoryLine Pro* technical support, contact the company as follows:
Windows 95 and Windows 3.1 users, call (818) 861-6003
Macintosh users, call (213) 223-9652

For installation questions only, contact Sybex at (800) 227-2346.